LEARNING ANOTHER LANGUAGE THROUGH ACTIONS

by

James J. Asher, Ph.D.

Recipient of the
OUTSTANDING PROFESSOR AWARD
from San Jose State University, Founded 1857
Historic as California's Oldest Public Institution of Higher Learning

Recipient of the First Annual
Western Association for Human Development
JAMES J. ASHER AWARD
For Creative Contribution to the Field of Education

With Classroom-Tested Lessons by Carol Adamski

The problem is that about 95% of the students drop out of second language programs before achieving basic proficiency. Why do they give up? The answer you will find in this book could dramatically change the rest of your teaching career.

First Edition
1st Printing 1977, 2nd Printing 1979
3rd Printing 1981

Second Edition
ISBN 0-940296-02-0
1st Printing 1982, 2nd Printing 1983

Third Edition
ISBN 0-940296-50-0
1st Printing 1986, 2nd Printing 1988

Fourth Edition
ISBN 1-56018-494-9
1st Printing 1993

Fifth Edition
ISBN 1-56018-301-2
1st Printing 1996

Sixth Edition
ISBN 1-56018-502-3
1st Printing 2000

Published by
Sky Oaks Productions, Inc.
P.O. Box 1102, Los Gatos, California 95031 USA
Phone: (408) 395-7600 • **Fax:** (408) 395-8440
E-Mail: tprworld@aol.com • **Web:** www.tpr-world.com

Free TPR Catalog upon Request.

Dedication

First Edition
To Ginny, Jeff, and Melissa

Second Edition
"There is nothing permanent but change itself."
In memory of James J. Asher, Sr.

"The best gift a father-in-law or mother-in-law
can give is the gift of non-interference...
There is no regret in saying nothing."
In memory of Vernon Gardner

Third Edition
"If you want to make a friend, you have to be a friend."
In memory of June and Earl Jandron

Fourth Edition
In memory of a gentle, sensitive, loving woman—
my mother, the movie actress.

Fifth Edition
To my grandchildren—Russell, Sam, Katelyn Lee and Morgan Marie.

If we were to overhear God humming a composition written by angels, we would be so touched by the beauty of the Voice that tears would be streaming down our faces. The closest I have come to this experience is to answer the phone and hear the small voice of a child say, *"Hello, Grandpa."*

Sixth Edition
To the real star of the family—Virginia Lee Asher

"Everything in moderation."

TABLE OF CONTENTS

Page

PART I TPR: A PERSONAL STORY 1-1
Pre-TPR 1-1
The Teaching Machine 1-3
Guessing by the Learners 1-3
Power of Guessing: An Explanation 1-7
The First Trial Learning Hypothesis 1-7
One Trial Learning 1-10
A High Velocity Logic Theory of Information Processing 1-14
The Crucial Test: A Cause-Effect Theory of Learning 1-18
Another Discovery: Zero Trial Learning 1-20
The Laboratory 1-21
Let's Get a Research Grant 1-22
Maybe a Motion Picture is the Answer 1-23
My First Motion Picture 1-24
What's in a Name? 1-26
Another Attempt to Persuade Washington 1-27
The Search for the Secret Behind TPR 1-30
The Myth of Children's Superiority in Language Learning 1-31
The "Thick Tongue" Phenomenon 1-33
The Search Continued for the Secret Behind Language-Body Learning 1-33
MAKING DOCUMENTARY FILMS 1-35
The Film in Japanese 1-35
The Film in German 1-37
The Adult Film in Spanish 1-40
The Children's Film in Spanish and French 1-41
The Lost Film of Nava 1-45

PART II THE PROBLEM 2-1
An Instructional Strategy that Produces High Motivation 2-3
Summary 2-4
The Evidence 2-4
Classroom studies with children 2-5
Laboratory studies with children 2-6
Laboratory studies with adults 2-7

TABLE OF CONTENTS

Page

Classroom studies with adults 2-11
Learning German in night school 2-11
Learning German: The University of Texas Experience 2-13
Learning Spanish 2-14
English as a second language 2-15
Why It Works 2-17
Infant Development 2-17
Summary 2-19
Brain Lateralization 2-19
Application to Language Acquisition ... 2-24
Playing to the Right Hemisphere 2-25
TPR 2-25
The Learnables 2-26
The Sens-it Cell Model 2-26
Interactive Tape and Teacher Technique 2-27
Suggestology 2-28

PART III MOST OFTEN ASKED QUESTIONS 3-1

PART IV CLASSROOM LESSONS 4-1

1. How to orient and motivate the students ... 4-1
How to start the training
The importance of novelty

2. How to expand basic structures 4-5
Hints on pacing
The rule of three in introducing vocabulary

3. How to cope with the fast-moving pace 4-11
The value of novel commands that are playful, silly and even bizarre

4. Why there is no tedious repetition of sentences 4-13
The first reading experience

5. How to increase your sense of timing 4-17
The first experience of role reversal
Using video tape to enhance the student's sense of achievement

6. The first experience of directing questions to students 4-18

TABLE OF CONTENTS

Page

Why students should not be interrupted as they speak in role reversal
What can be expected from new students entering the class for the first time

7. Learning numbers **4-20**
Contrasts such as "long" and "short"
Students utter commands to direct the behavior of a teacher's aide

8. Introduction of the present continuous **4-24**
More with numbers
Short answer questions

9. Preparation to visit a department store **4-25**
More on the present progressive
Introduction of "Who is . . .?"
Reading

10. Introduction of "Where is . . .?" **4-27**
More on the present continuous
A slide presentation of a clothing store
Writing personal information
Introduction to possessive pronouns

11. Asking questions of students **4-29**
Demonstrating the present continuous with personal pronouns
Introduction of days of the week
More with the question word "Who."

12. More practice with the days of the week **4-31**
Review of the present continuous with personal pronouns
More on possessive pronouns
The first experience of reading a story

13. Slide presentation of a clothing store **4-33**
Review of the present continuous
A general review

14. Field trip to a clothing store **4-34**

15. Review of the clothing store experience **4-35**
Review of the present continuous
Review of short-answer and long-answer questions

TABLE OF CONTENTS

Page

16. Using commands to review contrasts (e.g., tall and short) 4-36
    Using short answer questions to review contrasts
    Introduction of affective (i.e., emotional) states as angry, sad, happy and so forth
    General Review including parts of the body, colors, numbers, clothing, opposites, prepositions, possessive pronouns, and the present progressive
17. Review of opposites 4-38
    Review of emotional states
    New vocabulary
    Role reversal
18. Fast-moving review 4-39
    Pancho Carrancho
    Role reversal
19. Reading a second story 4-40
    New vocabulary
    Review of question words—what, who and where
20. Using commands to review verbs and verb inflections 4-41
    Introduction of the past tense
    New vocabulary about occupations
21. More with the past tense 4-42
    Review of occupations
    Reading
22. More with the past tense 4-43
    A new twist with the past tense
    Review of occupations
    Reading and writing personal data
23. Review of the past tense 4-44
    Different sentences, but the same grammatical cue
    Introduction of negation combined with the past tense
    Reading and writing personal data

TABLE OF CONTENTS

Page

24. Review of the past tense **4-46**
Questions to be answered in the past tense
Reading
Making clocks

25. Telling time through commands **4-47**
Fine detail in telling time
More with the past tense

26. Reading and writing **4-47**
Review of all content
Pancho Carrancho

27. Consumer behavior: buyer-seller
transactions.......................... **4-49**

28. Slides of a supermarket **4-49**
Role playing in a supermarket
Introduction of places (hospital,
bank, etc.)

29. More on places.......................... **4-50**
Reading sentences created by students

30. Review of student-constructed sentences **4-51**
Review of the past tense
Pancho Carrancho with vegetables
Introduction of the past form of the
verb "to be"

31. More on the past form of the verb
"to be" with new verbs **4-52**
More with places (home, school, store, etc.)
Short-answer questions
Practice with ordinal numbers

32. Reading................................ **4-53**
Review of the past tense
More with demonstrative pronouns

33. Slides of a supermarket **4-54**
Role playing transactions in a supermarket

34. Reality-testing (students uttered commands
to move visitors) **4-55**
Discussion groups

TABLE OF CONTENTS

Page

35. Review of the verb "to be" **4-55**
    Reading
    Pancho Carrancho
36. Reading **4-57**
    Introduction of restaurant vocabulary
    Role Playing
37. More restaurant role playing **4-58**
    Ordinal numbers
38. More with ordinal numbers **4-58**
    Everyday dialogues
39. Role playing restaurant situations **4-59**
    Practice with the relative clause
    Review of everyday dialogues
40. Travelogue **4-60**
    Some follow-up geography
    A tactile experience
41. Object descriptions **4-61**
    Family vocabulary
42. Family vocabulary **4-63**
    Introduction of the future tense
    Role reversal
43. Review of family vocabulary **4-63**
    More with the future tense
44. Review of the future tense **4-64**
    New commands
    Field trip to a house
45. Review of the future tense **4-65**
    Pancho Carrancho with verb cards
    The future tense with the Michigan Cue Cards
46. Role reversal **4-65**
    Field trip to a house
    Reading
47. Verb review **4-66**
    House review
    Introduction to "there is"

TABLE OF CONTENTS

Page

48. Review of house vocabulary **4-67**
    Review of "there is"

49. Continuation of "there is" **4-67**
    Adjectives

50. Review of "there is" **4-68**
    Introduction of "there are"
    A guest speaker

51. Reading review of "there is"
    and "there are" **4-69**
    Introduction of "can"
    More with opposites

52. Review of opposites **4-70**
    Introduction of "I can't"
    An imaginary car

53. Acting out what was read **4-71**
    Slides of a gas station
    Role playing gas station transactions

PART V SELECTED REFERENCES **5-1**

PART VI UPDATE TO THE FIFTH EDITION **6-1**
Interview: A Conversation with Dr. James J. Asher about Total Physical Response (TPR) and Education

Experiences of Classroom Teachers - The application of TPR to Higher Order Thinking Skills **6-5**

PART VII FROM MY MAIL BAG **7-1**

TPR PRODUCTS .... *Please see the back of this book.*

BOOKS

GAMES

STUDENT KITS

TEACHER KITS

CLASSIC VIDEO DEMONSTRATIONS

FOREWORD

FIRST EDITION

Well, it's finally completed. This book is intended for language teachers of children or adults who want a guideline for applying the "total physical response" in their day-to-day classroom instruction.

The book is based on the concept that the assimilation of information and skills can be significantly accelerated through the use of the kinesthetic sensory system—which, incidentally, is *underused* except for the instruction of pre-school children and impaired children. As normal children progress from grade to grade, there is less and less utilization of the kinesthetic sensory system. There is less physical action and increased learning through reading and writing. This may be a serious mistake especially for the two most difficult learning tasks in school—acquiring a second language and mathematical understanding. It may be that both languages and mathematics are perceived as being unlearnable by most people because the instruction depends on the senses of vision and audition to the exclusion of the kinesthetic system.

The book is divided into three parts. In Part I, I tried to present the problem that people experience in their usually unsuccessful attempt to acquire a second language, and one possible solution in an instructional strategy based on the kinesthetic sensory system. After that, the evidence is summarized documenting the powerful effect that the kinesthetic sensory channel has in making a second language learnable for most children and adults. Perhaps no other single idea in second language acquisition has been as thoroughly explored.

Part II is a *question-and-answer* section in which I attempted to anticipate most questions which teachers ask about the approach. For questions I may have missed, you are cordially invited to write me. I promise to respond promptly.

Part III is a lesson-by-lesson plan that is based on a training log kept by Carol Adamski as she applied the approach to teach English as a second language through 150 hours of classroom instruction. Since I revised the basic log, any mistakes in the printed version are mine alone.

Appreciation is expressed to the fine teachers who worked with me through the years in the experimental research conducted in their classrooms. Without their support, little could have been accomplished .

SECOND EDITION

In the first edition of this book I did not refer to my approach as the Total Physical Response (TPR) because I thought the term was somewhat esoteric. However, since then, I realize that most people who have applied my stress-free model for language acquisition think of it as TPR. Hence, in the second edition you will see learning through actions also called the Total Physical Response or TPR.

In the second edition I have updated the research findings, especially by showing how our approach is a right brain instructional strategy. There are other effective right brain instructional approaches for language acquisition. I have described each of these and where to write for further information.

In the five or so years since the first edition appeared, thousands of instructors in most languages, including English as a Second Language and the sign language of the deaf, have applied the TPR approach to children and adults. From letters that I have received and the conversations with instructors in workshops throughout the country, I have expanded the section entitled, "Most Often Asked Questions."

Since more and more instructors are publishing TPR lessons that have been used successfully in their classes, I have cited these in the Appendix under "Other TPR Training Materials," Also, I have reprinted in the Appendix (with the permission of Ziff-Davis Publishers, Inc.) an article which appeared in *Psychology Today.* It is entitled, "Fear of Foreign Languages." As a result of that article I have received letters of inquiry from every "nook and cranny" in the U.S.A. and overseas. The letters have poured in from people of every occupation (including prison inmates) who want to acquire another language. They ask me to recommend instructors in their local communities who are skilled in TPR. If you are such a person, please let me know what TPR training you are willing to offer to the people of your community.

I would like to express a special thanks to the fine people from preschool teachers to university professors who have given me, through the years, their encouragement and support. My appreciation also to Emi Nobuhiro for her conscientiousness in preparing typed materials and Harry McCluskey for his problem solving skill in printing.

THIRD EDITION

This is a high risk edition since I will start out with the intimate behind-the-scenes story of how the *Total Physical Response* (TPR) came to be. I am a private person by nature, but the self-revelation in Part I may inspire future researchers to build upon my work, sidestep mistakes that I have made, and discover how to join a rather elite group of researchers—perhaps only 5% whose work was actually applied in the daily lives of thousands of people.

Enjoy the book in good health and have a ball applying the concepts with your students.

If I can help you along the way, let me know.

FOURTH EDITION

I am pleased to tell you that in the past twenty-five years, my Total Physical Response—known world-wide as TPR, has been used successfully in thousands of classrooms around the globe in European, Indian, Asian, and Semitic languages. Enthusiasm for the approach seems to increase geometrically every year.

In response to popular demand, my documentary films demonstrating the effectiveness of TPR are now being transferred to video cassettes. After viewing one of my video demonstrations in London, a British language instructor commented: "Thank Goodness, these are not new films. Since they were made years ago, it tells me that the approach has been 'time tested' and therefore merits serious attention." So, for American audiences that are attracted to anything "new," relax and enjoy the classics...

FIFTH EDITION

As an update, I am including a reprint of an interview conducted by Dr. Roberta Stathis that was published recently in the IDEAS for Excellence Newsletter. It is entitled, ***A Conversation with Dr. James J. Asher about Total Physical Response (TPR) and Education.*** Also you will find a note from classroom teachers commenting upon the "tremendous potential of using TPR to successfully develop students' ***higher order thinking skills...***" You will find the update in the back of this book starting at 6.1.

Since I introduced the concept of TPR about thirty years ago, thousands of language instructors worldwide have discovered the magic of TPR. With few exceptions, this phenomenon is not the result of instruction in colleges and universities, but from individual teachers recom–mending the approach to other teachers. I believe it is a fair conclusion that the validity of this stress-free learning strategy has been thoroughly demonstrated in carefully controlled research studies and in successful classroom experiences with many different languages acquired by several hundred thousand children and adult students.

Therefore, it is time for colleges and universities to create courses of study with hands-on experiences that produce skilled practitioners of the Total Physical Response. It is unfair to new language teachers— and the students they will instruct— to graduate from programs in education, applied linguistics, and second languages with a cursory awareness of TPR. Usually the textbook about "methodology" will only have a paragraph or two about TPR which is lost in a labyrinth of other approaches that are, frankly speaking, ineffective.

Of course, the university experience should be organized around my book, ***Learning Another Language Through Actions*** and Ramiro Garcia's ***Instructor's Notebook: How To Apply TPR For Best Results.*** Our classic video demonstrations are an excellent way to motivate keen interest in the approach.

In the back of this book, you will find scores of books that will help shape the skills of the new language teacher to guarantee a successful experience in the classroom no matter what the ages of their students and no matter what the target language.

SIXTH EDITION

I have expanded the Q & A chapter and created a new chapter called, ***From My Mail Bag***. From hundreds of letters and e-mail messages, I have selected those that you will find most helpful in your work. Whenever possible, I have also included e-mail addresses so that you can follow-up by communicating with other TPR instructors throughout the world.

In this sixth edition, I have included the latest right-left brain research, which is my model for explaining the amazing results of TPR instruction. Since the Nobel-prize winning brain lateralization experiment of Roger Sperry, 4,000 research studies have been published. We know now, for example, that the brain (a) is independent of us (in that it can processes information without intruding upon our awareness), and (b) the brain has the answer to any question we may ask at least one-half second (or more) before we do. For more details, see Part III, Most Often Asked Questions and Answers.

PART I

TPR: A PERSONAL STORY

Some of the most frequent questions people ask me are, "How did you get the idea for TPR?" and "How has TPR changed through the years when you first introduced it in the 1963 film, 'Demonstration of a New Strategy in Language Learning'?" From my recollections, I would like to recreate the story of TPR as I experienced it.

PRE-TPR

When I graduated with a doctorate in psychology from the University of Houston in 1957, I accepted a position of assistant professor in the psychology department of San Jose State College in San Jose, California. In San Jose (which was an agricultural small town then, tucked away peacefully in the lush Santa Clara Valley —the prune capital of the world), I enjoyed teaching courses in business and industrial psychology because here was an opportunity to apply theories of psychology to solve complex problems.

Although I was intrigued with the difficulties in matching people with jobs to help individuals achieve successful work experiences (and later I published the results of many research projects designed to improve personnel selection) — I was especially fascinated with problems of training, particularly skill learning.

I should mention here that my master's degree was also from the University of Houston in radio and television — specifically television journalism. Television in 1955, the year I graduated, was an infant medium. For example, video tape had not yet been invented. Almost all programming was "live" — the remainder was on film.

My mentor at the university, in media journalism, was a very warm and skillful professor named Richard Uray who offered me at graduation my first job as a photojournalist working for a local TV station in Houston. I also had an opportunity to join the faculty in the radio-television department at Lehigh University in Pennsylvania.

I turned down these attractive job offers to continue working for a doctorate in the psychology department. I worked under the guidance of Dr. Richard Evans, a well-known social psychologist whom I met when I worked as an apprentice on the television crew of a program in which Dr. Evans was presenting a course in psychology on the educational channel, KUHT. (Incidentally, the person who took the photojournalist job was Tom Jerrel who is now a nationally known correspondent for the ABC Television Network.)

Those three years in Houston were productive and fast-moving. When I arrived in Houston with my wife Ginny, the Korean War had just ended and I was a returning veteran ready to use that "scholarship" from Uncle Sam, called the G.I. Bill.

Living in Texas at that time was a grand experience. For example, working at the educational television station which broadcasted from the University, I met visiting celebrities (all of whom were invited to come on the air for personal interviews) from Mrs. Eleanor Roosevelt to the then Vice-President, Richard Nixon.

While I worked on my doctorate in psychology I was a part-time instructor on the faculty and also a research assistant to Dr. Richard Evans on a range of interesting projects from the design of an escape route for metropolitan Houston in the event of an atomic attack to measuring consumer preferences for programming on the novel toy called television. Dr. Evans was an energetic and knowledgeable mentor who was extremely generous with his time and most considerate in his guidance of graduate students.

At graduation time I sent out letters of inquiry and resumes to several universities. With one resume left over, a fellow student, Loren Corotto, suggested that I try his alma mater, San Jose State College, which I did, and I was hired. I discovered that San Jose State was founded in 1857 and was the oldest public institution of higher learning in California. Few people know that both "Berkeley" and UCLA were branches of San Jose State when they first started. The psychology department at San Jose State had at that time about 40 full-time Ph.Ds and was expanding rapidly. It was one of the largest psychology departments in America.

As I mentioned, I had an interest in skill learning and as a researcher I wanted to select a problem to explore that was complex and could be applied to the "real" world. Foreign language seemed to be ideal because (a) it was a complex problem in skill learning, and (b) most psychologists had abandoned this area as barren of productive research because the complexity of behavior made "clean," well-controlled experiments difficult; hence, the competition for research support was minimal. Also, I had a personal interest in foreign languages for this reason: In school, I had tried courses in Latin, Spanish, French and German. With acute stress, I managed to pass these courses, but my competency in languages was almost zero. This was puzzling since my general intelligence seemed to be high enough to master other school subjects from mathematics to the clarinet. There must be, I felt, a secret to foreign language acquisition that I had not yet discovered.

The Teaching Machine

Before Professor B.F. Skinner of Harvard published his programmed learning articles which inspired the teaching machine movement, I toyed with the idea of a machine that would accelerate foreign language learning. My ideal machine would have all the features of optimal learning as, for instance, the student views a vocabulary item in print, pronounces it, then hears a native speaker pronounce the utterance. Theoretically, this model "guaranteed" success because there was immediate and specific feedback information which allowed the learner to match a pronunciation attempt with the correct pronunciation so that one could rapidly "shape" (to use Skinner's term), the verbal response until it was perfect.

In addition to feedback information to the learner, the model made good theoretical sense for two other reasons. First, two sense channels—vision and audition—were involved; and secondly, there was an immediate reward in perceiving how one's pronunciation matched with the ideal response. I brainstormed the designing of this machine with one of my students, Colin Wright, who attempted to build a prototype.

The construction of the prototype was abandoned when we discovered that a similar machine called the Language Master was commercially available. I purchased one through the college for research that I was planning.

Audition and Vision in Learning Languages

My first research project in foreign languages was entitled "Sensory Interrelationships in the Automated Teaching of Foreign Languages," and it was supported by a small research grant which I was awarded from the U.S. Office of Education in 1960-61. The results, using an intricate research design (Asher, 1961, 1962a, and 1964) showed that the sensory channel of *vision* produced more efficient learning and retention when contrasted with the sensory channel of *audition.* The findings were not especially striking, but something quite unexpected happened in the context of those experiments.

GUESSING BY THE LEARNERS

In the vision experiment, adults viewed a display such as this:

WORK

TRABAJAR TRAMITAR

Each person then made a guess as to whether *work* meant "tramitar" or "trabajar" by writing the Spanish that was thought to be correct. The experimenter then said "right" if the choice was correct or "wrong" if it was incorrect. Notice that in the first exposure to Spanish, each person "guessed" the Spanish equivalent to the English from two choices and notice also in Table 1 that each pair of items in Spanish were almost identical since there was usually only a one phoneme difference.

TABLE 1: Sample Items†

THOSE WHO	LOS QUE	BOSQUE
WE GAVE	DIMOS	DAMAS
TICKETS	ENTRADAS	ENTRE DOS
COURTESY	CORTESÍA	CONDESA
(THEY) LEARN	APRENDEN	ATIENDEN
BAD HUMOR	MAL HUMOR	PUNDONOR
TO	A	AHÍ
TO WORK	TRABAJAR	TRAMITAR
WE SAY	DECIMOS	DECÍMO
WE GIVE	DAR	MAR
HE KISSED HER	LA BESÓ	LA PESO
WHO	QUE	AQUÍ

†*From Appendix A, pages 75-77 in Asher, James J. "Sensory Interrelationships in the Automatic Teaching of Foreign Languages," Final Report Title VII Project No. 578, National Defense Education Act of 1958, Grant No. 7-04-091, Sept. 1, 1961.*

The adults in the audition experiment *listened* to a word in English such as "work," then listened to the choices of "tramitar" and "trabajar." In the first exposure to the task, each person guessed which of the target language utterances matched the meaning of the English. The person's selection was made by pronouncing the Spanish utterance thought to be correct and as in the vision experiment, the experimenter responded with either "right" or "wrong." Remember that the people participating in the experiments were carefully screened to insure that all had no prior training or exposure to Spanish.

Now, here is the puzzle: As you can see in Table 2, for those who learned either visually or aurally, their guesses were highly correlated with almost every measure: initial acquisition practice, relearning through a different sense channel, retention, and transfer-of-learning.

The higher one's guessing score on the first exposure for the

50-items, the faster one learned vocabulary items, the more one retained, and the more flexible one was in transferring to a different task to be learned (i.e., understanding sentences and stories).

For another group of learners who had no prior exposure to Spanish, we administered the 50-item guessing measure. Then each person had a demanding task in which they viewed an English word

TABLE 2

Correlations Between the **Guessing Score** and Each of the Performance Measures†

	Visual Subjects N=20	Aural Subjects N=20
Initial Vocabulary Learning	.820***	.782***
Relearning of Vocabulary (through a different sensory mode)	.543**	.683***
Sentences Understood (after initial learning of vocabulary)		
#words correct	.510*	.466*
#meanings	.385*	.424*
Sentences Understood (after relearning)		
#words correct	.626***	.364
#meanings	.696***	.240
Story Understanding		
Reading	.699***	.533**
Listening	.665***	.472**
Retention		
Recall	.698***	.544**
Recognition	.612***	.562***

Note: Significant beyond *.05, **.01, ***.005

†(Adapted from Table 11, page 32, Asher, James J. Final Report for "Sensory Interrelationships in the Automated Teaching of Foreign Language," Sept. 1, 1961.)

such as "work" and then wrote the Spanish equivalent which was "trabajar." Still another group listened to the English and pronounced the Spanish equivalent. Notice that this task was more difficult than merely selecting which of two Spanish words was the correct meaning for an English word. Nevertheless, the results were amazingly similar: The more accurately one guessed the meaning of a word, the more rapidly one learned vocabulary items, the more one retained, and the more flexible the person was in learning other tasks (i.e., understanding sentences).

TABLE 3

Correlations Between the **Guessing Score** and Each of the Performance Measures†

	Visual Subjects N=17	Aural Subjects N=19
Initial Vocabulary Learning	.578**	.740***
Relearning of Vocabulary (through a different sensory mode)	.594**	.660***
Sentences Understood (after initial learning)		
#Words correct	.088	.701*
#Meanings	.373	611*
Sentences Understood (after relearning)		
#Words correct	.491*	.880***
#Meanings	.253	.701*
Retention		
Recall	.176	.721***
Recognition	.572**	.058

Note: Significant beyond *.05, **.01, ***.005

†(Adapted from Table 26, page 61, in Asher, 1961.)

The Power of Guessing: An Explanation

Why should guessing have a powerful relationship to learning, retention, and transfer-of-learning to future tasks? Some critics suggested that the participants in our studies did not guess but had a positive transfer from prior exposure to a Romance language such as French, Italian, or Latin. We found no evidence to support that explanation.

Other critics thought that incidental learning from the Hispanic culture (i.e., street names) in California accounted for the phenomenon. But, when we interviewed the participants, most were confident that their choices on the first exposure were "pure guesses" (Asher, 1961).

The First Trial Learning Hypothesis

My explanation for the strong relationship of "guessing" to performance is what I called the *first trial learning* hypothesis. That is, the more times one must be exposed to the learning problem (for whatever reason) before it is internalized, the more difficulty one will have later in retaining the task.

Evidence to support this idea would be to examine the relationship of exposures before learning (prelearning exposure) to retention. I expected to find that the more times one must experience the problem before it is internalized, the lower the probability of recall later. To test the hypothesis, I asked different groups of college students to learn vocabulary items in Spanish, Japanese, or Russian. Then I correlated the number of exposures each person needed to learn the items with their retention measured immediately after learning and later at intervals of 24 hours, 48 hours, and one month.

As may be seen in Table 4, all of the correlations were extremely high and negative which is interpreted to mean that the *less* practice each person required before they were learned, the *higher* the retention.

TABLE 4

Correlations Across *Subjects* for Practice-before-learning and Retention†

Language	N	Sensory Mode	Time Delay	r
Japanese	20	A	None	—.87
Japanese	20	V	None	—.85
Japanese	20	A	48 hours	—.66
Japanese	20	V	48 hours	—.61
Spanish I	20	A	48 hours	—.63
Spanish I	20	V	48 hours	—.85
Spanish I	20	A	96 hours	—.48
Spanish I	20	V	96 hours	—.68
Spanish II	15	A	over one month	—.79
Spanish II	16	V	over one month	—.57**
Spanish III	19	A	None	—.65
Spanish III	16	V	None	—.78
Spanish III	19	A	48 hours	—.76
Spanish III	16	V	48 hours	—.69
Russian	20	A	None	—.56
Russian	20	V	None	—.65
Russian	20	A	48 hours	—.34(NS)
Russian	20	V	48 hours	—.95

N = number of people who learned different language items.
A = auditory presentation V = visual presentation
Note.—All coefficients are at the .005 level except r = —.57 for which p = .01 and the r = —.34, which is not significant at .05.
†(From Table 2, page 102, in Asher, James J. Evidence for "genuine" one-trial learning. *International Review of Applied Linguistics,* 1963, vol 1/2, 98-103.)

Based on this evidence, I believed that the optimal conditions for learning was in one-trial on the *first exposure* to the information that was to be internalized. The super-learners were those people who needed the fewest exposures before assimilation because the process of acquisition seemed to be that minimal input of effort in practice resulted in maximum retrieval later. Those who required more exposures to learn were least efficient in retrieval.

The puzzle was this: Why can some people acquire something (information or the making of a novel response as in producing a foreign utterance) on the first exposure while others must experience the input over and over before intake occurs. Some people are "quick studies" and others are "slow learners." Intelligence is the first explanation that comes to mind; but intelligence is no explanation but rather a conclusion — a label saying merely that people learn at different rates.

I tried a different strategy. Instead of exploring factors within people such as "intelligence" or "aptitude," let's look *outside* of people. Let's look at the structure of the task.

TABLE 5

Correlations Across *Items* between
Practice-before-learning and Retention†

Language	N	Sensory Mode	Time Delay	r
Japanese	40	A	None	—.75
Japanese	40	V	None	—.74
Japanese	20	A	48 hours	—.64
Japanese	20	V	48 hours	—.44*
Spanish I	30	A	48 hours	—.53
Spanish I	30	V	48 hours	—.55
Spanish I	20	A	96 hours	—.57
Spanish I	20	V	96 hours	—.79
Spanish II	20	A	over one month	—.72
Spanish II	20	V	over one month	—.66
Spanish III	20	A	None	—.81
Spanish III	20	V	None	—.39*
Spanish III	30	A	48 hours	—.72
Spanish III	30	V	48 hours	—.62
Russian	40	A	None	—.65
Russian	40	V	None	—.61
Russian	20	A	48 hours	—.69
Russian	20	V	48 hours	—.81

N = number of paired items presented for learning

A = auditory presentation V = visual presentation

†(From Table 1, page 101, in Asher, James J. Evidence for "genuine" one-trial learning. *International Review of Applied Linguistics,* 1963, Vol 1/2, 98-103.)

For example, the closer an *item* in Japanese, Spanish, or Russian is to being internalized *on the first exposure,* the better should be the retention immediately after learning, and later at intervals of 48 hours, 96 hours and one month. This is exactly the finding in Table 5 with extremely high inverse correlations, meaning that the *fewer* times an item must be exposed to a learner before internalization, the *higher* the retention.

The explanation I believed to be true, was first trial learning, but before that could be accepted with confidence, it was necessary to eliminate rival hypotheses. For instance, can it be that the more difficult the foreign utterance is to pronounce, the slower the learning? When the factor of *pronunciation difficulty* for Japanese was removed with the statistical technique of partial correlation, the original correlations were almost unchanged.

Another rival explanation was *length* of the foreign utterance. The rival hypothesis was that the shorter the foreign utterance, the fewer repetitions necessary to internalize the items. Again, when this factor was removed statistically, the original correlations were unchanged.

Other rival explanations eliminated were (a) the more *pleasing* the foreign utterance was perceived by learners, the fewer repetitions necessary; (b) the more *associations* evoked by the foreign utterance, the fewer the repetitions, and (c) items "easier to learn" as judged by a linguist's contrastive analysis would require fewer exposures before learning occurred. All of those alternative hypotheses were eliminated.

But now we had a *fact* without an explanation. The fact was that the *closer* items were to being learned on the first exposure, the more likely it was that those items would be retained — either immediately after learning (short-term) or hours, days — even a month later (long-term).

ONE TRIAL LEARNING

How can we alter the task to produce one trial — preferably first trial learning? Although *first trial learning* was a novel idea, *one trial learning* had been explored and debated for years by two opposing groups of psychologists.

One group, the so-called associationists (often referred to as S-R Psychologists) believed that learning was incremental. That is, with each exposure to the task to be learned, one made a stronger and stronger association. Each trial was a stamp that made the imprint in the mind more and more distinct. With each exposure, the "bond" between items was "cemented" and a "habit" was formed.

The opponents were the Gestalt Psychologists who believed that when learning happened, it occurred suddenly in one trial. For example, the famous Gestalt psychologist, Wolfgang Köhler, demonstrated the "aha" phenomenon with this problem that he presented to an ape: Bananas were placed outside the animal's cage just out of reach. Inside the cage was a stick. The ape stretched his hand through the bars and tried again and again to grasp the bananas—but always without success. Then he withdrew into the cage, picked up the stick, and toyed with it—sometimes banging it on the floor or on the bars. Then, suddenly, in a seeming burst of insight, the animal thrust the stick through the bars and pulled the bananas within his reach.

In another of Köhler's experiments, bananas were hung on the ceiling of the cage, out of the animal's reach. On the floor were several wooden boxes. The ape tried in vain many times to reach the bananas. His rage increased with each unsuccessful attempt. Then the ape withdrew to a corner of the cage and seemed to have given-up when suddenly, in a burst of activity, he stacked the boxes on top of each other and clambered up the boxes to reach the bananas.

The Gestaltists believed that when learning happened, it occurred in a flash, in a burst of insight signalled often with a person exclaiming, as did Archimedes leaping from his bathtub, "Aha, I've got the answer!" Learning happened in one-trial. Further, they believed that mere frequency of exposure to "associate" two items of information was superficial. For example, as the Gestalt psychologist, Max Wertheimer, illustrated in his classic book, *Productive Thinking,* for authentic learning to take place, a person must understand the "inner structure" (the pattern) of the solution.

Wertheimer (1959) used problems in mathematics to demonstrate his concept of "inner structure." For example, consider this geometric figure called a parallelogram:

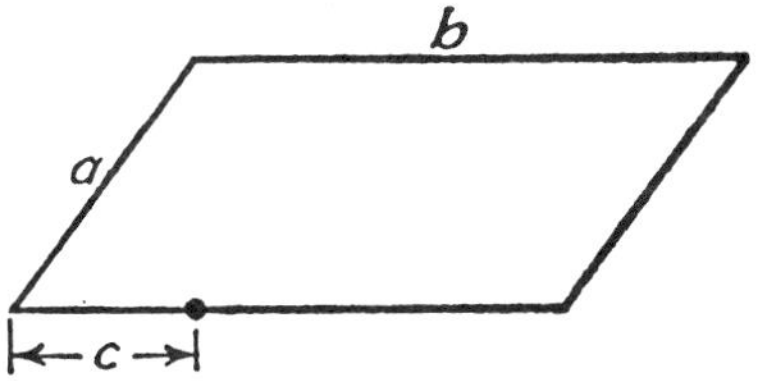

Figure 1*

*(From Wertheimer, M. *Productive Thinking,* 1959, 14.)

You can teach children to find the area of any parallelogram in the world using "frequency of association." For instance, show the children how to use their rulers to measure a, b, and c. Then show them step-by-step how to find the area by performing the arithmetic operations in the formula of $b\sqrt{(a+b)\ (a-c)}$. Have the children repeat the procedure with many parallelograms of different sizes and "voila," the children now have the skill to solve the problem of finding the area for *any parallelogram in the world.*

"But," Wertheimer said, "this is not true learning because the children do not understand the 'inner structure' of the problem. As proof, come into the class the next day and tip the parallelogram on its side by drawing this on the board:

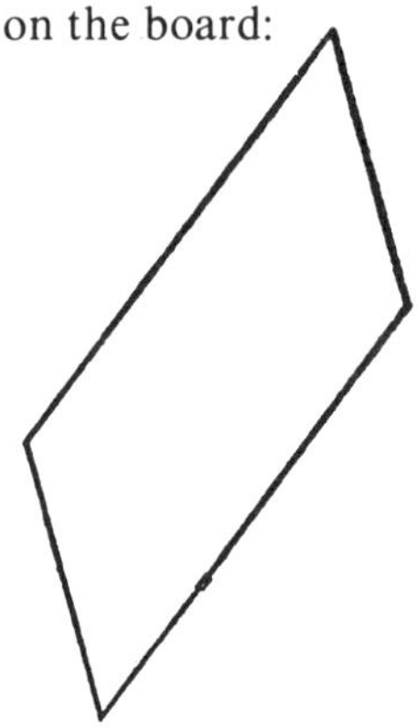

Figure 2

Then ask the children to find the area without calling it a parallelogram. Their response will be, "We can't do it!" If you ask, "Why not?" they will answer, "because we have never seen that problem before." The "inner structure" is still a mystery to the children.

Incidentally, the inner structure is this:

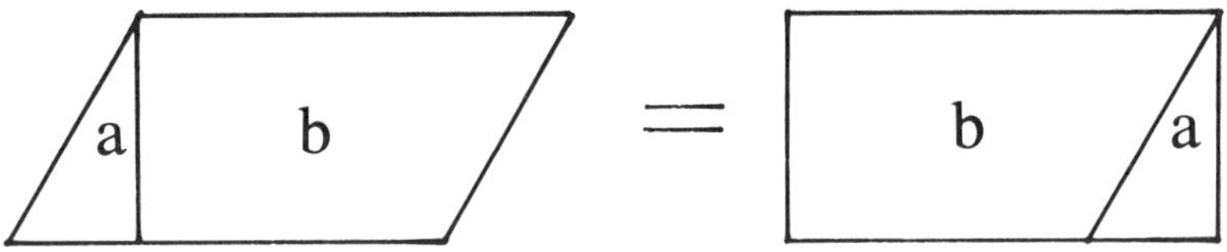

Figure 3

In Figure 3, when you cut off the triangle labeled "a" from the left side of the parallelogram and paste it on the right side, you now have the familiar rectangle. The area of a rectangle in the length multiplied by the width.

The argument between the Associationists and the Gestaltists raged for 25 years. Now it seems clear to me that the argument was specious because the Associationists used *verbal tasks* almost exclusively in their learning experiments while the Gestalts used *non-verbal tasks* such as pictures, patterns, and experiences. One group was exploring left brain input while the other group was looking at right brain input.

Input to the left brain in *verbal tasks* is a slow, incremental multiple exposure process because the left "resists" the novel. Input to the right brain is a *pattern* which is understood usually in a flash —in one-trial or one exposure. Each group was looking at different sides of the brain. No wonder their conclusions were irreconcilable.

But of course, the concept of an independent left and right brain is only a recent finding which won Professor Roger Sperry of the California Institute of Technology a Nobel Prize. Twenty-five years ago, our picture of the brain's role in learning was limited to the concept of "equipotentiality," — an idea developed by Harvard psychologist, Karl S. Lashley. Lashley conducted many ablation experiments in which an animal learned a task, then a portion of the brain was removed to discover how the impairment affected the animal's performance on the task previously learned. From this work, Lashley concluded that any part of the brain could assimilate and store learning. No matter what part of the brain was excised in animals, the animal could still demonstrate retention for a learned task. *Location* in the brain was not important, only *how much* of the brain was intact. The more brain that was untouched by the surgeon's knife, the more capable the animal was in making an appropriate response to a learning problem.

Curiously, almost ignored in this controversy of incremental versus one-trial learning was the extraordinary demonstration of memory by people with mnemonic skills. For example, one individual was introduced to 500 people in an audience on a popular night-time television talk show. Immediately, after only one exposure, the mnemonic expert was able to call each person in the audience by name (first name and surname).

Books written by experts in mnemonics suggest that information we want to recall should be integrated into a picture we create in our mind. For instance, if I am introduced to Joe Simmons, I may create a picture of Mr. Simmons reclining on a mattress (since Simmons is a famous mattress manufacturer). Given our current understanding of brain lateralization, the memory experts were recommending that we shift from the left to the right side of the brain where information is processed in pictures and patterns. Instead of attempting the *direct* storage of words and numbers through repetition (left brain input), the mnemonic experts recommended *indirect* storage by inserting the symbolic information into imaginary pictures we create in our minds (right brain input).

It always amazed me that learning psychologists seemed to dismiss the suggestions from mnemonics as trivial and irrelevant in deciphering the puzzle of how people learn. The problem was that learning theorists had no model which allowed them to assimilate observations from the field of mnemonics. Mnemonics were an interesting curiosity from the field of entertainment that did not fit comfortably with learning theories of that time. (As a parallel example from the late 1800s, Sigmund Freud observed that hypnosis was dismissed by the medical profession as a stage trick of entertainers —a parlor toy which had no place in the serious business of healing.) Mnemonics were seen as "magic tricks" that we could not expect ordinary people to master.

A High Velocity Logic Theory of Information Processing

As I mentioned, my work in the nineteen sixties convinced me that practice before learning was detrimental to the retention of information. The optimal conditions would produce learning in one exposure. But what are the optimal conditions for first trial learning?

At this time I was also working on a problem solving model which I thought could be helpful in solving the mystery of how to achieve first trial learning (Asher, 1963b).

The model worked like this: Learning, I believed — and still do believe — is the *reverse* of problem solving. For example, learning means to internalize an existing concept. Problem solving means that one *repairs* an existing concept that has a tension-producing flaw. Often we are unaware of flaws in an existing concept until someone, usually an inventor, presents an alternate concept for comparison. The invention of the microcomputer is a classic illustration. Before the computer, people were content to perform accounting tasks with a pencil and a pad of legal-size paper. Once a person performs the data analysis on a computer with a spreadsheet, pencil-and-paper instantly becomes a stressful and unacceptable procedure.

Once a concept has been internalized (that is, learned), there is what I have called "concept constancy" (CC). The concept has its own life and it resists any threat to its existence. Literally, a concept once internalized, becomes reified. Using a contemporary brain lateralization model, the left brain will resist the introduction of a novel concept, but once the idea is incorporated, the left brain will resist any threat to remove or change the idea.

Problem solving is the *reverse* of learning because it is an intrusion to change or even replace an existing concept. Problem solving is a process which I call, "concept disruption." (CD). It is "difficult" for the left brain to accept a new concept but once the concept is accepted, it is "difficult" for the left brain to accept any modification or replacement. Therefore, strategies are needed to produce concept disruption.

Here are some examples of strategies designed to disrupt an existing concept. Perhaps the most famous strategy is brainstorming. The procedure is to suspend critical thinking while a group of people suggest many, many possible solutions to a problem. The instructions to the group are to "think wild" and "the more ideas the better—we want quantity, quantity, quantity" and "the more fantastic and far-fetched your ideas, the better because later we can evaluate your ideas for practicality." Notice the conscious attempt to silence what I call "the automaticity of the left brain." That is, the left brain is like the cruise control of your car—it remains on continually during our waking hours unless we intervene to shut it off. For example, when we experience anything novel such as viewing a movie, the utterance that spontaneously comes out of our mouth as we walk out of the theater with a friend is, "How did you like the film?" or "What did you think of the movie?" The left brain automatically evaluates any new input.

Alex Osborn (1957), the creator of brainstorming, realized 40 years ago—long before the left-right brain research, that the *judicial mind,* as he called it, must be quieted before the *creative mind* was free to operate without inhibitions. People with a natural inclination for creative thinking spontaneously respond to new ideas by thinking of reasons why it will work. Most people, however, are ready to explain persuasively *in detail* why the novel idea will not work. Most people are able immediately to produce a flow of critical thoughts to block or destroy any suggestion that threatens to disrupt an existing concept.

Incidentally, I do not consider puzzles to be a genuine problem solving activity. Puzzles are concepts intentionally engineered with flaws that can be repaired with *ready-made answers* to be discovered by the puzzle-solver. This activity is entertainment because the participant knows that a resolution exists and is available. In genuine problem solving, existing concepts have flaws that create two sources of tension. *First,* the imperfections within the concept are tension-producing and *secondly,* answers are not apparent and are not readily available which means a situation of ambiguity which is also tension-producing.

I wanted to apply concept constancy and its nemesis, concept disruption to language learning. My idea was this: When we internalize (that is, learn) a concept, the conditions of learning can make it either easy or difficult later to modify or even replace the internalized concept. Using psychological terms, the context of learning can produce, in the future, either positive or negative transfer. If positive, then a future concept can be assimilated in fewer exposures; if negative, then the assimilation will require more exposures. What then, should be the ideal context of learning?

As a clue in solving the problem of the ideal context for learning, I recalled an idea that I wrote in an unpublished 1959 paper entitled, "A Symbolic Logic Theory of Perception." In that paper I suggested that visual illusions, which I will illustrate next, can be explained by a high velocity logic which the mind uses to process incoming data. For example, consider this illusion:

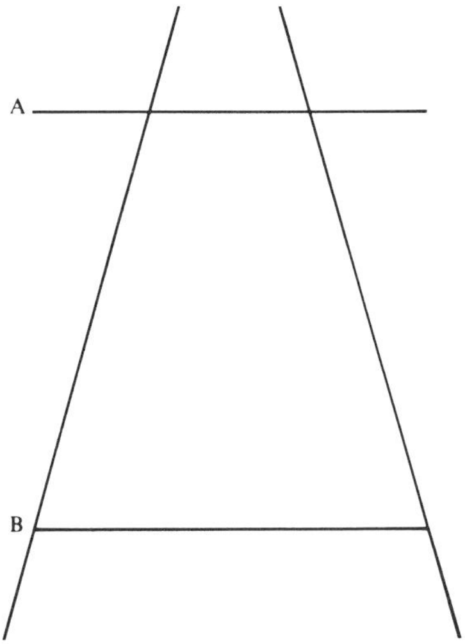

Figure 4

Most people see the horizontal line A as *longer* than line B. This is an illusion since A and B are identical in length.

I hypothesized that the pattern in Figure 4 is processed by the mind at lightening-fast speed with a logical analysis like this:

The vertical lines appear to converge in the distance; hence, they must *actually* be parallel.

If crossbar A is *actually* identical with crossbar B, then both will appear to be flush with the vertical lines. Since the crossbars do not appear to be flush, A is *not actually* equal to B in length.

If A is *actually* shorter than B, then A should appear well within the limits of the vertical lines. Since this condition is not met, A is *not actually* shorter than B.

Finally, if A is *not actually* equal to or shorter than B, then the only remaining possibility is that *A must be longer than B.* Thus we see A as longer than B even though by physical measurement, A is equal to B.

If the mind has a high-speed logic processor mechanism for evaluating incoming data, then it probably functions in verbal learning. As a direct test of the logic hypothesis, I asked one of my graduate students, Brad Fallentine, to collect data for his master's thesis using this design: Students would associate pairs of nonsense syllables* under three conditions. Some nonsense syllables would be "closed." That is, whenever the learner would see, for example, **WEV**, the person wrote **WAK.** The internal logic, I hypothesized, would be that the person learns that **WEV** means **WAK** and nothing else. The concept is "closed"—there is concept constancy. It will be theoretically more difficult to associate a new response to **WEV** other than **WAK** since the mind has registered that **WEV** means **WAK** and nothing else.

In the second condition, other nonsense syllables were "open" to accept modifications since the context of learning was this: When the person sees, for instance, **LAF**, the individual responds by writing **CEN** or . . . The internal logic of the mind is that **LAF** means **CEN** or something else. The mind associates **LAF** with **CEN** but it is open to another possible response.

In the third context of learning, when the person saw **PIL**, the individual wrote **LIV** and . . . The logic was that **PIL** means **LIV** and something else. Again the concept learned is open to assimilate additional information.

Then we asked the learners to associate new pairs of items as for instance when they saw **WEV**, they wrote a new response of **BEC**; when they viewed **LAF**, they wrote **GUL**; and in response to **PIL** they wrote **KEN**. I expected that if logic was operating at high velocity

*To the non-psychologist, something that is named *nonsense* must be a misprint because why should anyone take seriously anything labeled as "nonsense"? Nonsense syllables were invented in 1885 by the great German researcher, Hermann Ebbinghaus. The idea was to use symbols that were empty of meaning such as **MEV, ALZ,** and **DVR** because the intent was to simplify the learning task to skeletal components (much like the reduction of meaning in linguistics to the phoneme) so that the underlying principles of learning could be made visible.

below the level of conscious awareness, then it would require many more exposures for concept disruption of closed concepts than the open concepts. In fact, there should be no disruption of open concepts and hence, fewer trials to internalize new associations.

The results confirmed my hypothesis: Those concepts that were "open" when initially learned, required on the average about 30% fewer exposures to assimilate concept changes compared with concepts that were "closed." As further proof that high velocity logic was operating in each learner, I expected that future concept changes would be easier for the "open" concept of the form **A** means **B** *or* **C** compared with the "open" concept of the form **A** means **B** *and* **C.**

The reason was that in the first context of learning, the individual anticipates that *either* **B** or **C** can follow **A,** but in the second context of learning, one expects that *both* **B** and **C** should be present. Since both **B** and **C** were not present in the follow-up concept changes, there was more "noise" (i.e., resistance to inclusion) from an unconscious high velocity evaluation of the input which blocked "intake."

The results again confirmed the hypothesis, since on the average, the "open" form of **A** means **B** *or* **C** required about 30% *fewer exposures* to assimilate concept changes compared with the "open" form of **A** means **B** *and* **C.**

The Crucial Test: A Cause-Effect Theory of Learning

It seemed to me, as I explained in a 1964 paper published in the *Journal of Humanistic Psychology,* that if the target to be internalized was structured so that the incoming raw data was validated by the high velocity information processing mechanism, then the sensory input would be converted into information on the *first exposure* and placed in long-term storage for retrieval anytime in the future. This meant to me that the incoming raw data had to be evaluated as "truth" or "believable" or "usable" by the cognitive file clerk. One way, I thought, to establish the believability of incoming data would be to demonstrate a cause-effect relationship.

For this demonstration, I enlisted that aid of a graduate student from Japan whose name was Shirou Kunihira and my secretary, Alice Dickie. The plan was this: Shirou would utter a direction in Japanese, then Alice and I would *repeat* the command, and then act it out. The idea was that the command form was the ideal cause-effect relationship because language produced (or caused) an action in the learner.

After five minutes of hearing Japanese commands, repeating

them, and then acting them out, it was obvious to me that the procedure was not working. Each new command seemed to erase the memory of the previous command. Nothing was retained. Of course, I included production in the model because, at that time, it was assumed by all living linguistic authorities that production was the primary skill to be learned. "Language was talk; talk was language." All other skills were secondary.

But something was not working. At this point, I suggested that the three of us sit down, and relax. While we were resting, I turned to Shirou and said, "Can you give us a simple one-word direction in Japanese that will get us up from the chairs, but we will not repeat what you say. You say something in Japanese, do the action yourself and we will silently follow you." Shirou replied, "Shall I use the polite form in Japanese which will involve more than one word?" "No," I said. "Keep it simple . . . let's have one word only, if possible."

Shirou grimaced and objected with, "I can use the imperative you hear in the military, but it is harsh and considered rude in ordinary conversation." I thought about it for a few moments; then I said: "If the military command form is simple one-word commands, please use it. Our objective is to internalize Japanese. Later we can work with the more complex polite form."

So, we started with: "Tate" uttered by Shirou as he stood up and we also stood up. Then I motioned for him to direct us to sit down which he did with "suware" and we all sat down. "Again," I said. "Let's try it again." So we did. Then I motioned for him to say something in Japanese to get us walking which he did with "aruke" and we all walked across the room. Then I held up my hand to stop and Shirou said, "tomare." Then he said "maware" and we turned. I swirled my finger for a repeat performance of maware followed by a turn. Then we did it again.

To this routine we added: "Tobe" for jump, "kagame" for squat and "sagera" for walk backwards. After four or five more trials with Shirou uttering a direction in Japanese and acting with us, I then asked Shirou to be seated, utter the Japanese directions and we would attempt to perform the physical actions on our own. To our amazement, it worked!

We were excited. I said: "Now, Shirou, let each of us try it alone. I'll go first." I did it without making a mistake. Then Alice tried it alone. We both performed perfectly. It seemed like a miracle.

"Let's stretch the directions," I said. "I will point to a location in the room and you direct us in Japanese to walk to that location." What followed were expansions such as these:

To ni aruite ike. (Walk to the door.)

Isu ni hashitte ike. (Run to the chair.)

Tsukue ni hashitte ike. (Run to the desk.)

Again, a perfect performance from each of us for the expanded directions in Japanese. The expansions continued with the complexity as illustrated with these examples:

Kami to hon to enpitsu o motte isu ni suware.
(Pick up the paper, book, and pencil and sit on the chair.)

Tsuku ni aruite itte enpitsu to hon o oke.
(Walk to the desk and put down the pencil and book.)

Mado ni hashitte itte hon o motte tsukue ni oite isu ni suware.
(Run to the window, pick up the book, put it on the desk, then sit on the chair.)

Incidentally, when I typed, from earlier publications (Asher, 1964; and Kunihira and Asher, 1965), the Japanese examples you have just read, it was the first time in over twenty years that I have seen the Japanese in print; but those utterances are so thoroughly internalized that I can still hear Shirou uttering each direction as if he was in the room reading over my shoulder as I typed.

As the directions in Japanese became more and more complex, I realized that we were internalizing the target language in *chunks* rather than word-by-word, and I also realized that retention was *long-term.* (The Japanese utterances did not disappear from memory. Our bodies could respond accurately to a direction ten minutes later or hours later.)

Another fact: The more complex the direction in Japanese, the easier it was to understand. There was still another interesting twist. As we went along, our sense of time disappeared. We "worked" for hours with no awareness that time was passing. And the more we worked, the more exhilarated we were.

Another Discovery: Zero Trial Learning

I continued to urge Shirou to recombine the constituents to create surprise directions — ones we had never heard before nor seen modeled. We were thrilled that either Alice or I could respond perfectly to Japanese utterances we had never heard before. Our output in performance was *greater* than the input from the "instructor." Certainly this was even better than my goal of one-trial learning on the first exposure to the material to be learned. This was *zero trial learning* since we could respond perfectly to novel utterances — ones we had never heard before.

After several hours of successfully internalizing one Japanese direction after another in more and more elaborated and convoluted patterns, we sat down to rest and debrief about a most extraordinary intellectual adventure. We were on a natural "high." Shirou seriously suggested, "Let's pack our suitcases tonight, move to Japan and open a language school to teach English with this approach. The Japanese will love learning English in this manner."

To illustrate the difficulty that Japanese students were experiencing in trying to acquire English, Shirou told us this story: Diligently for twelve years he had studied English in school in Japan. On his first trip to America, the American customs inspector boarded the ship, approached Shirou and asked, "What is your name?" Of course the inspector blended the words together in a natural speech rhythm that sounded like: "Whachyurname?" Shirou knew this must be English but he could not decipher it. The inspector repeated the question, "Whach yur name?" Again, no glimmer of understanding. Undoubtedly Shirou had heard in school: "What - is - your - name?" But never "Whachyurname?" This must be something simple the man is asking me, Shirou thought, but what is it? Did I waste twelve years in school studying English? He was flooded with feelings of failure, and tears began streaming down his face.

The Laboratory

We did not leave for Japan to open a language school, but instead I persuaded the University to let me use as a laboratory, a small classroom which was located directly across from the men's room. It turned out to be an ideal location because everyone that came out of the men's room was invited into the laboratory to learn a sample of Japanese. We had an unending supply of subjects to try this strange language-body experiment in which the learner was silent, listened to the "noise" coming from Shirou's mouth, then performed the action he observed Shirou doing.

One of the people that came out of the men's room was a professor's son, 12-year-old Harold Keely, Jr. I asked the boy for a few minutes of his time to help me with a language experiment and he agreed. After working with him for about ten minutes using my language-body learning strategy, the boy asked to stay longer and I consented. So he worked the entire afternoon absorbing Japanese through body movements. "Would it be all right if I came back tomorrow for more Japanese?," he asked. It was the summer holiday from school, but Hal insisted that he wanted to return every day (which meant a long bus ride from his home to the University) for more Japanese, and he brought two other neighborhood friends with him.

It was becoming clear that the language-body strategy worked with people of all ages. It was also clear that the approach worked with any language since I invited foreign students who spoke many different languages to play the role of the language instructor uttering "noises" to direct the movements of students."

Then I made another fascinating discovery. I arranged with three foreign students at the University to come to the laboratory and play the instructor's role. For example, learners would acquire a scenario by following directions uttered in Japanese. Then play-out the scenario again, but with someone directing the person in Persian. Finally, there was a third replay except this time the directions were in Portuguese.

When learners were comfortable in acting out a situation in three languages, I tried this: At a prearranged, secret-signal one of the three foreign instructors would utter the next direction to the learner. In other words, the learner would hear a direction in Persian to stand; then the next direction to walk may be in Portuguese, and then the person may be directed to stop in Japanese. One direction followed another rapidly and unpredictably in Persian, Portuguese, or Japanese. The result was astonishing because every person who experienced body movements in many tongues, perceived and responded as if the person was hearing only one language. There was no confusion. There was no hesitation. There were no mistakes.

The Rosetta Stone of language acquisition was in a choreography of language and body movements. Nature had revealed, I believed, one of the great secrets of learning.

Let's Get a Research Grant

The results were so sensational that I wanted to get a federal research grant to continue the work. But, I had learned a lesson which was this: When I attempted to explain to people how the language-body principle worked, they did not understand. They would say, "Oh, yes. That's just like the Army Language School" or "That's just like Berlitz" and I would say, "No . . . NO. this is different. Let me explain again."

The only way I could effectively communicate what this was about would be a "live" demonstration. Now here's the problem. The federal agencies in Washington insisted that proposals for research grants be in writing. I tried to by-pass the written medium by requesting: Look, I've discovered something exciting about language learning which cannot be communicated effectively on paper. Please send a representative to San Jose and I will demonstrate. They replied: "We're busy people. Write it down and send it to us like everyone else does."

Well, I tried, but it did not work. They didn't understand. Each of my proposals was rejected. After the disappointment diminished, I toyed with a different plan. It was this: Since the only effective way to communicate this idea is a demonstration, and since I couldn't get agency people to leave Washington to witness a demonstration, why not send the demonstration to them. (Remember, these were the days before the existence of television tape.) I had a master's degree in radio and television which involved some incidental training in the expensive medium of making motion pictures. More and more, my thinking focused upon motion pictures as the ideal way to communicate the language-body principle.

Maybe a Motion Picture is the Answer

My small laboratory was on the third floor of a classroom building. In the basement of that building was the college motion picture expert, Richard Szumski. His work was to assist faculty with slides, photographs, and tapes that could be used to improve instruction. When I visited Szumski in his basement office, I said, "Dick, I want to make a 16 millimeter sound motion picture, perhaps thirty minutes in length."

Dick removed the pipe from between his teeth and replied, "Do you know how expensive it is to make a 16 millimeter sound motion picture that is thirty minutes long?"

"I don't care how expensive it is. I have something important I want to communicate to people and I think film is the most effective way to do it."

Dick relit his pipe, exhaled smoke and said thoughtfully: "Tell me what the film is about."

I said, "Dick, I can't tell you what the film is about."

Lines of perplexity radiated across his face. He told me later that he wondered about my sanity. "Listen," he said, leaning forward and pointing the stem of his pipe at my chest for emphasis, "You want me to help you make a film but you won't tell me what it's about. I'm fairly bright. Explain it to me."

"Dick, you don't understand. It has nothing to do with brightness or dullness. An explanation will not communicate the idea."

"Then how in the world can we proceed?"

There was a long pause and then I asked him, "Do you have any children?" He explained that he had a son who was three and a daughter who was eight. "Can you," I asked, "bring your daughter to my laboratory tomorrow at 1:30? I won't tell you what will happen, but I would like you to discover what this is all about for yourself."

At precisely 1:30 the next afternoon, Szumski appeared in my laboratory with his 8-year-old daughter who was wearing a colorful party dress. "Dick," I began, "do you trust me?" He nodded, so I followed with: "OK, then I would like you to leave your daughter with my research assistant, Shirou Kunihira, for twenty minutes. You and I will go across the street and get some coffee while Shirou works with your daughter. We'll come back in twenty minutes and see how much Japanese your daughter understands."

We had a cup of coffee and were chatting when Szumski looked at his watch and said, "Your time is up. Shall we return to your laboratory?" When we returned, I said to Shirou: "Show us what Valerie understands in Japanese."

Shirou began uttering directions in Japanese. As he spoke, the child responded confidently, and without hesitation. As the directions increased in intricacy, the expression on Szumski's face was incredulity.

When the demonstration was over, Dick turned to me and whistled. "You know," he confided, "if that wasn't my own daughter I wouldn't have believed this if you tried to explain it to me." Then he added, "You can count on me to help you make a 16 millimeter motion picture."

My First Motion Picture

We began work on the film with me as the writer, director and narrator, Shirou as the instructor of Japanese, and Richard Szumski as the technical expert responsible for the photography and production.

I wanted to demonstrate three thoughts: The first was the fact that average American students can rapidly acquire an understanding of spoken Japanese in chunks rather than word-by-word. Secondly, once students have internalized a complex sample of Japanese, there is long-term retention which is at least a year in length. And thirdly, output-is-more-than-input which means that learners can understand novel directions—ones they had not previously heard in training. This, to me, was the essence of fluency because if learners can only understand the exact utterances used in training without being able to comprehend utterances recombined into unfamiliar sentences, the training has low efficiency.

Again, the three messages I wanted to communicate in this 16 millimeter black-and-white film were: rapid comprehension of a target language, long-term retention, and fluency as demonstrated when learners understand novel utterances—ones they had never heard before. The final product was a fifteen minute motion picture entitled, *"Demonstration of a New Strategy in Language Learning."* In the film (see page 5-16), I introduced for the first time, a name for this new strategy for language learning. I called it, "The Total Physical Response" — a name I lived to regret.

In the summer of 1964, after completing the film in Japanese, I decided to increase my understanding of linguistics by attending the sessions sponsored by the Linguistics Institute of America at the University of Washington in Seattle.

This was "basic training" in linguistics which I thoroughly enjoyed. For a psychologist whose training was limited to verbal learning, it was exciting to expand my understanding to dimensions of natural language such as phonology, morphology, syntax and semantics.

During that summer in Seattle with its picture-postcard weather, students were invited to a demonstration by linguist, Kenneth Pike. I was seated in the gallery of a huge auditorium which was filled to capacity. On stage were four or five chalkboards, a chair, and a table on which were a few items such as a feather, a pencil, and a book.

Dr. Pike, who was unknown to me at the time, was introduced and, accompanied by a thunderous ovation, strolled on stage dressed casually in slacks and a short-sleeved Hawaiian shirt. He bowed graciously to acknowledge the applause.

Then a comely, bronze-skinned woman dressed in a colorful sarong was ushered on stage to be met by Dr. Pike, whose task was this: With no information about where the woman was from or what her native language was — decipher, within a few hours, how the language works. It was explained to the audience that Dr. Pike would show that he had successfully deciphered the target language when he produces one novel sentence after another.

For me it was a "wowsville" demonstration because he deciphered the language through a **reverse** *language-body* communication. For example, Dr. Pike would perform an action and gesture for the woman to tell him what he had done. He, for instance, picked up the feather and pointed to it, gesturing for her to identify it. When she did, he wrote the vocabulary item on the board in phonetic script.

Then he *dropped* the feather and gestured for her to tell him what he had done which he quickly wrote on the board. Next he *picked up* the feather; she spoke in her native tongue, and Dr. Pike translated the "noise" into phonetic script.

Clearly he was searching for the *pattern* of the language in utterances as:

put down . . .
pick up . . .
touch the . . .
open the . . .
close the . . .

As I recall, in less than three hours, Dr. Pike could reverse roles with the "informant" and utter a novel direction, then act it out himself and the woman would nod with approval. By novel, I mean that he was recombining constituents to produce sentences he had not used in deciphering the target language.

Always, he would write the novel sentence on the board — he filled all the chalkboards and would race from one to the other to examine and compare items — then read what he had written and perform the appropriate action.

I thought to myself, if students had the skill of listening to a "strange" language and transcribing into phonetic script, we would use the Total Physical Response for rapid internalization of comprehension, then students could transcribe the scenario using phonetic script, and almost immediately be in the production stage of language acquisition. The problem, of course, is that most people do not have Dr. Pike's skill with phonetic script.

What's in a Name?

Critics made me feel that this name which I coined, called "The Total Physical Response" was a mistake for two reasons. The first was that the name is esoteric since most people, would not understand it; and perhaps more importantly, the word, "physical" had low prestige. For example, notice that Physical Education is now called in many places, Human Performance. In academic circles, the mind is celebrated as an instrument of beauty, power, and even spirituality, but the body was perceived as something to be tolerated, but not revered.

For instance, notice the associations we have with the body such as "sins of the flesh," "weakness of the flesh," and "temptations of the flesh." We hide the body in clothing and we are encouraged to resist instincts, impulses, and impurities of the body.

Only in recent years have we witnessed a renaissance of interest in the body as a beautiful instrument of health, energy, and power. But in the 1950s and 1960s, academicians were dedicated to the development of the mind and, if possible, the denial of the body's existence.

Academicians operated with a classic dichotomy between mind and body. Hence, I was advised by colleagues to find another name—one that did not contain the word, "physical."

This bias — almost a taboo for anything physical, delayed for years, in my opinion, the consideration of TPR as a possible learning tool. Even now it is difficult for traditional theorists to fit TPR into the scheme of language acquisition because traditional linguistic theories are mind-orientated (often called cognitive learning) in which the body disappears as trivial in the learning process.

Another Attempt to Persuade Washington

Now I had a short 16 mm film that demonstrated the power of language-body learning in rapid understanding of a target language and long-term recall—over a one-year duration. I wrapped up a print and sent it with a brief cover letter and my resume to the Office of Naval Research in Washington, D.C. Simply, my message in the cover letter was that previously the Navy responded to my proposals as interesting, but at that time funding was unavailable for new projects. The enclosed film illustrates an exciting new learning principle that I would like to explore further with support from the Navy. How about it? (Of course, my cover letter was not that blunt.)

About 72 hours later, I received a long-distance call from the head of the Behavioral Science Division of the Office of Naval Research, a small, elite agency that pioneered support for research in the behavioral sciences. I was astonished to hear the voice on the other end of the line tell me that they had previewed my film and liked the idea very much. The agency had $50,000 left in their budget for this year and perhaps I could use the funds, the man explained, to continue my research.

But there was one small reservation. The Navy liked my film so much that they took the liberty of making a copy to show around the country as an illustration of the kind of research the Navy was supporting in the behavioral sciences. If I objected, the voice explained quietly, they would of course, burn the copy. Objection? Of course not. I was excited that the Navy liked my film and I appreciated their support to continue my work.

When Shirou uttered, "Tobe!" my son Jeff and Valerie Szumski enjoyed performing the action.

Shirou is directing Valerie in Japanese to catch the ball.

The Search for the Secret Behind TPR

I used the funds from the Navy to search for the secret behind language-body learning. The mystery was this: When noises coming from someone's mouth are followed by a body movement, the learner is able immediately to decipher the meaning of the noise at many levels of awareness including phonology, morphology, syntax, and semantics. Not only is there immediate understanding of the strange noises coming from someone's mouth, but the patterning of the target language is internalized in such a way that the learner is able effortlessly to reorganize constituents to understand novel sentences.

Certainly this phenomenon was the Atlantis of Linguistics because in a few exposures to a language sample in the context of body movement, we could witness in children and adults (a) the comprehension of novel sentences — ones the learner had never heard before, (b) unusually long-term retention which seemed to have the permanency observed in skill learning as when one acquires the capability to ride a bicycle or to swim with the butterfly stroke, and (c) the linguistic achievement was accomplished seemingly without effort—in a stress-free activity. When language and body movements were arranged into a choreography, this was analogous to people floating in a gravity-free environment.

But, what was there about this mysterious combination of language and body movements that produced such astonishing results? Was this an exciting discovery about human learning or an illusion created by an unknown artifact. The history of science is, after all, littered with illusions that seemed at first to be real. For example, there is a high correlation between certain types of cholesterol and heart attacks. Although most physicians are aware that a correlation does not necessarily imply a cause-effect relationship, the medical recommendation is to change one's life style to minimize cholesterol.

However, a recent finding by researchers at the Lawrence Berkeley Laboratory (Chui, 1986) suggests that some people may inherit a single gene that becomes activated after the age of 40 and then raises the levels of a harmful form of cholesterol in the blood.

Another example of illusions in science is the autonomic nervous system which was believed to be operating *automatically* beyond the conscious control of an individual. Evidence now suggests that people can achieve voluntary control of many functions once thought to be mechanical, and biologically programmed. The technique called "biofeedback" is to let a person monitor body functions such as blood pressure when changes occur with either a visual or auditory signal.

Language and body movements seem to be a beneficial combination for the internalizing information, but exactly what was the factor that enhanced learning? Was it motion? Was it a change in arousal or alertness? Was it an increase in believability that comes from personal experience? Was it an activation of a particular part of the brain that is inoperative when one is seated as in a lecture hall?

While I was thinking about how to explore the language-body phenomenon in an attempt to decipher exactly how it worked, I was intrigued with another mystery. It was this: With language-body learning, adults seemed to demonstrate a peak performance that matched the performance of children. This contradicted a universal belief that when people acquire a foreign language, children can always be expected to outperform adults.

The Myth of Children's Superiority in Language Learning

Was the belief in children's superiority a myth—another illusion? To find out, I designed an experiment (in collaboration with one of my fine graduate students, Ben S. Price) which we later published in *Child Development* (Asher and Price, 1967). The idea was simple: The belief in children's superiority seemed to be the result of observing that when a family immigrates to a foreign country, the children acquire the new language rapidly and effortlessly while their parents struggle for years, often to achieve only marginal intelligibility. What else can one conclude other than children have some unknown gift for language acquisition?

But, could the observation be explained by the context of language learning? For example, young children acquire the target language when caretakers speaking the foreign language utter one intimate direction after another for the infant to follow. Thousands of these caretaking directions move the infant through activities such as bathing, eating, dressing, going to the bathroom, and playing. Older children acquire the target language in the context of play in which other children initiate the movement of peers with directions such as, "Throw me the ball . . . Don't step on the line . . . Come here."

But what about adults? These poor creatures attempt to acquire the target language in a *non-play* context in which language is disembodied. Adults are like statues in which balloons of language appear above their heads much like the comic strips. Adults "converse" with dialogues such as this: "Hello, it's a beautiful day, isn't it?" The other person replies, "Yes it is. I hear that there may be rain this weekend."

With children, most utterances are rich in body movements that are intimately synchronized with languages; but adults have an impoverished context of learning because body movements only rarely cue the meaning of utterances.

Our hypothesis was this: If adults have an opportunity to acquire a sample of Russian in a learning context in which language is synchronized with body movements, will they understand and retain the Russian at a level equal with children? In other words, if adults are given the same opportunity as children to acquire the target language, will the "superiority of children" disappear?

The results were definitely "yes" because, as you will see in Figure 5, when adults had the opportunity to acquire language through body movements, they did not equal children, but actually surpassed children of all ages that we observed. These adults outperformed the children with dramatic differences rarely seen in human learning.

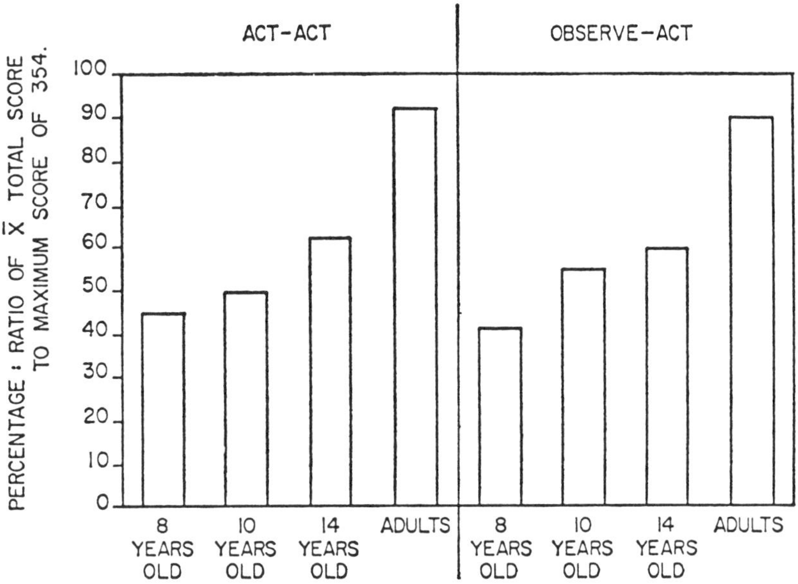

Figure 5

The "Thick Tongue" Phenomenon

"Adult Superiority" was demonstrated for understanding spoken Russian, but how about other skills such as pronunciation? In a follow-up study with Ramiro Garcia, we explored whether children had an advantage over adults in pronunciation. (Asher and Garcia, 1969).

Garcia, then a graduate student in linguistics at San Jose State University, had painstakingly collected data from a carefully selected sample of Cuban immigrants who had settled in the San Francisco Bay Area. The immigrants represented people who entered America at different ages from infancy through adulthood. The research design had a marvelous simplicity because the idea was to visit the people in their homes and record their reading of several sentences in English that contained all of the English phonemes that Hispanic speakers typically have difficulty pronouncing. Although the design was simple, the execution was extremely time-consuming because Garcia would arrange to travel, often great distances, to a person's home; and then, to quiet the fear of a stranger entering their home to "gather information," Ramiro would often sit and converse for several hours before people felt comfortable enough to proceed with the data collection.

This study is now recognized as a classic—the first of the genre which explored the relationship of age to pronunciation for people immigrating to a foreign country. The study by Asher and Garcia has been cited so frequently by researchers in the past twenty years that it was featured as a *Citation Classic* (Asher and Garcia, 1986).

The results, which have been independently confirmed in recent years by other researchers (Krashen, 1981), were that puberty seems to be the biological marker for pronunciation. That is, if a person immigrates to a foreign country before puberty, the probability is extremely high that the individual will achieve a near-native pronunciation of the target language. After puberty, only rarely will the person have a near-native pronunciation of the target language, no matter how many years the person lives in the foreign country. Our recommendation is that with equal opportunity, adults can outperform children in understanding the target language; but for fidelity of pronunciation, start the language training early in childhood—preferably *before* puberty.

The Search Continued for the Secret Behind Language-Body Learning

By 1969, I had completed thirty or forty experiments in an attempt to discover (a) the conditions in which TPR worked best, and (b) the reasons why this language-body learning strategy produced such spectacular results.

As I explained in an article entitled, "The Total Physical Response Approach to Second Language Learning" (Asher, 1969), with samples of Russian and Japanese, TPR produced a highly significant acceleration in comprehension no matter how complicated or novel the foreign utterance and no matter how long the time interval after training, from 24 hours to two weeks.

Secondly, during training, it did not matter whether learners acted or observed a model act, but it was critical that *each* person later demonstrate comprehension by physically acting in response to directions in the foreign language. This was verified when those who *acted* in the demonstrations of retention outperformed those who *wrote English translations* to show their retention. The conclusion seemed to be that one could observe a model act in response to commands during training, but it was critical that each person follow-up by physically performing in response to directions in the target language.

Thirdly, we analyzed the language-body interaction in an attempt to pinpoint exactly what produced the extraordinary acceleration in acquisition and retention. Four features of language-body interaction could explain the impact of TPR. One of these factors was **position** which refers to the location of the learner in the room as an action is completed. For example, if the Russian command is to pick up the pencil and book, the person may expect that the next command will have something to do with the pencil, the book, or both.

Another factor is **concurrency** which means that the learner may be in motion before hearing the entire direction in the foreign language. For instance, if the command is, "Run to the door, pick up the flower, and sit in the chair," the person may be in motion running to the door immediately after hearing that part of the utterance which may simplify the problem of comprehension.

The next factor was **cue** which refers to the location of objects in the room. As an illustration, if the individual has been instructed in Russian to "... put the pencil on the chair ..." then the location of the pencil will give some information about future commands. Any future mention of pencil should direct the person's attention to the chair.

Finally, **sequence** may be a salient factor because utterances may signal with a high probability the next utterance that will follow. For example, if the Russian command is "sit!" the next will probably be "stand!" If the command is "run!" the next would be "stop!"

Sequence would be important early in training but diminish in later units when the target language becomes complex and new.

We conducted exhaustive experiments to assess the impact of position, concurrency, cue, and sequence. No single one of these components could explain the acceleration in TPR learning. Apparently, the *intact* kinesthetic event when the person performs is important. Future researchers may discover that some other factor in the complex motor act will account for the impact on learning, but our research did not isolate such a factor.

We did demonstrate in this series of laboratory experiments that people who focused only on comprehension skill using a language-body strategy, outperform on all measures, those people who attempted to comprehend *then pronounce* the utterance in the target language (Asher, 1969).

MAKING DOCUMENTARY FILMS†

The Film in Japanese

I discovered in making presentations that my short motion picture with Japanese as the target language was almost magical in arousing many jaded foreign language teachers from their "dogmatic slumbers." The concept of comprehension skill as a graceful, stress-free way to produce readiness for speaking, reading and writing was initially perceived as heresy. After all, every living linguistic authority from Nelson Brooks to John B. Carroll believed that *production* was the logical starting place for language training since "language was talk" and "talk was language."

It was easy for audiences in the 1960s and even the 1970s to deny my message since I was a lone voice contradicting a choir of impressive and distinguished academic people. Only when the lights went out in the lecture hall and my film flashed on the screen did my message have a chance of penetrating the intellectual Maginot Line constructed in the mind of the audience.

There were a few exceptions in those early days. For example, I am appreciative of support from the late Paul Pimsleur who graciously invited me in August 1969 to make a presentation with my film at the International Congress of Applied Linguistics at Cambridge University in England. He recognized the validity of my message and he would have been influential in changing prevailing thought patterns if it had not been for his sudden death while he was still in his forties.

Scenes from my first film, "Demonstration of a New Strategy in Language Learning."

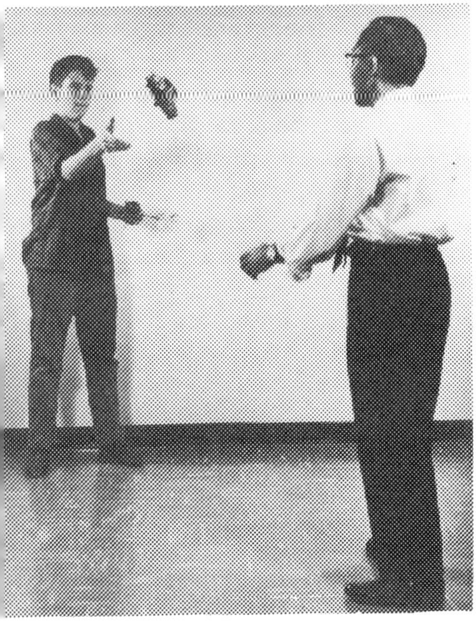

Hal Keely, Jr., demonstrates almost perfect retention of Japanese one-year following TPR training.

Shirou uses TPR to help 12-year-old boys internalize Japanese.

Without a motion picture to demonstrate in a few minutes the power of the total physical response, I am sure that my research would never be applied today on a large scale with thousands of students in many different countries. Probably 95% of all research is never applied in the daily lives of people. Most research ends up stored and forgotten in the dusty archives of libraries.

I was so impressed with the power of film in opening up even the most skeptical language teacher, that I decided to make a documentary film, *no matter what the cost,* for every research project that I attempted in the future.

The Film in German

The first classroom study with the *total physical response* was with Sylvia deLangen teaching German to adults in night school at Cabrillo College in Aptos, California. The intent was for the students to be *silent* for the entire semester as they assimilated an *understanding* of spoken German through our language-body training.

But after two or three weeks, the students refused to remain silent. They complained to Mrs. deLangen that the German was "on the tip" of their tongues. They wanted to talk.

"No! Hold them off!" was my direction to Sylvia, but student pressure each week continued to intensify until I relented when the instructor explained that if we didn't give the students a chance to speak in German, we would certainly have a mutiny.

From the beginning of this classroom experiment in TPR (which is described in my *Modern Language Journal* article of 1972), I collaborated with one of my former students, Allan Beyer, who had started his own motion picture business. Allan and I would visit the class periodically throughout the semester and under my direction, he would capture student progress on 16 mm color film.

When the semester was over and student skills were compared with students in production-oriented traditional classes, I had the raw material to write a script along with the article that later appeared in the *Modern Language Journal.* I found that my earlier training in radio-television was invaluable in producing an effective documentary film. The end-product looks so easy to the novice viewing it that there is a temptation to believe that anybody can make a high-quality documentary film.

Based on my experience, I would definitely encourage every researcher to make a film (or video tape) in conjunction with a research project. The secret is in writing a script that *tells* an *interest-*

Scenes from my second film in which adults between 17 and 65 enjoy internalizing German with TPR.

ing story. Storytelling is a talent but it is also a skill that can be developed with practice. A story should have a beginning, a middle, and an end. It should have suspense, a fast-moving pace, and if possible, a surprise ending.

It is important in movie-making to work with people *you can work with*. For example, Allan and I were an excellent team because with only a few words or a gesture, Allan could sense what I wanted to capture on film and he did a brilliant job of unobtrusively registering on film those magical moments in a TPR learning experience. I was fortunate, too, to have other excellent people on the team such as Sylvia deLangen and my research assistant, the hard-working and conscientious Jo Ann Kusudo.

The end-product was a 16 mm color film called, *"Strategy for Second Language Learning,"* which has been enjoyed by thousands of people around the world.

The Adult Film in Spanish

The next classroom experiment with TPR was at San Jose State University in which students with no prior training in Spanish met once a week for three hours for one school year. The intent was to explore how to make the **transition** from comprehension skill to other skills such as speaking, reading, and writing. A unique feature of this study was that although the students only met once a week, there was no homework.

My team for this project (supported by the U.S. Office of Education) was Jo Ann Kusudo, who was my most capable research assistant, and a talented instructor of Spanish, Rita de la Torre. Periodically during the year, Allan Beyer and I would visit the class with motion picture equipment and unobtrusively, film student progress.

Student achievement in skills of comprehension, speaking, reading, and writing as measured by standardized tests such as the Pimsleur measures were so spectacular that no one, I felt, would believe the results on paper unless you could see for yourself in a documentary film.

Nevertheless, I did publish our findings in *The Modern Language Journal* (Asher, Kusudo, and de la Torre, 1974) and concurrently, I produced the 16 mm color film, *"A Motivational Strategy for Language Learning"* which has been seen by thousands of viewers in the past ten years.

At about this time, I received a phone call from Dr. Janet King Swaffar who was on the faculty in the German Department at the

University of Texas at Austin. She explained that she had been assigned the task of reviewing the literature in second language learning to find ways of rejuvenating language training at the University of Texas. Many students would start training in German but more than half would give-up by Level 2.

Dr. Swaffar had found my articles in the *Modern Language Journal* and she wanted more information including a preview of my documentary films in Japanese and Spanish. Frankly, she was skeptical. Could the results in my articles be as dramatic as I presented them?

What could I do to persuade her other than comply with reprints of other TPR articles that I had written and films for her to view? After studying the articles and films, she called me again with the news that she was collaborating with her colleagues to apply TPR to all students in Level 1 and Level 2 classes in German at the University of Texas at Austin.

The results of that daring venture you may read for yourself in the article by Swaffar and Woodruff entitled, "Language for Comprehension: Focus on Reading, a report on the University of Texas German Program" (1978). Incidentally, for their work, Dr. Janet King Swaffar and Dr. Margaret S. Woodruff were awarded the coveted *Paul Pimsleur Award.* Also, the content of the Level 1 course in German is now available in both German and English (Woodruff, 1986).

The Children's Film in Spanish and French

Language-body learning seemed to work beautifully with adults, but how about children in elementary school through high school? With a research grant from the U.S. Office of Education, I collaborated with these fine language teachers to explore how children would respond to the TPR approach : Suzette Ross-*Preschool French,* Sister Eva Wormell-*1st and 2nd Grade Spanish,* Pat Overall-*5th Grade Spanish,* Elena Schwab-*6th Grade Spanish,* Leonard Hill-*7th Grade Spanish,* and Ramiro Garcia-*High School Spanish.* Also working with us every Saturday morning for about a year was Carol Adamski, a teacher of ESL for adults. Other language teachers periodically joined the group including: Wilma Ann Filinick, Lazaro Garza, Elaine M. Kurilla, Richard Pugh, Jeri Robles, John Tweeten and Silvia Tweeten.

At each Saturday meeting, which convened at my home, we prepared TPR lessons, exchanged ideas and shared problems. It was an exciting year for all of us because we recognized that we were on

Publicity photos for the film "A Motivational Strategy for Language Learning." (In the upper right, Rita is directing me and Jo Ann in Spanish, to act out a scenario.)

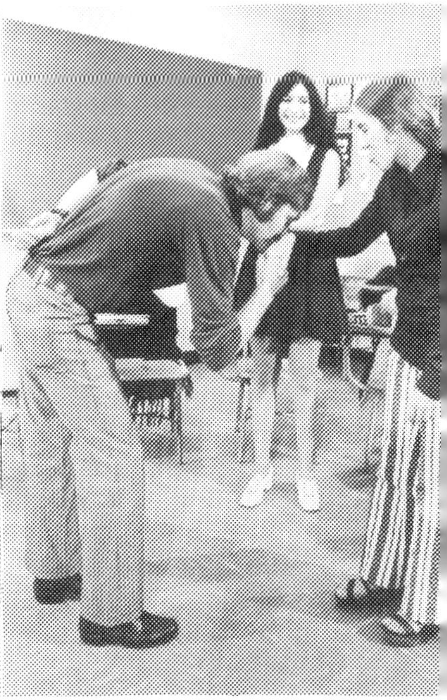

University of Texas at Austin. She explained that she had been assigned the task of reviewing the literature in second language learning to find ways of rejuvenating language training at the University of Texas. Many students would start training in German but more than half would give-up by Level 2.

Dr. Swaffar had found my articles in the *Modern Language Journal* and she wanted more information including a preview of my documentary films in Japanese and Spanish. Frankly, she was skeptical. Could the results in my articles be as dramatic as I presented them?

What could I do to persuade her other than comply with reprints of other TPR articles that I had written and films for her to view? After studying the articles and films, she called me again with the news that she was collaborating with her colleagues to apply TPR to all students in Level 1 and Level 2 classes in German at the University of Texas at Austin.

The results of that daring venture you may read for yourself in the article by Swaffar and Woodruff entitled, "Language for Comprehension: Focus on Reading, a report on the University of Texas German Program" (1978). Incidentally, for their work, Dr. Janet King Swaffar and Dr. Margaret S. Woodruff were awarded the coveted *Paul Pimsleur Award.* Also, the content of the Level 1 course in German is now available in both German and English (Woodruff, 1986).

The Children's Film in Spanish and French

Language-body learning seemed to work beautifully with adults, but how about children in elementary school through high school? With a research grant from the U.S. Office of Education, I collaborated with these fine language teachers to explore how children would respond to the TPR approach : Suzette Ross-*Preschool French,* Sister Eva Wormell-*1st and 2nd Grade Spanish,* Pat Overall-*5th Grade Spanish,* Elena Schwab-*6th Grade Spanish,* Leonard Hill-*7th Grade Spanish,* and Ramiro Garcia-*High School Spanish.* Also working with us every Saturday morning for about a year was Carol Adamski, a teacher of ESL for adults. Other language teachers periodically joined the group including: Wilma Ann Filinick, Lazaro Garza, Elaine M. Kurilla, Richard Pugh, Jeri Robles, John Tweeten and Silvia Tweeten.

At each Saturday meeting, which convened at my home, we prepared TPR lessons, exchanged ideas and shared problems. It was an exciting year for all of us because we recognized that we were on

Publicity photos for the film "A Motivational Strategy for Language Learning." (In the upper right, Rita is directing me and Jo Ann in Spanish, to act out a scenario.)

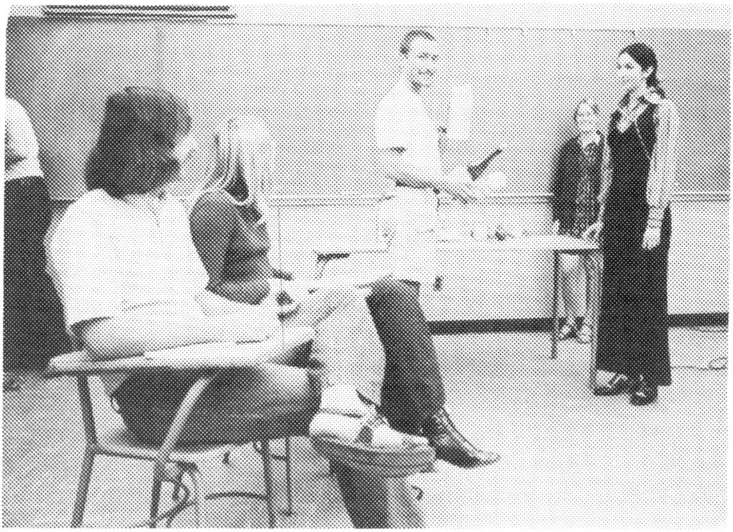

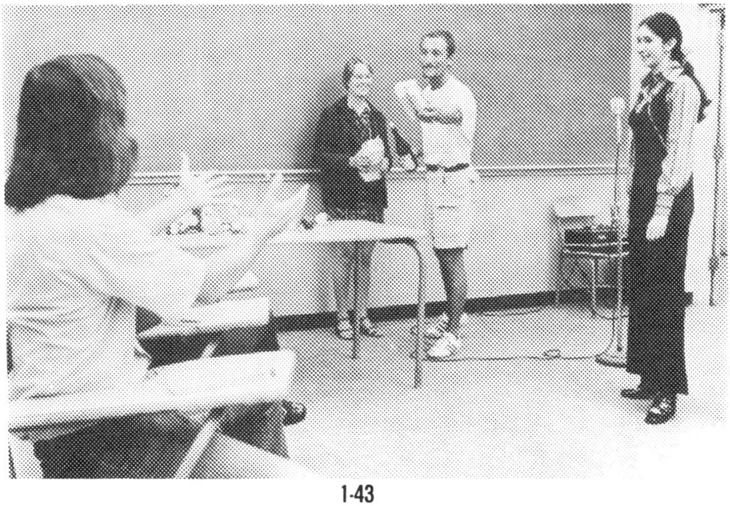

the "cutting edge" of a movement that had the potential of helping most children experience a successful and exhilarating experience of internalizing a second language.

I learned from this that TPR flourishes in a team venture in which ideas flow generously from member to member sparking more ideas. Every instructor who has tried TPR has discovered a new twist—something unique because the territory of language and the body plays to the right hemisphere of the brain—the creative side.

As the year progressed, we discovered and invented many new ways of measuring comprehension skill, speaking, reading, and writing.

During that year, I compared the progress of students in TPR classes with those attempting to acquire a language in traditional production-oriented classes. You may read the results in this article: "Children learning another language: A developmental hypothesis" which was published by *Child Development,* 1977, *48*, 1040-1048. (The findings are also described in Part II of this book.)

Periodically during the year, Allan Beyer and I visited the TPR classes and systematically collected on 16 mm film, samples of students performing. Then at the end of the school year, I wrote a script to integrate all of the filmed samples to tell a story which you may see in the 16 mm color motion-picture, *"Children Learning Another Language: An Innovative Approach"* (See page 5-13). The last sample that we filmed was preschool children acquiring French with TPR. The classes were taught in San Francisco by Suzette Ross. This meant that Allan and I drove in his VW truck from San Jose to San Francisco which was about a one-hour trip.

During the morning of the filming, I noticed that Allan was having difficulty concentrating on the task and he was perspiring profusely. A number of times I asked whether he was feeling well enough to continue, and he assured me that he was fine. I did not realize that Allan who was a healthy, handsome young man in his late twenties had already made the decision to take his own life.

We finished the filming and drove back from San Francisco to San Jose which is a 60 mile trip. During that time, Allan said very few words, but I didn't think anything of it since he was a quiet person by nature.

Later that evening, I received a phone call from our graphic artist who worked with us on film projects. She was sobbing when she told me that Allan was dead. Never in my life have I felt such shock. I dropped the telephone receiver and screamed.

It didn't make any sense. If Allan, with everything going for him—youth, intelligence, talent, physical appearance and a wholesome family background—couldn't make it, what chance did the rest of us have?

After his funeral I remember talking with his girlfriend, searching for an explanation. I asked her why he didn't give his friends a chance to help. Her explanation was that he was too proud to ask for help.

"You know, Jim," she confided, "I would be with Allan in his home and he would be crying—sobbing uncontrollably. The phone would ring and he would go to the phone and talk to you in his business-as-usual voice, finish the conversation, hang up the phone, and continue weeping unconsolably. He was the world's greatest actor."

Allan was too proud to reach his hand to me across the seat of his truck that morning and say, "Man, I'm dying. Help me!"

★ ★ ★

The Lost Film of Nava

While I'm on the topic of film-making, I would like to share another experience that I had with John Sperling who was a Professor of Political Science at San Jose State University. John is now president of his own university in Arizona.

John Sperling is one of those extraordinary people who is as comfortable repairing the brake shoes on his car as he is delivering a lecture to college students. John, in the early seventies, viewed himself as a "people organizer" because, according to John's theory, unless one can organize people to focus in on a task, nothing of significance can be accomplished.

He had a devoted, almost cult-like following of students whom he trained, by his personal example, to be expert "people organizers." Being a futuristic thinker as well as a practical man of action, John thought that a superb training exercise for his young followers (tomorrows leaders) was to transport them to a foreign country and let them practice their people-organizing skills in a "strange" environment with people who spoke a different language.

To appreciate John, I should tell you that he was, by his own account, "a poor boy from the Appalachian Mountains unable to concentrate in school because of hunger and a constant buzzing in his head." He ended the pain of abysmal failure-after-failure in school by dropping out at sixteen to join the Merchant Marine.

On board many ships that undulated rhythmically day-after-day in the endless vastness of water, suddenly the "buzzing" in his head ceased—and to fill the time, he visited the ship's library and was thrilled to discover a novelty called "books." He became an addict—reading every book on board the ships and investing all of his earnings in more and more books.

After several years of working on ships, John was so well-read that, after leaving the Merchant Marine, he zoomed through several universities accumulating degrees including a doctorate from Cambridge University in England.

However, John Sperling, a rather short man, never lost the "common touch." He always wore Levis, a colorful, plaid shirt, cowboy hat and boots. And the students loved him. They would follow him anywhere to pursue any adventure that he suggested—no matter what the risk.

His plan was to move forty or so students into a tiny Mexican town called Nava where almost no English is spoken, and persuade the townspeople to let them work for two weeks in local jobs such as bartender, deputy sheriff, store keeper, assistant to the village priest, concessionaires at the park, and assistant to the mayor.

Naturally, the students needed survival skills in understanding and using at least basic Spanish—which is where I came into the picture. John had heard about my research and he was quick to see how the idea could be applied to achieve his goal.

The planning and execution of this unusual exercise was a team effort by the students which they worked through with enormous exuberance. This project was detail-rich because it involved inoculations, passports, a cultural orientation, 40 hours of language training[1], arranging a place to quarter the people and the acquisition of an air-conditioned bus—just to mention the obvious details.

"How in the world," I asked John, "will you acquire an air-conditioned bus which costs several hundred thousand dollars?" John looked at me with an amused expression. "You college professors," he said kindly, "are so provincial. Out there beyond the ivy-covered boundaries of this university is a community—ready to help us do anything if we approach them in the proper way—and that, my friend, is what I'm preparing my students to do."

We decided to document this unusual adventure in two ways. First, I would assess, using standard paper-and-pencil tests, student progress in acquiring Spanish with TPR during a crash 40 hour training period. (Asher 1973). Then I would go along with the group,

[1]If we were to do it again, I would insist on 200 hours of TPR language training.

and shoot a film which I would assemble later to tell the story. John assigned me to work with a motion-picture photographer whom I will call Henry*—selected by John because his rates were "reasonable." Under my direction, Henry shot thousands of feet of motion picture film.

It was one of the most productive and illuminating experiences of my life—and I believe the students shared that feeling. We established such a warm, family relationship with the people of Nava that almost the entire town turned out to bid us farewell when we left—tears were streaming down everyone's face.

When we returned home, I immediately began to edit the raw film footage to fit a script I had written to tell the story of Nava. One day, Henry asked to remove the film for cutting—a process involved in editing, and then he suddenly disappeared leaving a note that he got a job making a film aboard a yacht that was going around the world.

He left no forwarding address and no message as to where the uncut film was stored. That was more than thirteen years ago.

I had long ago given-up hope of ever seeing the film again when a few months ago, I came to my office and there in front of the door was a box crammed with the uncut film and a cryptic, unsigned note which read: "Film shot in Nava, Mexico."

Everyday when I go to my office and see the mysterious box of uncut film, I wonder whether it will ever be worked into a polished documentary film.

*Not his real name

The main street of Nava.

A student working in the park.

A local business.

The cantina.

John making repairs on the bus.

My son, Jeff and I in Nava.

The pool room.

A fiesta for the children.

The fruit stand.

The air-conditioned bus.

PART II

THE PROBLEM

The most difficult learning task for children and adults may be the attempt to acquire a second language in school. This conclusion is supported by the attrition rate of students in foreign language programs. For example, John Lawson (1971), a school superintendent in Shaker Heights, Ohio reported that the dropout rate may be more than 85% by the third year and more than 95% by the fourth year. Few students—less than 5% who started in a second language—continue to proficiency. Similar findings were reported recently in California (Wollitzer, 1983)

Even for the students who stay in a language program for at least two years in high school studying Spanish, French, or German, proficiency as measured by standardized tests is, according to John B. Carroll (1960), less than satisfactory. A college senior majoring in a second language is presumably among the select group of 5% who continued language training and therefore, because of high aptitude for language learning and four years of schooling in a specific language, should have keen proficiency. However, Carroll stated that the average college senior majoring in a second language has "limited working proficiency" in speaking and comprehending the foreign language (p. 200, 1967).

Since there is a severe dropout rate for students in language programs, there may be a temptation to infer a cause-effect relationship. The reasoning would be that somehow the constraints of the classroom produced difficulty in language learning. If not, why is school so ineffectual in language training especially when one observes that a normal six-year-old child *without schooling* has mastered all the essential parts of the individual's native language including phonology, syntax, and semantics? Evidence for this accomplishment is the fact that the six-year-old can utter and comprehend thousands of sentences the child has never heard before (Carroll, 1966).

The language achievement of the six-year-old *without schooling* in comparison with students in school is striking. Does this mean that schools have failed? Not necessarily since the differences in achievement may simply be the result of exposure time.

For example, by the age of six, a child has listened to his or her native language for 17,520 hours, which is a conservative estimate based on eight hours a day for 365 days for six years. During those six years, let us estimate that the child has produced vocalizations only one hour per day, which amounts to 2,190 hours. In comparison, the student in the classroom in one year has listened to a foreign language for 320 hours[1] and has produced vocalizations for 27 hours, assuming the student talks 10 minutes per class meeting (Asher, 1972a).

The figures are not impressive until they are converted into a different frame of reference. For instance, if we expect the student in the classroom to have the fluency of a six-year-old child, the student should listen to the foreign language for 55 years of college instruction[2] and the student should have the opportunity to vocalize in the foreign language for 81 years[3] of college of instruction.

When foreign language instruction is viewed from a time perspective, the mystery is that so much is accomplished in a highly condensed period of time. It is probably a realistic conclusion that almost any existing school program can produce at least basic fluency if the student remains in the program long enough—and long enough means at least four to eight years.

The problem is this: few students—less than 5%—are able to endure the *stressful* nature of formal school training in languages. The task is to invent or discover instructional strategies that reduce the intense stress that students experience. The goal is to develop an instructional strategy that has enough motivational power to persuade 75% of students who start language study, instead of the current 15%, to continue into the third year of language training. If students get through the third year, the probability is extremely high that they will continue for advanced work.

[1] This is a generous calculation based on 32 weeks multiplied by 5 hours a week in class plus 5 hours a week listening to tapes.

[2] 17,520 divided by 320 = 55.

[3] 2,190 divided by 27 = 81.

AN INSTRUCTIONAL STRATEGY THAT PRODUCES HIGH MOTIVATION

Next we will present the case for an instructional strategy that not only makes a second language learnable for most people, but enjoyable. This strategy is based on a model of how children learn their first language. For example, there are three critical elements in the way children learn their first language (Asher, 1972b).

The first element is that listening skill is far in advance of speaking. For instance, it is common to observe young children who are not yet able to produce more than one-word utterances, yet they demonstrate perfect understanding when an adult says, "Pick up your red truck and bring it to me!" As far back as 1935 teams of investigators as Gesell and Thompson or Bühler and Hetzer have reported that when children learn their first language, listening comprehension of many complex utterances is demonstrated before these children produce any intelligible speech.

We infer from these observations that it is no accident that listening precedes speaking. It may be that listening comprehension maps the blueprint for the future acquisition of speaking. Evidence by Ervin (1964) supports this hypothesis. For example, Ervin found that young children had no difficulty understanding model sentences spoken by adults. But, when these children were asked to imitate a sentence immediately after it was uttered by an adult, they were unable to do this accurately. Their attempts at imitation were not copies of what the adult said but were distorted according to a concept the child had about the nature of English. This concept, we would suggest, was acquired through listening comprehension.

Not only is listening critical to the development of speaking, but children acquire listening skill in a particular way. For instance, there is an intimate relationship between language and the child's body. Utterances, usually commands from adults, are used to manipulate the orientation, location, and locomotion of the child's entire body. This phenomenon can be observed in a massive number of commands as:

"Come here!"

"Stand still!"

"Don't make a fist when I'm trying to put on your coat!"

"Pick up the red truck and put it in the toy box in your room!"

Finally, listening skill may produce a "readiness" for the child to speak. Speaking may be like walking in that attempts to speed up the appearance of this behavior before the child is ready, may be futile.

As listening comprehension develops, there is a point of readiness to speak in which the child spontaneously begins to produce utterances.

A reasonable hypothesis is that the brain and nervous system are biologically programmed to acquire language, either the first or second, in a particular sequence and in a particular mode. The sequence is listening before speaking and the mode is to synchronize language with the individual's body. In a sense, language is orchestrated to a choreography of the human body.

From this analysis of children's first language, there are clues for second language learning. Basically, the premise is that if you want to learn a second language gracefully and with a minimum of stress, then invent a learning strategy that is in harmony with the biological program.

Summary

Again, the three key ideas in the instructional format for children or adults learning a second language are:

- Understanding the spoken language should be developed in advance of speaking.
- Understanding should be developed through movements of the student's body. The imperative is a powerful aid because the instructor can utter commands to manipulate student behavior. Our research suggests that most of the grammatical structure of the target language and hundreds of vocabulary items can be learned through the skillful use of the imperative by the instructor.
- Do not attempt to force speaking from students. As the students internalize a cognitive map of the target language through understanding what is heard, there will be a point of readiness to speak. The individual will spontaneously begin to produce utterances.

THE EVIDENCE

This section is a rather technical account of research findings. If one is not experienced in deciphering the details of research, this section can be omitted without loss of meaning. The reader may then wish to skip to Part III, the ***MOST OFTEN ASKED QUESTIONS.***

This synopsis of the research findings does not follow a chronological progression beginning with the first experiment, then the second, and so forth. Rather, the research was organized as follows: classroom studies with children, laboratory studies with children, laboratory studies with adults, and classroom studies with adults. Most of the work was supported by research grants and contracts from the Office of Education-Title VI and Title VII, the Office of Naval Research, and the program of small grant awards from San José State University.

Classroom Studies with Children

Asher (1972b) designed a pilot study, carried out by Silvia de Langen, to determine how fast understanding of spoken German can be assimilated by American children when the learning is based on the imperative.

The children (N=5) were members of a Girl Scout group who volunteered to learn German in an after-school class two days a week. The 11-year-old girls were moved continuously through commands in German by de Langen. The results of this pilot study indicated that the children with no prior training in German understood the same amount and content of German that is assimilated through memorization of dialogues by adults during the initial two months of training at the Defense Language Institute (DLI). This was a striking demonstration since the DLI training is six hours a day for five days a week which is 240 classroom hours for a two-month period.

One important implication is that a pre-learning period of listening understanding through the imperative could possibly accelerate student's progress in a traditional program. Theoretically, if students have listening fluency for all the content they would hear in the training program, (a) stress would be reduced, (b) more attention units would be available to focus on learning other skills such as speaking, and (c) there should be a large amount of positive transfer from listening-understanding to speaking, reading, and writing.

In a series of classroom studies to follow up the pilot demonstration, children in the first, second, fifth, sixth, and seventh grades had experienced teachers uttering commands in Spanish to manipulate the movement, orientation and action of the students (Asher, 1976). The language training for one school year was usually 20 minutes a day three times a week with no homework.

The results may be seen in the documentary film, *"Children Learning Another Language: An Innovative Approach"*

The first finding was that all groups of children made rapid progress in understanding Spanish when compared with groups. Secondly, there was substantial transfer-of-learning from understanding spoken Spanish to reading, writing, and speaking. This means, of course, a large savings in instructional hours. And thirdly, the children showed their most dramatic gain in the comprehension of novelty. That is, the students had an accurate understanding of what was said in Spanish when elements learned in training were recombined to create unfamiliar sentences. For example, let's say the children in training experienced, "Sit on the chair!" and "Walk to the table!" A novel sentence would be to recombine learned elements to produce the unexpected and unfamiliar command, "Sit on the table!"

The linguistic flexibility in understanding recombinations may be the skill often referred to as "fluency." If students only understand the exact content experienced in training, they are non-fluent. Only when students can comprehend unfamiliar sentences—the recombinations — there skill in fluency.

Laboratory Studies with Children

The important advantage that a "laboratory" study has over a classroom study is the control of variables which means that conclusions tend to be more clear-cut. The essence of a laboratory study is the simplification of an experience to eliminate everything but the variables under study. Sometimes laboratory studies are called experiments.

For an honor's thesis, Mary Hamilton conducted an experiment to test the hypothesis that 6th grade children (N=16) who acted in response to Russian commands would have better retention than children (N=16) who sat and observed a model act (Asher, 1966). To reduce differences in ability for sixth graders in the experimental and control groups, Hamilton matched the children in both groups on the *California Test of Mental Maturity,* the *California Achievement Test,* and teacher ratings on classroom performance. None of the children was bilingual and none had prior exposure to the Russian language.

The results showed that the retention of children who acted in response to Russian commands was far superior (beyond the .01 level) compared with the children who sat and merely observed a model act. The greater retention of the children in the experimental group held whether the Russian commands were short or long, familiar or unfamiliar (i.e., novel commands in which elements learned in training were recombined).

In the Hamilton study, the children in the experimental group listened to a command in Russian, then *acted* with a model during training, and later demonstrated retention by *acting* individually in response to commands. The control children listened to a command in Russian, then observed a model act during training, but later demonstrated retention by writing English translations in response to commands. It is possible, therefore, that acting in response to a Russian command during training did not produce the great increase in retention. It could be that acting rather than writing during *retention tests* was responsible for the difference in retention. As a test of this hypothesis, Benjamin S. Price designed a study for his master's thesis using children in the second, fourth, and eighth grades (Asher, 1966; Asher & Price, 1967). To control the factor of ability to learn, sixteen pairs of children in each grade level were matched on the *California Test of Mental Maturity,* the *California Achievement Test,* and teacher ranking on classroom performance. This was a replication of the Hamilton experiment except that during the retention tests the children in both the experimental and control groups listened to each Russian command, then *acted out the response.* In the Hamilton study, the controls wrote English translations in the retention tests.

The results were about equal retention for either the experimental or control groups from the second, fourth, and eighth grades. The implication was that during the training phase, children could either act with the model or observe a model act. Acting or observing during training was not a crucial difference, but it was important how children responded during retention tests. Acting during the retention tests either facilitated learning or allowed more competency to manifest itself. As a test of the hypothesis that acting rather than writing in the retention phase facilitated a greater retrieval of information, a follow-up study was conducted with eighth graders.

Approximately two months after the eighth graders in Price's initial study had completed their training in Russian, another retention test was administered. This time, half of the eighth graders in the experimental and control groups *acted* during the two-month retention test while the other half *wrote* English. The results for complex Russian utterances showed better recall for the children acting out their responses.

Laboratory Studies with Adults

For a master's thesis, Shirou Kunihira conducted an experiment to teach a sample of Japanese to college students (Kunihira & Asher, 1965).

Procedure. An experimental and three control groups learned a sample of Japanese which began with simple commands as "tate" (stand) and "aruke" (walk), but within twenty minutes the complexity of the utterances was increased, for example, to this: "Mado ni hashitte itte hon o motte tsukue ni oite isu ni suware" (Run to the window, pick up the book, put it down on the desk, and sit down on the chair).

The experimental group (N=16) listened to the Japanese commands played on a tape recorder, and after each utterance, acted with the instructor as their model. If the utterance was "To ni aruite ike" (Walk to the door), the students and the model walked to the door. If the command was "Kami to hon to enpitsu o motte isu ni suware" (Pick up the paper, book, and pencil and sit down on the chair), students and the model picked up a paper, book, and pencil, returned to their chairs and sat down. Students, who worked in groups of four or five, were instructed to be silent, listen to the Japanese, and do exactly what the instructor does.

The first control group (N=15) was treated the same as the experimental group except that these students sat and observed the model perform during training. The second control group (N=18) listened to the English translation from the tape after each Japanese command, but they did not observe the model perform. The third control group (N=18) read the English translations in a booklet after they heard a Japanese utterance. They also did not observe the performance of a model.

Scoring of the retention tests. The retention tests were given immediately after training, 24 hours later, and then following a two-week interval. These retention tests were scored in behavioral units as, for example, if a student in the experimental group heard "Isu ni hashitte itte hon o oke" (Run to the chair and put down the book), the individual received one point for running, another point if the person ran to a chair, another point if an object was put on the chair, and a point if the object was a book. Therefore, for the utterance "Isu ni hashitte itte hon o oke," the total possible score was four points. The same scoring procedure was used for students in the control groups except that these people wrote down the English translation for the Japanese.

As to scoring categories, a *single word* was, for example, "aruke" (walk); a *short utterance* was a thought unit as "To ni aruite ike" (Walk to the door); a *long utterance* was more than one thought unit as "Tsukue ni aruite itte enpitsu to hon o oke" (Walk to the desk, and put down the pencil and book); and a *novel utterance* was a recombination of utterances used in training so that, in this sense, novel commands were heard for the first time in the retention tests.

Results The experimental group who acted in training and acted individually in the retention tests had significantly better recall ($p < .001$) than each control group. The experimental group's superiority in retention held for complex Japanese utterances and also held for different time intervals after training from 24 hours to two weeks. When the study was repeated by Asher (1965) using Russian as the target language, the results were quite similar to the findings obtained with Japanese by Kunihira.

A Further Exploration

For adults learning a sample of either Japanese or Russian, optimal retention was achieved by an *Act-Act Group* who acted along with a model during training and then each subject acted alone during the retention tests. The comparison was always an *Observe-Write Group* who sat and observed a model act during training and then wrote English translations during retention tests.

The conclusions were still not clear-cut since understanding Japanese or Russian may be associated with the format of the retention tests rather than the conditions of training. To decipher what was happening, further experiments were conducted with college students learning samples of Russian (Asher, 1969). We had already observed the performance of the *Act-Act group* and the *Observe-Write group.* To complete the set, we needed an *Observe-Act Group* who observed a model in training, but acted individually in the retention tests, and an *Act-Write group* who acted with a model in training, but wrote English translations in the retention tests.

The first hypothesis was that it did not matter whether students in training acted with the model or sat and observed a model act in response to commands in a foreign language. Indeed, the results confirmed the hypothesis since we obtained no significant statistical difference in understanding of Russian for students in the *Act-Write Group* compared with the *Observe-Write Group.*

The second hypothesis was that retention (either short or long) was accelerated when each student *acted alone* to demonstrate understanding of the foreign utterance. The hypothesis was confirmed when students (N=37) who acted or observed in training but *acted in retention* tests were contrasted with a group (N=34) who also acted or observed in training but *wrote English translations in the retention tests.* For either short or long term recall (i.e., two weeks after training), students who acted alone to demonstrate understanding of the target language outperformed students who were not required to act individually to show their comprehension. Their differences in recall were striking, usually significant beyond the .001 statistical level.

Another way of interpreting the results is this: When students acted or observed a model act *in training,* the input was to the right brain. To retrieve the input, the maximum retention occurred when the performance measure also played to the right brain, (as when each person *acted* alone in response to directions in the target language). If we input to the right brain, but later ask the left brain to retrieve the information, the results will be significantly *less* than if both input and output are from the right brain.

Often in school, students complain that they *knew more* than was measured on a paper-and-pencil test. Probably the students are quite accurate in their perception. The school experience is a *mix* of right and left brain input, but output is almost always measured from the left brain exclusively.

Concluding Remarks

There are two distinctly different phases in the learning process. The first is *modeling* (usually by the instructor with a few students) to communicate the meaning of utterances. The second is a *demonstration* by the individual student acting alone to show that the utterances were understood. These modeling and demonstration stages may be analogous to comprehension and performance, learning and retention, or input and output.

The results seem to indicate that it is *not* important that the individual student models along with the instructor so long as the *individual* student later demonstrates comprehension through action.

It should be explained that the laboratory studies were conducted somewhat differently from the classroom studies to be presented next.

In the classroom studies, the procedure was to alternate the modeling by the instructor and the demonstration by the individual student for a few utterances at a time until the student's behavior indicated understanding, then to recombine constituents in utterances to increase student skill at flexibility of comprehension. In the lab, there was a 50:50 split in time between modeling and demonstration, but in the classroom the split was 25:75. There was minimal time in the modeling—the fewest trials to achieve communication of meaning—then students individually demonstrated comprehension of familiar and unfamiliar (recombined constituents) utterances.

The ideal in language learning is to achieve minimal input with maximum output. We strive for the fewest input trials (modeling) that are necessary to communicate meaning. Then, the students, under the skillful direction of the instructor, expands the input to produce maximum output. By recombining elements of the input, the student demonstrates immediate understanding of unfamiliar utterances. This process of recombination maximizes output and moves the student in the direction of genuine fluency.

Classroom Studies with Adults

The classroom studies with adults learning German, Spanish, and English as a second language attempted to explore three issues:

1. Can the entire linguistic code of the language be learned with a format in which the students physically responded to commands?

2. Can listening comprehension of the target language be achieved without using the student's native language?

3. When students achieve understanding of spoken language will there be a large amount of positive transfer-of-learning to other skills as speaking, reading, and writing?

Learning German in Night School

In a classroom study, which has been thoroughly detailed by Asher in the March 1972 issue of the *Modern Language Journal*, night school adults experienced about 32 hours of training in German with an instructor who used commands to achieve understanding of spoken German.

Results. The first finding was that most grammatical features of German could be nested into the imperative form. With creativity from the instructor, almost any aspect of the linguistic code for the target language could be communicated using commands. For example, the *future tense* can be imbedded into a command as, "When Sam runs to the door, Edna *will* write Sam's name on the chalkboard!" The *past tense* is incorporated into the command structure when the instructor says, "Abner, run to the table!" After Abner has completed the action, the instructor continues with, "Josephine, if Abner *ran* to the table, run after him and put your book on his head!" As to the *present tense,* nesting it in the imperative is illustrated with this command: "When Sam *runs* to the door, Edna will write Sam's name on the chalkboard!"

The second finding was that basic understanding of spoken German could be achieved without using the student's native language. For certain abstractions, however, the German was written on one side of a cardboard card and English on the other. Then abstractions as "honor," "justice," and "government" were manipulated as objects. For instance, the instructor said in German, "Luke, pick up 'justice' and give it to Josephine!" "Abner, throw 'government' to me!"

However, later classroom studies in other languages suggest that abstractions should be delayed until students have internalized a detailed cognitive map of the target language. Abstractions are not necessary for people to decode the grammatical structure of language. Once students have internalized the code, abstractions can be introduced and *explained* in the target language. As one ESL instructor expressed it, "If you have to use translation, you are swimming across a river in mid-winter without noticing that there is a bridge."

Thirdly, the achievement of understanding for spoken German by the night school students with only 32 hours of training was significantly better than the listening comprehension of college students who had completed either 75 hours or 150 hours of formal college instruction in German.

The fourth finding was that the internalization of understanding resulted in a large savings in instructional hours through transfer-of-learning to reading, writing, and speaking. After 60 hours of training, the spoken German was spontaneous and uninhibited, but there were many errors in pronunciation and grammar. Our expectation was that if the students were willing to talk and talk in German without anxiety about making mistakes, eventually, when their confidence was extremely high, they could be "fine tuned" to produce the subtleties of speech that approximate a native speaker. Our goal here was a spontaneous shift from understanding to a level of production in which the student's vocal output was intelligible to a native speaker.

The experience with the night students learning German has been captured on a documentary film in color entitled, "Strategy for Second Language Learning," which is available from Sky Oaks Productions *(See Classic Video Demonstrations at end of book).*

Learning German: The University of Texas Experience

In an exciting paper* presented at the American Association of Teachers of German, Dr. Margaret Woodruff reported how the first year German language course under the direction of Dr. Janet King Swaffar at the University of Texas at Austin was converted to the TPR instructional strategy recommended in this book. About 350 students learned German using the concepts I have described. A scientific report has been published by Swaffar and Woodruff in *The Modern Language Journal* (1978, 62, 27-32). The title is, "Language for comprehension: Focus on reading. A report on the University of Texas German Program." The findings will be summarized next.

Results. First, listening and reading were assessed with the *Modern Language Association Cooperative Foreign Language Tests.* After only *one semester* of German in the experimental TPR program based on commands, the average listening and reading skill in German was about the same as students completing the *second semester* of German in a traditional audio-lingual program.

Secondly, the proportion of students who went from the first to the second semester was historically only 50%, but with the innovative TPR program, about 75% elected to continue into the second semester.

Thirdly, the motivation of students was appreciably increased as shown by student ratings. In the past, the mean student ratings for the course were average, and slightly above average for the instructors. In the TPR program, the mean student ratings were *above average* for the course and between *above-average* to *excellent* for the instructors.

For the detailed TPR lessons used in Level 1, see the book by Dr. Woodruff entitled, "Comprehension-Based Language Lessons: Level I," (1986).

*A copy may be obtained by writing ERIC (Center for Applied Linguistics, 3520 Prospect Street, N.W. Washington, D.C. 20007). Ask for, "Comprehension and communication, fine; but what do you do about grammar?" and "The role of listening and speaking in a reading program; activities and games for foreign-language learning."

Learning Spanish

The adults in this class were college students (N=27) with no prior training in Spanish who attended class for three hours one evening a week for two semesters. There was no homework.

The procedure using the imperative for the internalization of understanding for spoken Spanish has been thoroughly detailed by Asher, Kusudo, and de la Torre (1974). After about ten hours of training in which the instructor spoke commands in Spanish to manipulate the behavior of individuals in the class, the students were invited, but not pressured, to reverse roles with the instructor. Those students who felt ready to try speaking, uttered commands in Spanish to the instructor who performed as directed by the students.

From this time on, about 20% of the class time was role reversal in which individual students had a chance to speak Spanish to move the instructor or peers. Later on, students demonstrated their creativity by inventing skits which they performed in Spanish. Still later in training, students role-played in problem-solving situations. For example, a student had to pretend that on a visit to Mexico, he found himself locked inside his hotel room when the key broke in the lock. His task was to use the telephone to resolve the difficulty.

There was no systematic training in reading and writing. For a few minutes at the end of each class meeting, the instructor wrote on the chalkboard any structure or vocabulary item requested by the students. These items in Spanish, with no English translations, were almost utterances the students had heard during the class. As the instructor wrote on the chalkboard, the students wrote in their notebooks.

Results (Midway through training). The midpoint in training was about 45 hours of instruction in which class time was 70% understanding spoken commands, 20% was speaking, and 10% was reading and writing.

The first finding was a keen level of listening understanding since the experimental class with only 45 hours of training excelled comparison groups of high school students with 200 hours of instruction and other college classes with either 75 or 150 hours of class time in Spanish with the audio-lingual method.

On the *Pimsleur Spanish Proficiency Tests-Form A* (First Level), the average student in the experimental class achieved the 70th percentile rank in listening skill, the 85th percentile rank for reading, and the 76th percentile rank for writing. Speaking skill for the average student was in the "good" category on the Pimsleur test.

Results (At the end of training). After 90 hours of training, proficiency was assessed with the *Pimsleur Spanish Proficiency Tests-Form C* (Second Level). This measurement was stringent because it was designed for students who had completed the second level of audio-lingual training which is 150 hours of college instruction. Nevertheless, the experimental group performed beyond the 50th percentile rank for listening, reading, writing, and speaking.

The changes in student attitudes and skills as the students progressed through one year of experimental training in Spanish were recorded on motion picture film. The 16 mm film in color entitled, "A Motivational Strategy for Language Learning," is available from Sky Oaks Productions *(See Classic Video Demonstrations at end of book).*

English as a Second Language. The Metropolitan Adult Education Center in San Jose, California has, for years, offered an English as a Second Language program for immigrants whose native languages were Spanish, Chinese, Japanese, Greek, or Russian. When a student enrolled for ESL classes at the Center, the individual was assigned on the basis of a placement test, to a class designed for Level I, II, III, or IV. Most classes met three hours a day for five days a week.

All classes, except one, were taught with an audio-lingual approach which included the repetition by students of what was uttered by the instructor, dialogue memorization, pattern drill and exercises in reading and writing.

One Level I class did not experience the audio-lingual format, but instead acquired understanding of spoken English through commands by the instructor. Then later, they reversed roles and spoke English to manipulate the instructor and their peers. Still later, they responded to the commands on flash cards. And later yet, they began to write English sentences. The hour-by-hour experience of the students will be presented in this book as a guide for teachers.

Results. At the end of the school year, the Metropolitan Adult Center used a 40 item measure of reading skill developed by John Fleming (1973). The results, in Table 1, showed, first of all, that the *Fleming Reading Test* had content validity. For example, since the classes in Set A were all trained in the audio-lingual approach and all had 96 hours of training, we would expect that students in Level IV should, if the test had content validity, perform the best; Level III should be next best; Level II should be third best; and Level I students should be the lowest scorers. Indeed, the results matched our expectations with Level IV scoring an average of 90%; Level III was an average score of 58%; Level II with a mean score of 54% and Level I with only 24% on the average.

TABLE 1

Results of the Fleming Test Given to Adult ESL Classes

Level of Entry Skill	Hours of Training	N	$\overline{X}$	s
Audio-lingual Classes A				
I	96	22	24%	18%
II	96	19	54%	21%
III	96	29	58%	20%
IV	96	13	90%	7%
Audio-lingual Classes B				
II	120	26	41%	13%
III	240	14	54%	17%
IV	120	17	86%	11%
The Experimental Group				
I	120	30	52%	17%

N is the number of students in a class.
$\overline{X}$ is the average or mean.
s is the standard deviation.

Secondly, the experimental group who experienced the innovative format of a command strategy performed at about the same proficiency on the Fleming test as the advanced audio-lingual students in Level II and III. Thirdly, it should be noted that the performance of the experimental class was even more striking than shown in Table 1 since nine students included in the analysis were relatively new to the class. If those nine are eliminated from the data, the average score increases from 52% to 61% (s=11%).

The Whisman School Project. A three year research project supported by a federal grant was completed by Jackson (1979) and her colleagues at the Whisman School District in Mountain View, California. Children in elementary school with deficiencies in English language skills were matched on vocabulary, language comprehension and expressive skills. Then for one hour a day, children in the experimental group were removed from classes and tutored, individually or in small groups. to enhance their comprehension skills using Asher's Total Physical Response approach. Gradually the students were advanced from comprehension into production. The matched students in the control group experienced for one hour a day, a traditional audio-lingual production-oriented training program.

After three years, the experimental group had the following gains when compared with the control group: (a) on the average, a 1.5 year advantage in vocabulary, (b) 80% more comprehension on the average, and (c) an average comparative increase in expressive skills of 130%. All gains were statistically significant using multivariate analysis of variance.

A unique by-product of this research project is a placement test for comprehension so that training for each child starts at where the student is in understanding the target language. For more information, write: Pat Jackson, 1975 San Ramon Avenue, Mountain View, California 95043. Also, a book has been published entitled, *Beginning English Through Actions (Addison-Wesley Publishing Company, Reading, MA 01867).*

WHY IT WORKS

Since the first printing of this book ten years ago, I have developed several theories to explain why the approach seems to enable children and adults to enjoy rapid, stress-free assimilation of *any* language (including the sign language of the deaf) followed by long-term retention. I offer these explanations to you as tentative models that have been helpful in clarifying the underlying process involved in language acquisition.

Infant Development

The approach simulates, at a speeded up pace, the stages an infant experiences in acquiring its first language. For example, before the infant utters anything more intelligible than "Mommy" or "Daddy," that child has experienced hundreds of hours in which language was imprinted upon body movements. The infant may only be able to decode the language through the medium of body movements such as looking, laughing, pointing, reaching, touching, and eating. Understanding of the target language was achieved in thousands of intimate caretaking transactions in which adults gently directed the infant's behavior with sentences such as:

Look at Daddy.
Look at Grandpa.
Smile for Grandpa.
Point to Autie.
Touch your nose.
Stick out your tongue.

Notice that these transactions do not demand speech from children. The child responds exclusively with a physical action initially and later in development with simple one-word utterances such as "yes" or "no.".

The Swiss psychologist Jean Piaget called this process of language acquisition *constructing reality*. It was not enough that someone *tell* the infant about reality or *explain* reality to the infant. Translation for the infant will not work. The child must, according to Piaget, *construct reality* through first-hand experience. For children with physical handicaps such as paralysis, the observation of language "causing" changes in the behavior of others is apparently enough to decipher and internalize meaning.

As far back as 1929, child psychologists Gesell and Thompson observed that infants develop a sophisticated understanding of what people are saying before the infant attempts to speak. Talk from the infant may be released once the child has internalized a rather intricate map of how the language works. Then, throughout the child's development, production always shadows comprehension. Production lags far behind the child's understanding of spoken language.

Once the child achieves fluency in the native language, the "biological" pattern for acquiring language does *not* disappear. Hence, if a person wants to acquire another language without stress, the sequence should be—first, acquire comprehension of the target language, and as comprehension becomes more and more sophisticated, there will be a point at which the individual spontaneously is *ready* to produce the language.

With infants, talk cannot be forced. Even coaxing and rewarding will not speed-up the appearance of talk. Talking is like walking—unless the infant is ready, all attempts at teaching will be futile. As understanding of spoken language expands and expands, people become ready to talk. Readiness to talk is an interesting concept because it contradicts the notion that one person can *directly* teach someone else to talk.

When talk appears it will *not* be perfect. There will be many distortions, but gradually pronunciation and grammar will shape itself in the direction of the native speaker.

The home is an "acquisition enriched" environment since communication with the infant is achieved when language is used to direct the child's physical behavior. Caretakers create a choreography in which language directs body movements.

By contrast, school is an "acquisition impoverished" environment for non-speakers of the target language since the instructor's behavior is to explain, explain, explain. When the instructor explains, declarative sentences are used which tend to be empty of information for the non-speaker.

For example, without a translation, this explanation in geography is meaningless to a non-speaker of English:

Alaska is a recent addition to the United States. The Alaska Highway System extends 1,523 miles from Dawson Creek, B.C., to Fairbanks in Alaska's goldrush country.

Classroom instructors can help children with limited English by transforming lessons in social studies, mathematics, etc., from the declarative into the imperative. Meaning will then be transparent to *all* students in the class. (For illustrations, see page 3-32.)

Summary. Children and adults can achieve understanding of a second language through the imperative faster than an infant acquiring its first language. The reason is that the infant's repertoire of responses is limited to a *few primitive behaviors* such as looking, reaching, grasping, pointing, touching, smiling, eating, and eliminating. By contrast, the student has a vast network of complex behaviors that can be evoked in response to directions uttered in the target language. Hence, the understanding of language that the infant achieved in thousands of hours can be condensed into a few hundred hours of training for the student acquiring a second language.

Brain Lateralization

Caretakers communicate with the infant when spoken language is uttered to direct physical behavior. We have discovered that the language-body communication also works for students—children or adults who are attempting to acquire a second language.

When the instructor skillfully uses the target language to direct the student's behavior, understanding of the utterance is transparent, often in only one exposure. Also, the understanding is achieved without stress and then retained for weeks, months, and even years.

Language-body communication is a fascinating and powerful principle of learning.

We observed the phenomenon with infants acquiring their first language and students acquiring a second language. It seems to be a universal principle that holds true for *any* language including the sign language of the deaf. It seems to hold true for *any* age group that has been studied from children to senior citizens.

The language-body principle of communication can be more clearly understood using recent findings from brain lateralization research (also known as the split-brain research). This work was pioneered by Nobel prize winner Roger Sperry and his colleagues at the California Institute of Technology. These researchers wanted to explore this issue: Does each hemisphere of the brain process information independently and then relay messages to each other across a narrow switchboard of neural tissue called the corpus callosum? Since the only connection between the two walnut-shaped halves of the brain is the corpus callosum, the plan was to cut this tissue to disconnect any communication between the left and right cerebral hemispheres of cats.*

*The optic chiasm was also cut.

Next, a black patch was placed over the cat's left eye so that everything the cat experienced through the right eye was transmitted only to the right hemisphere of the brain. The cat was then placed in front of two adjacent doors that swung inward when nuzzled by the cat. One door was marked with a "V" behind which was food; behind the other door with an inverted "V" was nothing.

Each time the cat was released with a patch over the left eye, it had to decide which door to select for a reward of food. Of course, on each trial, the door marked with a "V" would be varied randomly so that to find food, the cat had to learn to differentiate the symbols. When the cat consistently went to the door with the "V," learning had taken place.

Now, what would happen if the patch was placed on the right eye and the problem is reversed with food behind the door with the inverted "V"? In the normal cat, we would expect "negative transfer" which means that it will require substantially more trials to learn the reversal than it did to master the original problem.

But for the split-brain cats there was no negative transfer. It was as if the cat had never experienced the problem before. It was as if the left brain did not know what the right brain had experienced. Once the corpus callosum was cut, the left and right hemispheres of the brain seemed to function independently.

The split-brain research with cats and higher mammals stimulated the creative thinking of surgeons who reasoned as follows: Since epileptic seizures in many people seem to originate in one hemisphere of the brain and radiate like an electrical storm to the other hemisphere, the severity of an attack can perhaps be diminished by cutting the corpus callosum. Theoretically, this would contain the seizure to one hemisphere only. The result should be a decrease in the massive trauma that people experience in a seizure, and if both halves of the brain function independently, there should be no serious disruption in normal everyday behavior.

The operation was successful. There were diminished epileptic seizures and, in addition, we were able to explore further in humans the working of the right and left brain. The findings were exciting and have, I believe, important implications for learning other languages. The case history of P.S. as reported by Gazzaniga, LeDoux, and Wilson in 1977 illustrates how each hemisphere processes information.

P.S. is a right-handed, 15-year-old boy who experienced severe epileptic attacks at about the age of 2. His development was normal until the age of 10 when the seizures started again and became intractable. In January of 1976, the entire corpus callosum was surgically divided.

In one series of demonstrations after the operation, P.S. was seated a few feet from an opaque screen and instructed to fix his gaze on a dot in the center of the screen. Then a rear view projector flashed words or pictures on either the right or left sides of the screen and the person was asked to tell what he saw. Here's what happened.

When a picture of an ordinary object such as a *pencil* was flashed on the right side of the screen, P.S. immediately said, "I saw a pencil." But if the object on the next trial was an *orange* which appeared for an instant on the left side of the screen P.S. would report, "I didn't see anything." Curiously, P.S. correctly named all objects projected into the left brain (those appearing on the right side of the screen) but reported seeing nothing that was flashed to the right brain. *It was as if the right hemisphere was blind.*

In the next demonstration, words for common objects such as safety pin, tire, bicycle and playing card were flashed on either side of the screen. Again, a perfect score in naming items projected into the left hemisphere and "blindness" for items flashed into the right hemisphere. But the blindness was an illusion. The individual *did see* the pictures and words projected into the right hemisphere but he was not conscious of it—that is, he could not express the experience in words.

How do we know that? Even though the subject reported seeing nothing when, for instance, "orange" was flashed on the left side of the screen, if the researcher said, "Please pick up a pencil with your left hand and write the word that just appeared on the screen," P.S. scribbled the word, "orange." Researchers were astonished to discover that even though P.S. reported seeing nothing for an item flashed to his right brain, he could *write, spell, point to* or *pick up* the appropriate item with almost perfect accuracy.

They made the tests more complex. For example, P.S. was told, "When you see a word flashed on the screen, please say a word that is opposite. If for instance, you see 'man' then you would say 'woman.' If you see 'black,' you would say 'white.'" The results: Again, "blindness" for words flashed to the right hemisphere, but on every trial he could *point to* the correct item from a set of four words. The same results were obtained when P.S. was asked, "This time when you see a word, give me a word that is associated. For instance, if you see 'clock,' you might say 'time.' If the word is 'porch,' you might say, 'house.'" When P.S. only had to *point to* an associate from among three choices, there was a perfect score by either the left or the right hemisphere.

They tried this variation: "P.S., when you see a word, tell me another word that rhymes. For instance, if you see 'canoe,' you would say 'new' or 'who.'" Again, if there were three choices to select from, P.S. had almost a perfect score for either hemisphere.

Clearly, the right hemisphere is mute—*unable to talk*—but is is processing information and can express itself if you provide a "voice box" such as touching objects, pointing to a choice from alternatives, or even spelling.

The right brain understood action verbs because P.S. could point to a picture from a set of pictures that represented words such as "sleeping," "laughing," and "drinking." Remember, when each of those words were transmitted to the right hemisphere, P.S. reported, "I didn't see anything," yet he was able with almost perfect accuracy to point to the correct item in a set of choices.

In an infant's development of understanding, I suggested that the child decodes when the parent directs the infant's movements in caretaking situations such as dressing and feeding. I was most interested in how a split-brain patient processes commands. The directions to P.S. were, "When you see a word such as laugh, please laugh. If you see cry, then cry."

When the command "rub" was flashed to the right hemisphere, the subject rubbed the back of his head with his left hand.

He was asked, "What was the command?"

He said, "Itch."

It appeared as if a command was received in the right brain, followed by a change in behavior. The rubbing, for example, *was observed by the left hemisphere* which made an interpretation that P.S. was *itching* his neck. Notice that the left brain was not aware of what caused the movement in P.S., but it attempted to describe the behavior it observed.

This process was further shown in this demonstration: "P.S., assume the position of a ________" and the word "boxer" was flashed to the right hemisphere. Immediately, P.S. shifted his body into a pugilistic stance.

"P.S., what word did you see?"

Without hesitation, he said, "Boxer."

Later the demonstration was repeated, but just after "boxer" was projected to the right brain, P.S. was restrained from moving. Then he was asked, "What word did you see?"

He said, "I didn't see a word."

Moments later, when he was released, he assumed the pugilistic position and said, "O. K., it was boxer."

When a direction was flashed to the right brain, that hemisphere performed the appropriate action. Since the left brain did not receive the command, it was unaware of what "caused" the person's behavior. The left brain merely observed the change in behavior and attempted to make sense out of it. It is as if there is a "double consciousness" with each brain processing information independently, then selectively communicating with messages transmitted across the corpus callosum.

Further evidence of a "double consciousness" may be seen in the fascinating research in hypnosis by Ernest R. Hilgard, formerly the Chairman of the Psychology Department at Stanford University. As an illustration of Hilgard's work, when a person was asked to place a hand in ice water and verbally report the amount of pain on a scale of 0 to 10, the maximum pain was usually reached in less than a minute. Then, when the individual was hypnotized and instructed "to feel nothing in the water," the person verbally reported *no pain* while the hand was in ice water. However, the individual was further instructed while in hypnosis that the "hidden observer" would pick up a pencil with the other hand and signal the level of pain by *writing* a number on a scale of 0 to 10.

Results: Although the *left brain* was saying that the person was experiencing no pain while a hand was immersed in ice water, the *right brain* was *writing* with the other hand that the person was indeed experiencing pain that escalated rapidly from 0 to 10 (maximum pain) within one minute. Professor Hilgard's experiments with hypnosis (1977) are provocative because they are, in my opinion, an independent confirmation of findings from the split-brain research of Dr. Roger Sperry.

Is the left hemisphere able to understand commands? The evidence suggests, in the case of P.S., that when a command such as "laugh" was flashed to the left hemisphere, the individual often uttered the word aloud. The right brain then heard the direction and executed the command. Both hemispheres can recognize the correct response to a command when the individual is only required to point to a picture in a set of pictures, but *only the right hemisphere seems able to express appropriate behavior in response to commands.*

Application to language acquisition. The right hemisphere is mute but can express itself by listening to a command in the target language, and then performing the appropriate action. The left hemisphere can express itself by talking. The left is verbal while the right is non-verbal which means that it can communicate through physical behavior such as pointing, touching, drawing, singing, gesturing, and pantomime.

As a hypothesis, I believe that the infant deciphers the meaning of language in the right hemisphere. The target language is decoded when spoken commands by caretakers "cause" changes in either the infant's behavior or other people the infant observes.

The infant's left hemisphere cannot speak, but for hundreds of hours it observes language "causing" different actions in the infant and others—until the left brain is ready for its feeble attempt to talk. Gradually, the left becomes more and more aware that through talk, it has the power to "cause" events to happen. But throughout the child's development, the left shadows the right. The child's understanding as demonstrated in body expressions is far in advance of speaking.

I believe that nature's design continues to operate when an individual—child or adult—attempts to learn a second or third language. Therefore, it seems clear that a logical starting point for any instructional program that intends to teach another language is to structure the content especially for the right hemisphere.

Playing to the Right Hemisphere

The optimal starting point in acquiring another language is to enter the strange language through the right hemisphere. In the past 20 years, we have explored one way to achieve this by simulating relationships in adult-child caretaking transactions.

The instructional strategy, which I call TPR, is to seat a few students on either side of the instructor and request, "When I say something in the target language, listen carefully and do what I do. For example, if I say 'Tate!' and I stand up, you stand up. Just listen and act rapidly without trying to pronounce the words yourself."

Then, with the instructor as a model, the students start responding with actions to one-word commands such as "stand, sit, walk, stop, turn, and run." Most everyone is surprised that they can demonstrate perfect understanding with body movements in a few trials. Then the one-word sentence is expanded into:

"Stand up; point to the door; walk to the door; touch it; and open the door!"

Students are impressed that within a few minutes their comprehension can be expanded rapidly. Within a few hours, students understand grammatical constructions that are nested in the imperative such as:

When Maria walks to Juan and hits him on the arm, Shirou will run to the chalkboard and draw a funny picture of the instructor."

By entering the right hemisphere when language "causes" changes in the student's behavior, individuals can rapidly decipher the language code. As the student expands an understanding of how the target language works and what it means, there is a point when the person is ready to talk. This cannot be forced. This will occur spontaneously. And when talk appears, it will *not* be perfect. There will be many flaws, but gradually it will shape itself in the direction of the native speaker.

In comparison, a left hemispheric entrance is slow-motion learning. Each detail of production—which the student is *not ready* to make—is practiced before the student has internalized a holistic pattern of how the language works. By practicing surface features of production prematurely, the learning process is slowed down to a tedious, monotonous pace that extinguishes attention and retention. The consequence is stress.

Other effective right hemisphere instructional strategies have been developed by Harris Winitz, James R. Nord, Norman Gary, the late Judith Gary, and Georgi Lozanov.

The Learnables

Harris Winitz from the University of Missouri has developed an approach called "The Learnables," in which the student listens on a cassette to a direction in the target language, then *looks* at a picture. The meaning of the utterance is transparent from the context of the picture. The voice on the cassette moves the student from picture to picture, without translations, as the complexity of the target language increases and increases.

By listening and looking in response to spoken utterances, the student internalizes a more and more sophisticated understanding of the target language. "The Learnables" is a self-instructional program that is available commercially in English, French, German, and Spanish. (See *Order Form for TPR Training Materials on page 5-11.)*

A recent theoretical article by Dr. Harris Winitz was published in *The Annals of the New York Academy of Sciences* under the title, "Input considerations in the comprehension of first and second language." Also see his chapter in the book, *The Comprehension Approach to Foreign Language Instruction (Ed.: H. Winitz), 1981.*

Sens-It Cell Model

Another right brain approach that starts by training in comprehension skills has been developed by James R. Nord. The approach, called the *Sens-it Cell Model,* is based on a concept developed about thirty years ago by I. A. Richards (1968) and is illustrated in Richard's *Language Through Pictures Series.*

The principle is this: *Comprehension* is to hear a spoken utterance and then select an appropriate situation. Reverse the process and the result is *speaking,* in which one begins with a situation and selects an appropriate utterance.

Notice that the "utterance" is not language but only the public representation of language. Language has a public and private representation which corresponds to symbols such as talk and meaning which is a situation.

As Nord explains, "Language is neither a sentence alone nor a situation alone. It is their combination that makes a language and, therefore, it is their combination which needs to be used as a basis for analysis." The problem to be solved is how to provide in the classroom both the sentence and the situation so that comprehension is transparent.

Nord and his colleagues have developed a variety of techniques to fine-tune comprehension while students are seated at their desks in the typical classroom setting. Basically, students listen to an utterance, see a picture, then select an appropriate response from among alternative choices. When the student makes the correct choice, there is immediate confirmation because the paper on which the responses are being made, changes color.

Nord feels that comprehension fluency can best be achieved by applying *all comprehension type instructional formats that are available.*

For more information on the Sen-it Model, see the articles by Dr. James R. Nord cited in the reference section. Also see the chapter he has written in this book: *The Comprehension Approach to Foreign Language Instruction (Ed.: H. Winitz), 1981.*

Interactive Tape and Teacher Technique

Norman and the late Judith Gary from Cairo University in Cairo, Egypt have tested comprehension training in English with more than "2000 adult students in large classes under widely varying conditions for more than three years in Egypt." The students were mostly non-academic young adults in the lower ranks of occupations such as hotel employment, housekeeping, security, cook's assistant, and maintenance work.

Gary and Gary believe, as they explained in an article published in *The Annals of the New York Academy of Sciences,* that comprehension activities should make up the bulk of an instructional language program, "perhaps as much as 80 percent."

The authors have observed that literate adults acquiring understanding of a spoken language prefer having access very quickly to a visual representation of what they hear. Therefore, after students have internalized an understanding of several lessons, let them see the lessons in print. This gives the students easy access to lessons which increases their confidence since they can check to be sure that they understood all parts of each message. The lessons in print are *not* provided before all material is thoroughly internalized to prevent distorted concepts about the correspondence between sounds and the graphic representation, which is an especially difficult problem in English.

Gary and Gary in their article reviewed the research and concluded that the most important finding was that language learners should *not be required* to speak immediately — although students may produce utterances spontaneously if they wish. The results are more significant gains in reading, writing, and speaking as well as in listening comprehension when compared with students required to speak right away. This conclusion, they maintain, has more empirical support "than any other methodological issue which has been investigated."

According to the authors, the *last skill* to be introduced to the students *is speaking*. The *first* is *listening comprehension,* then reading followed by writing, and finally, speaking. They caution that reading, when introduced, should be limited "to what learners have already shown that they comprehend aurally. This is, they would read only what they have already heard."

I believe that Gary and Gary have developed an effective approach to expand the student's skill for flexible and complex thinking in the target language. The student becomes more and more sophisticated in understanding what people are saying in the target language.

For articles by Norman and the late Judith Olmsted Gary, see *Comprehension Based Instruction: Theory* by Judith and Norman Gary and *Comprehension Based Instruction: Practice* by Norman and Judith Olmsted Gary which was published in *The Annals of the New York Academy of Sciences.* At the end of the latter article, there is a sample lesson that illustrates the approach. Also read their chapter in the book, "The Comprehension Approach to Foreign Language Instruction" (Ed.: H. Winitz), 1981.

To contact Dr. Norman Gary, write him at: 401 S 15th Street, San Jose, California 95112.

Suggestology

Georgi Lozanov from Bulgaria has developed a right brain instructional strategy called *Suggestology.* The idea is to relax the resistance to language acquisition that comes from the critical thinking of the left hemisphere. The left brain seems to want to keep us "safe and sane." This is accomplished by critically scanning and rejecting, if possible, unfamiliar ideas. The left hemisphere constantly advises us that we should "stick to what we know."

Lozanov recognizes that we cannot expand the student's comprehension of the target language by merely explaining to the student the meaning of utterances. Content by itself is not enough. There is a lack of authenticity. There is a lack of believability.

An analogy would be an actor in a stage play. It is not enough for the actor to read lines from a script. There must be a performance in which the audience "believes" in the character the actor is playing. A convincing portrayal comes from the content of the dialogue integrated with appropriate intonations, gestures, facial expressions, costumes, and body movements.

Actors create a mood of believability in the audience—a relaxation of the critical thinking in the left hemisphere and heightened sensitivity of the right hemisphere. Actors construct a reality for the audience with talk, behavior, props, costumes, and music. The audience can then relax their normal skepticism and enjoy the assimilation of a new experience.

In Lozanov's approach, students are given a new identity including a name, an occupation, a geographic area in which they live, a family, and a background history. Each becomes a different person. This play acting with costumes, props, and music tends to bypass the left brain and permits the right brain to intake the target language.

For information about the educational applications of Lozanov's right brain approach (books, a newsletter, and a journal), write: The Society for Suggestive-Accelerative Learning and Teaching, Inc., P.O. Box 1216 Welch Station, Ames, Iowa 50011.

Actors create a mood of believability in the audience—a relaxation of the critical thinking in the left hemisphere and heightened sensitivity of the right hemisphere. Actors construct a reality for the audience with talk, behavior, props, costumes, and music. The audience can then relax their normal skepticism and enjoy the assimilation of a new experience.

In Lozanov's approach, students are given a new identity including a name, an occupation, a geographic area in which they live, a family, and a background history. Each becomes a different person. This play acting with costumes, props, and music tends to bypass the left brain and permits the right brain to intake the target language.

For information about the educational applications of Lozanov's right brain approach (books, a newsletter, and a journal), write: The Society for Suggestive-Accelerative Learning and Teaching, Inc., P.O. Box 1216 Welch Station, Ames, Iowa 50011.

Part III

MOST OFTEN ASKED QUESTIONS

To help you find the answers to specific questions, I have organized this chapter around the following topics:

Adults 3-36
Advanced Students 3-30
Attrition: How to reduce it 3-85
Austria: Teaching Methods 3-82
Beginning Students 3-14
Brain and comprehension 3-78
Brain and mathematics 3-89
Brain and meditation 3-90
Brain and prayer 3-90
Brain Research: New Findings 3-84
Brain and suggestion 3-88
Brain and the "unconscious" 3-79
Brainswitching 3-6
Children and language 3-25
Children and mathematics 3-90
Classroom 3-34
Class Size 3-83
Connecting With Students 3-80, 3-81
Crazy English 3-90
Discovery: Laws of Gravity 3-82
Goals (that motivate students) 3-10
Grammar: Some new ideas 3-36, 3-83
High School Students 3-36
Home School 3-53
Homework 3-49
How to Publish Your Work 3-68
Immersion: Research Findings 3-88
Internet: Meeting TPR aficionados 3-83
Introduction to TPR 3-2
Land Mines 3-53
Learning: A new theory 3-80
Mathematics 3-69
Music 3-69
Myth 3-29
Ninety-minute classes 3-85
Other Approaches 3-60
Personal 3-74
Policy-makers 3-59
Pronunciation 3-38
Research 3-3
Right-Left Brain 3-82, 3-84, 3-88, 3-89, 3-90
Science 3-69
Self-Teaching With TPR 3-52
Sign Language and Chimpanzees 3-79
TPR Storytelling ... 3-48, 3-49, 3-50, 3-78
Teacher Preparation 3-11
Testing 3-51
TPR Lessons 3-43
TPR Mentors 3-59, 3-83
TPR Student Kits 3-47, 3-48, 3-83
TPR Textbooks 3-48, 3-49
TPR Updates 3-68
TPR while Seated 3-47, 3-48
Transfer To Other Linguistic Skills 3-41
Vocabulary: Guidelines for selection 3-86
What's New .... 3-48, 3-49, 3-50, 3-78 thru 3-90
Workshop Presenters 3-72, 3-73

Note: Books, Student Kits, Teacher Kits, Games, and Video Demonstrations mentioned in my answers are described in the back of this book along with ordering information.

How would you summarize the basic characteristics of this approach?

It is based on the premise that people are biologically wired to acquire a language in a particular sequence. The sequence is visible from observations of how children acquire their first language. Before the child can utter anything more intelligible than "mommy" or "daddy," that individual has internalized a sophisticated understanding as shown when the infant accurately responds to commands as, "Dave, pick up your red truck and put it in your bedroom!" Further, we know that 1/3 to 1/2 of all utterances (Friedlander, 1972) directed at the young child are commands such as, "Don't make a fist when I'm trying to put on your coat!"

I hypothesize that to be in harmony with the biology of language acquisition, the sequence should be that understanding comes before speaking and is always further advanced than speaking. Understanding is probably a necessary condition for speech to appear. The achievement of understanding is accelerated by presenting the language through the imperative. When the child has internalized enough of the language code to be perceptually ready, speech will appear spontaneously.

Speech is like walking. Any attempt to force its appearance before the child is ready, is futile. And when speech occurs, there will be many distortions, but year by year, the distortions will gradually extinguish. The biological wiring as manifested in children's language development is still operative for learning a second language, no matter what the age of the learner. The only critical difference is pronunciation. Students beyond puberty who are trying to acquire a second language have a low probability of achieving a near-native pronunciation. The probability is high that most of these students will always have at least some accent (Asher and Garcia, 1969, 1982, 1986).

Can your TPR approach be applied to teaching any language?

Although all languages have not been explored, we believe the approach can be applied to any language. As of this time, my Total Physical Response has significantly accelerated the acquisition of English as a Second Language, Arabic, French, German, Hebrew, Japanese, Russian, Spanish, and the sign language of the deaf.

RESEARCH

How much research has been done to back up your TPR approach?

In presentations throughout the country, I often say that my Total Physical Response is perhaps the most thoroughly researched idea in the entire field of language acquisition. There are probably more experimental and field studies to support the principle than any other single concept in second language learning. I believe that is a fair and realistic conclusion, but you are invited to read the research documentation and decide for yourself. All research articles may be found in the list of references.

You mentioned that the latest electronic brain-mapping seems to confirm that comprehension activates the right hemisphere of the brain while speech activates the left. Why is this?

Why did nature decide to allocate the right side of the brain for understanding utterances we hear and the left for speaking? Here is my speculation: No editing is needed to receive a message but, indeed, before we speak, the string seems to be processed through an editor. The essence of socialization is to edit utterances before they become air waves carrying a message to another person. If we uttered every thought that flashed into our brain without editing, the result would be undecipherable messages that we hear from the lips of schizophrenics—a kind of James Joyce stream of consciousness.

If my editing hypothesis is correct, then of course speech would be on the left where the editor is located. Since there seems to be no editor on the right, it is capable of receiving and deciphering incoming messages. The brain seems to have its own intelligence and the more insight we have about how this brain-intelligence works, the better able we are to communicate with and motivate our students.

What about future research? What is still unknown?

Even though there is 25 years of research to support the Total Physical Response, much work remains to be done. For example, here are some unsolved problems which advanced students may wish to explore in a master's or doctoral thesis:

- When students experience language acquisition with TPR for four to eight years in school, will distortions in speech gradually extinguish?
- What is the correlation between student achievement when they experience TPR and individual differences such as learning style preferences, brain hemispheric dominance, grade point average, etc.?
- Under controlled conditions, how does the effectiveness of TPR compare with the Silent Way, Berlitz and the Direct Method as practiced at the Defense Language Institute and the Foreign Service?
- How will other innovations such as Blaine Ray's storytelling technique increase the learning impact of TPR?
- Specifically, how does body movement in response to commands facilitate long-term recall?
- Demonstrate with creative applications of TPR how to help native speakers of English correct the misuse of grammatical features such as pronouns (i.e. "Me and him went to the store.") This is especially challenging because the misuse is pervasive among the user's peer group and has often persisted for years.

What is still to be discovered about TPR?

Why it works so beautifully is still a mystery. Also, classroom teachers can make a contribution to our understanding of what we can expect from different age groups of students who acquire language skills with TPR.

For example, with children in the first and second grades, what skills can they acquire with TPR in 10 hours, 20 hours, 30 hours, etc.? We need *normative data* for different age groups at different stages of language acquisition. This means to measure systematically the skills of comprehension, speaking, reading and writing as people progress from level to level. The measurements can be standardized tests or teacher-made tests—providing that *each measure you use is reliable.* There are simple ways to determine the reliability of a measure. The most common are: test-retest with the same form, test-retest with a parallel form, or split-half. (Consult any basic text in testing for examples of how to do each.)

Another issue to be resolved is the optimal *blend* of exercises beyond Level 1. I believe that beyond Level 1, TPR is valuable for internalizing *any* new vocabulary item or structure.

Once people are into production, what left-brain exercises will enhance performance? Blaine Ray and his colleagues have reported success in the classroom with his storytelling technique in the *Look, I Can Talk!* series, but rigorous data showing the effectiveness of the approach have yet to be collected.

Language teachers (and instructors of mathematics and science) working with students day in and day out for years, have concluded that many concepts and skills are extremely "difficult" for students to master. What can TPR offer?

First, I believe that "difficulty" is an illusion. If someone tells me that learning is "difficult" for students, the message I get is that this is an unsolved problem requiring the creative application of brainswitching. It is an issue to be resolved in the area of research.

Because something is perceived as "difficult" does not necessarily mean that it is difficult. It means that we have not yet discovered a way of presenting the information or skill so that intake happens in one exposure. Also, I do know this: The chances of transforming the "difficult" task into an "easy" task are dramatically increased with the creative application of TPR which is a powerful brainswitching technique. The application may not be obvious, but my intuition is that it is definitely within the achievable range. Again, that is my strong feeling; not a dogmatical proclamation. It is a challenge for the young researcher to demonstrate how a "difficult" to internalize grammatical feature, for example, can be internalized in a few exposures.

BRAINSWITCHING

You talk about brainswitching from one hemisphere to another to help people internalize information on the first exposure. Have you got some practical suggestions for doing this?

My book ***Brainswitching*** is all about how to use both sides of the brain for learning, problem solving, counseling, motivation and so on, but I can offer you three ideas for persuading the ever-vigilant and blatantly suspicious gatekeeper which is the left brain to swing open a huge cathedral door on the right brain to let information gallop in unimpeded.

The first strategy is **body movement**. The student's body is our best ally for transmitting and receiving messages on the first exposure. You notice that I work the audience continually by reaching out, touching people, and inviting them to stand and join me in a demonstration.

The second brainswitching strategy is the **metaphor**. For example, I just used a metaphor when I talked about a suspicious gatekeeper swinging open a huge cathedral door on the right brain to let information gallop in. Another example: when a politician was asked recently about the US tax code, he said, "It is like an inner tube with a thousand patches." I think one of the most valuable skills any teacher can acquire is being able to find and create appropriate metaphors. This along with dramatic acting should be high priority skills in any teacher training program.

Incidentally, you notice that the metaphor is the secret of comedy. "Norm, how is the world treating you?" "...like a baby treats a diaper."

The third strategy is to **extinguish all critical responses** from our repertoire of teacher to student interactions. For instance, you will never hear me tell a student, "That's wrong!" or "Didn't you study at all?" The reason is that students (as well as the rest of us) are so self-critical that it is counterproductive to turn the heat up with any additional criticism, no matter how well intentioned, such as telling ourselves; "I'm doing this for the student's own good. Unless I give them feedback, how will the person learn?"

It takes enormous self-discipline on our part to eliminate negative facial expressions and remarks because we have experienced negative comments almost exclusively from our teachers. If you think about it, we are the victims of negative models.

Instead of, "That's wrong!" I may say, for example, "You're on the right track. Can anyone shape this up a bit?" or "You're never wrong in here; only off-target."

Often students will make an "off the wall" response which is an easy target for ridicule. I do not give in to the temptation. Rather, I will say, "That's very creative (which it is)."

If the student tells me, "I don't know." I may respond, "Say anything because anything you say in here is right. Give me a little piece—a little something to work with." Or I may say, "That's all right. Relax. I'll be back to you in a moment." Or I may say, "That's the left brain talking. Switch over to the right. I'll be back."

When I asked a question of a student in one of my statistics classes, the individual does not say, "I don't know." (which I gently extinguish from their repertoire) but rather, "I'm switching. I'm switching. Give me a moment."

If I play to the right brain of my students, are there any risks?

The only risk is that the left brain may be "jealous" since instruction is usually directed, in school situations, to the left brain. Therefore, the left may attempt to invalidate the right brain instruction with "inner talk" to the student such as, "This is so easy; I must not be learning anything." "I understand everything the instructor is saying in French, but I can't speak in French. Is this approach really worthwhile?" The left may attempt to sabotage the novel procedure just because it is unfamiliar and also because the left has nothing to do but "stand around and cause mischief." I believe that the left hemisphere should not be unoccupied for too long. One remedy is to permit the left to participate with the use of short dialogues which the students create based on constituents acquired through the imperative. Also, the storytelling exercises in the *Look, I Can Talk* series by Blaine Ray are helpful in engaging the left in productive activities.

Incidentally, by simply asking a question, you automatically brainswitch the activity from the right to the left hemisphere, especially if the expected response is either a written or spoken word, phrase, or sentence.

What's the difference between memorization and internalization?

It is the difference between processing information on the left side of the brain compared with the right. Traditional left brain instruction is verbal, either in spoken language or in print, and it is processed in serial order, word by word or sentence by sentence. The key characteristics are *verbal* and *serial order.*

By contrast, right brain instruction is non-verbal and processed in patterns. The key characteristics are *non-verbal* and *patterns.* This is something of an oversimplification because the right brain does process verbal information if it is presented in patterns such as a story, a drama, or an experience.

Activities associated with the left brain are work, study, multiple exposures to information, memorization, short-term retention, and stress. The classic example is the experience we have all had in school when we "studied (crammed) for the test." This means that we used repetition for short-term retention of information until it was called for on cue as in an examination. After that, the left brain had permission to erase.

For comparison, activities associated with the right brain are play, single exposure to information, internalization, long-term retention, and zero stress. A classic illustration of this is learning a new card game. Friends often want to introduce us to a new game by "explaining the rules." This is input to the left brain which rejects the verbal messages as nonsensical. We perceive the explanation as if we were looking at puzzling hieroglyphics. Hence, we instinctively do a brainswitch to the right hemisphere by saying, "Let's play a hand and we'll catch on."

Please keep in mind that the left brain responds to input such as:

analyzing	explaining
critiquing	judging
declaring	talking
discussing	telling

The right brain flashes on when you use:

acting	singing
drawing	storytelling
games or sports	touching, and
gesturing	tasks such as sewing, cooking,
metaphor	or small appliance repair.
pointing	

Where can I find more information about the right-left brain?

For a technical compilation of research findings from a three-day conference at UCLA, see the book: *"The Dual Brain: Hemispheric Specialization in Humans"* (eds.: Dr. Frank Bensen and Eran Zaidel), published by The Guilford Press. For an easy-to-read review of the right-left brain research with ***practical applications*** in language learning, mathematics, health, hypnosis, memory, etc., see my book, *"Brainswitching"*, published by Sky Oak Productions.

As the course develops, do the instructor's goals shift?

Yes, there is a shift from gross to fine detail. In the beginning, students are responding to chunks of language without focusing on the subtle features. As training advances there is more fine tuning to smaller and smaller details. You begin with a wide tolerance for student speech errors, but as the training progresses, the tolerance narrows.

An analogy is the tolerance parents have for distortions in their children's speech. What is rewarded at one age with remarks as, "How cute! How darling!" is punished at a later age with sharp parental comments such as, "It's not 'Me and Jeff brang in the groceries,' but 'Jeff and I brought in the groceries."' Remember, that as students progress in their training, more and more attention units are freed to process feedback from the instructor.

In the beginning, almost no attention units are available to hear the instructor's attempts to correct distortions in speech. All attention is directed to producing utterances. Therefore, the student cannot attend efficiently to the instructor's corrections.

Is goal-setting important for student learning?

It is absolutely critical. Part of student restlessness, lack of attention, and indifference is a by-product, in my opinion, of *having no goal.* People need goals to focus their attention, direct their energy, and persist with a task to completion. Please remember that it is important to promise students goals that are meaningful to them. For instance, a goal of internalizing the past tense at the end of the second year is a meaningful goal for the teacher, but not for the students who are apt to perceive as meaningful the goals of *reading a menu* or *understanding a television commercial* or *gossiping about a mutual friend.*

But how does one discover goals that are attractive to students?

One suggestion is to ask a focus group (i.e., a sample of students) to brainstorm goals in a small group of five or six students with one student elected to write down all ideas suggested no matter how fantastic or far-fetched. In brainstorming, all critical comments within the group are forbidden such as, for instance, "Aw, that won't work... That's silly... I don't like that idea... Let's get serious."

Rather than being critical, students are encouraged to "piggy-back" on other ideas, that is—expand on an idea, elaborate on it, suggest ways to enhance it. Encourage students to be crazy and think wild because later we can edit the list for practicality. (As an aside, notice that this activity quiets the judicious left brain by closing the door to critical comments while simultaneously swinging open the door to the creative right brain.)

Next, select the most promising ten or twelve ideas and present the list of goals to another group of students who rank the goals from most to least attractive; then organize the course to achieve the goals that students themselves tell us are interesting and motivate them.

TEACHER PREPARATION

What kind of teacher preparation is recommended?

A well-organized TPR workshop for teachers is excellent preparation. Successful TPR workshops have been structured with an introduction using either a live demonstration with members of the audience or show children and adults performing on video.

The presentation should include the rationale behind the TPR approach, and then each instructor should practice with students under the guidance of a master teacher experienced in the classroom applications of TPR with children or adults. There should be frequent follow-up sessions because once instructors begin their own classes, they become aware of many questions they would like to ask. This type of teacher training could be implemented easily by school districts, and the departments of teacher training in colleges and universities.

If no TPR workshops are available, I recommend that an instructor start by reading James J. Asher's Learning Another

Language Through Actions followed by Ramiro Garcia's *Instructor's Notebook.* With this information, one has a clear-cut conceptual blueprint together with a series of practical TPR lessons for a successful classroom experience.

Incidentally, if you are a novice to TPR, please try out the initial lessons with your neighbors and friends so that you can build your self-confidence in the approach and smooth out your delivery before you start with your students.

Finally, I recommend support groups similar to those of IBM and Macintosh, which meet to exchange tips and solve problems.

Are there any teacher preconceptions which could block the successful application of your TPR strategy?

There are three preconceptions which should be neutralized. The first is the *illusion of simplicity.* This seems to be an affliction of native speakers who have overlearned their language to such a keen state of perfection that it is perceived as a simple task. One then tends to move too rapidly and make large jumps that produce acute distress in students.

Secondly, the illusion of simplicity may result in a tendency to be *over-ambitious* for students. The teacher then pushes and rushes ahead, rather than moving systematically with a gradual transition from point to point. Perhaps the advice here is to relax and enjoy the venture along with the students. Let it unfold, develop and evolve.

The third difficulty, especially for native speakers, is a *narrow tolerance for errors in speaking.* Remember, we babbled before we talked and scribbled before we drew. In the development of any skill, there is a natural transition from gross to fine detail.

How does your TPR approach increase the teacher's creativity?

Since each student is continually emitting action responses, the instructor has an accurate "reading" of individual student progress at all times. Secondly, the massive feedback from student behavior seems to stimulate teacher creativity. For example, Pat Overall, who worked in the San Francisco Bay Area, developed a way of expanding the confinement of the classroom. She commissioned an artist friend to draw huge pictures on stiff cardboard. Each picture was a different environmental scene such as the living room, kitchen, bathroom, the street, and the inside of an office.

Then, some students were positioned at different locations in the room, each holding a different environmental scene. Other students would be directed in Spanish to a location such as the bathroom and responded to utterances as, "Touch the sink! Touch the tub! Turn on the faucet, wet your hands, put soap on your hands and wash your face!" Incidentally, you may see this innovation in our video demonstration:
Children Learning Another Language: An Innovative Approach.

Do you think that networking would be helpful in applying TPR?

Definitely.

Is this TPR approach exhausting for the teacher?

I used to think so until I observed the veteran TPR instructor, Ramiro Garcia, apply TPR with his high school students. Ramiro speaks in a low-key conversational voice, models once or twice, then utters directions to produce maximum action from students. The students do most of the physical work in response to his directions. With experience and observing many different instructors apply TPR, one acquires a pacing that is relaxed and comfortable. Some instructors such as Joe Moore and Gene Lynch are high-voltage personalities in constant motion, but others such as Ramiro Garcia and David Wolfe are mellow and low-key in their delivery of TPR. The approach seems to work no matter how it is filtered through the personality of the instructor.

If you had the responsibility of designing a teacher training program for language instructors, what would you do?

There are skills that I would definitely include in the program such as drama, storytelling, and voice training. Of course, these would be ancillary to the primary skill of helping students brainswitch from one hemisphere to the other and back again. Most people have experienced in school, class after class of left brain input but few illustrations of right brain input. Hence, teacher trainees need, in my judgment, intensive modeling of right brain input as, for instance, acquiring another language through TPR.

Other examples of right brain input would be storytelling, music, drama, pantomime, skits, and non-verbal communication using body language. Also, I would include play, sports, and practical skills such as cooking, plumbing, carpentry, electrical problem solving, and small appliance repair as right brain input.

BEGINNING STUDENTS

Must I start with, Stand up and Sit down?

No, it is not mandatory. It just happened, as I explained in Chapter 1, that I started with, Stand up, Sit down, Walk, etc. It is not a sacrosanct, magical entrance into the right brain.

To play to the right brain, visualize a bubble with a thousand points of entry. I entered with Stand up, Sit down, etc., but Ramiro Garcia has entered with, Walk to the chalkboard, pick up a piece of chalk and draw a house. Others have entered the right hemisphere with, Catch this ball, Throw the ball to me, etc.

Some guidelines for entry are these: physical movement, drawing, acting as in a skit, dramatizing a scenario (Stand up. Walk to the drawer. Open the drawer. Remove the pistol, etc.), playing a game such as a sport, performing a task such as cooking, sewing or small appliance repair, and singing.

What about the motivation of students?

For children and adults, motivation is superb. The three elements that generate intense student involvement and interest are (1) continual and fast-moving action, (2) surprises in unexpected novel commands that are often zany and bizarre (e.g., "When Henry runs to the chalkboard and draws a funny picture of Molly, Molly will throw her purse at Henry!"), and (3) students are aware that the second language is accessible to them as manifested in comments such as, "I can learn this language! I understand everything the teacher is saying!" For children in elementary school, the TPR instructional strategy based on the imperative could continue for many years with sustained student interest.

For adults, after 20 or 30 hours of training, some may express doubt that learning is taking place. Our explanation for this phenomenon is a *contrast effect.* An analogy is the experience of passengers on a jet airliner. As the plane ascends into the air, there is a distinct experience of acceleration and speed as one views the slant of the aircraft in relation to stationary buildings and objects on the ground. Once the plane has leveled off thousands of feet up in the air, there is no perception of velocity. There is the illusion that the plane is suspended motionless in space. To perceive movement, one needs to see the contrast of the vehicle in relation to the ground.

At the beginning of language training, students are euphoric because they can clearly *contrast* the massive internalization of the target language in comparison with their pre-training state. They are keenly aware of the sharp acceleration in their learning curve. Later in training, the learning curve is still steeply climbing, but it may be imperceptible to students. The input from the instructor is being internalized so easily that it seems the student is not moving. In the middle of training, with no point of reference, except prior fast learning, there is an illusion of no progress.

One solution is to collect, on video tape, samples of student skills at different stages of training so that when students have the illusion of "standing still" on the learning curve, you can show them where they were four weeks ago or eight weeks ago. Another solution, suggested by Ramiro Garcia, is to record on tape every command or other utterance you will present during a class meeting. In making your recording, speak rapidly with one utterance quickly following the next. Then at the beginning of the class, play the tape with this introduction: "At the end of today's class, each of you will understand everything you will hear next." When the class is over, play the tape again. If this is done at the beginning and end of each class, it could give your students a vivid realization of what they accomplished.

Can TPR be used as a supplement rather than the core of the entire course?

Definitely. The use of the imperative to accelerate the internalization of the target language has been used successfully as an adjunct to other approaches. For example, Richard Pugh in the Cupertino School District of California has taught Spanish to "gifted" 6th graders with this plan: He begins with the imperative for the first half of the course and then he follows up with the traditional audio-lingual textbook which has dialogue memorization, phonemic drills, reading, and writing exercises. Pugh reports that the 6th graders who start with understanding Spanish through the imperative, complete the textbook in about a fraction of the time needed by other "gifted" 6th graders who started immediately with the audio-lingual text. In other words, he observed large amounts of positive transfer-of-learning from the imperative training to a traditional approach.

Dr. David Wolfe who teaches Spanish and French in the Philadelphia Public School System (and supervises other ESL/FL instructors) reports a parallel experience. From the textbook, he extracts all the vocabulary that can be TPR-ed. For example, he organizes the words into columns under the heading of nouns, adjectives, verbs, adverbs, etc. Then, before students ever open a textbook, they internalize those words using TPR. The result is that three or four weeks later, when Dr. Wolfe passes out the books, the students are delighted that almost all the print on every page is familiar. Hence, students escape the experience of "textbook shock" that happens when students see page after page of hieroglyphics that triggers a rush of negative messages from the left brain such as, "Wow, this looks difficult. I don't think I can do it. I know I can't do it. What's the use of trying: I'll never get it."

By TPR-ing the vocabulary that students will later see in the textbook, you have created a comfort zone for students and I might add, a comfort zone for yourself because the textbook experience now becomes an attractive tool for learning rather than a source of dread and daily stress.

Why does your TPR approach produce long-term recall?

One possible explanation is the *motor skills hypothesis.* The procedure may have long-term recall for the same reason that any manual skill such as ice skating, bicycling or swimming has long-term recall. That is, in the initial learning, there was keen activation of the kinesthetic sensory system or "muscle learning," as it is sometimes called.

By contrast, in the usual foreign language classroom, the kinesthetic sensory system is only occasionally activated. Students most frequently sit quietly in rows, listen to the teacher and repeat what the teacher says, or mimic a dialogue they have learned by rote memory. The most powerful teaching aid available—the student's muscular response system—is rarely used.

A second explanation is the *believability hypothesis.* Student resistance to the assimilation, storage, and retrieval of information may be a function of "believability." For example, translating "Tate" into stand up and "Suware" into sit down has low believability. The high speed logic of the left brain may be this: How can "Tate" mean stand up when I have learned through thousands of previous experiences that when I heard the utterance, "Stand up," I have observed the physical behavior of myself and others standing up. Since the utterance, "Stand up" means to stand up, how can "Tate" mean to stand up?

The English utterance, "Stand up" has high believability while the Japanese utterance, "Tate" has low believability. The hypothesis is that when there is a conflict between high and low believability datum, the high will tend to dominate. The resistance generated by the left brain can be short-circuited, according to this hypothesis, by creating ***factual experiences***. For instance, if "Tate" does not mean to stand up why did my body perform this action every time the instructor said "Tate"? And if "Suware" does not mean to sit down, why am I sitting down after that utterance is spoken? It may be extremely difficult for the left hemisphere to deny factual input in the form of primary experiences, but easy to deny the validity of a statement by the instructor that an alien noise coming from his mouth means what he says it means.

Still a third explanation is the *right brain hypothesis.* Studies by Nobel prize winner Roger Sperry and his colleagues (Gazzaniga 1967, 1977) suggest that the right and left hemispheres of the brain process information independently and they selectively transmit messages to each other across a neural switchboard called the corpus callosum. The left brain seems to communicate through speech while the right brain is mute, but can communicate through physical behavior such as pointing, touching, drawing, singing, gesturing, and pantomime. TPR instruction may permit the student to process information through the right brain while traditional formats such as the audio-lingual or translation approaches may be oriented almost exclusively to left brain processing.

How fast should the instructor move students? What is the ideal pacing?

This will vary from group to group and student to student. One guideline is to move students fast enough for continual action but not so fast that they experience failure by making mistakes. You want each move to be successful. You should have a smooth, graceful transition from action to action. This is why a prepared script or outline is important.

Directing your actors for continuity and optimal movement is acquired through experience. The more you try it, the more proficient you become. I urge that instructors new to TPR try out lessons with friends and neighbors before coming into the classroom. This advanced sampling will enhance one's self confidence in the approach and smooth out the delivery.

How much repetition is necessary when the instructor models by uttering a command and acting along with students?

There is no universal rule. As a hint, the behavior of your students will continually signal you what to do next. For instance, if a student is hesitant or confused or rather slow to respond, the message to you is that more trials are needed. The ideal is to repeat until the student is confident, secure, and can successfully perform alone. There will be individual differences and with experience you will get more and more insight into pacing .

Is there some point in training when students themselves ask to memorize rules, grammar or idioms?

Strangely, that is exactly what happened with night school adults learning German through actions. After about 60 hours of TPR training, the students said they were ready to *memorize* fine points of grammar. They asked for grammatical explanations and were eager for rote learning of idiomatic expressions and other features.

Dr. Janet King Swaffar at the University of Texas observed a similar phenomenon. After 17 weeks (about 85 classroom hours) of internalizing German through the imperative, "classes expressed an independent desire to do regular memorization..." The students, at this point in training, recognized the value in "...rote learning of principle parts of verbs, mastering the rules of German word order, and learning idiomatic prepositional phrases. Therefore, a grammar text was assigned as supplementary reading. However, actual discussions of grammatical points remained limited to the five minute period at the end of the class hour or outside consultation between individual students and instructor." (Page 30, Swaffar and Woodruff, 1978.)

The important thought here is that when the students were ready, as indicated by their requests later on in training, memory exercises and rote rule learning were introduced. The implication is that when students are *ready*, rote learning can be a productive supplement to their TPR training.

I would like to try TPR, but my school system requires that I use a textbook they have selected. Any suggestions?

A Spanish instructor at Stanford University was required by her department to use the traditional left-brain type textbook. She did this: One day in her class, for five minutes only, she used a sample of TPR activities; then for the rest of the period worked with the book.

The next day, the students asked, "How about more of what you did yesterday? You know, you utter a direction in Spanish and we act it out." So, she applied ten minutes of TPR. This continued class after class with most of the time working with the book, but more and more with TPR. The results: a keener level of involvement by the students throughout the semester and a higher level of achievement in student proficiency. Even if you are "locked-in" with a required book, TPR can be an effective supplement to increase student motivation and achievement.

Dr. David Wolfe (instructor in Spanish and French) and Gene Lynch (instructor in German) have other excellent suggestions. For example, they recommend: 1. Comb the textbook to find all *action* verbs (i.e., scratch, look, walk, sit, sew, read, ride, throw, etc.). 2. Then, write TPR exercises that use the action verbs with other vocabulary in the book including nouns, adjectives, and adverbs. For example, consider the vocabulary item, "crooked." *TPR the item* with sentences that can be acted out by the students such as: Make your arm crooked. Draw a crooked line on the chalkboard. Now draw a straight line.

Wolfe and Lynch have discovered that *most* of the vocabulary in standard texts can be presented in a TPR format for easy assimilation by students long before they ever see the textbook. Then, when you distribute the book to each student, they are thrilled to discover that an enormous amount of the content is already understood. This reduces shock and enhances the student's motivation to work with the book.

How do you cope with abstractions without using translations?

When you cast material in the imperative, there is no translation. Abstractions may be an exception. Abstractions are simply vocabulary items that can be incorporated in several different ways. First, we recommend delaying abstractions such as *honor, country* and *government* until a large amount of structure in the target language has been assimilated with concrete vocabulary items.

Later in training, abstract vocabulary items have been taught with English on one side of a stiff cardboard flashcard and a foreign equivalent on the other side. Then the card is manipulated as a concrete item. For instance, if the target language is German, the instructor may say in German: "Maria, throw *government* to Eric! Eric, put *government* on top of your head and hand me *honor!* Sandy, put *justice* on top of the red book and take *honor* from me and give it *to* Cynthia!" (A demonstration of this technique may be seen in the video cassette, *Strategy for Second Language Learning.*

Another approach is to present the abstract concept in context. Later in training, you can explain an abstract concept *in the target language.* For instance, "Washington, D.C. is the center of government for America just as Ottawa is the center of government for Canada." Blaine Ray uses this approach in his storytelling technique and it seems to work

Frankly, I am not completely satisfied with the transition from a concrete level of reality with TPR to an abstract level of discourse. There must be new ways to achieve a more graceful transition, but this is an interesting problem for future researchers to discover.

Any suggestions for acquiring idioms?

Yes. I would suggest three steps. First, *delay* idioms until Level 2 when students have made a comfortable transition to production. Secondly, use the target language to explain the idiom in *simple terms* using vocabulary the students have already internalized.

As an illustration, the American idiom, "What is the hotel room running for?" can be explained in simpler terms as, "What does the hotel room cost?" Another example would be, "Don't let it throw you" which means in simpler terms, "Don't let it upset you." or "Don't let it distress you." or "Don't let it make you angry."

The third step is to invent and then act out a scenario in which the idiom is used. For instance, the scene is a hotel lobby in which the student plays a hotel clerk and the instructor is the customer. The customer approaches the hotel clerk and asks: "Can you tell me what the rooms are running for?" The clerk replies, "Yes, I can. For one person, the cost is $25 a night and for two people, it is $40."

Can your suggestions for acquiring idioms be applied to abstractions?

Yes, indeed. Use the three step model. First, delay the introduction of abstractions until Level 2 when students have made a confident transition to production. Next—this is Step 2—*explain* the abstraction in *context* using vocabulary the student has already internalized. For example, if the abstraction is *government*, then say, "Washington is the center of the American government just as Paris is the center of the French government and London is the center of the British government." The third step is to create sentences that signal the understanding of the abstraction with a physical action. For instance, "If San Jose is the center of California government, *raise your hand;* but if Sacramento is the center of California government, *stand up.*"

Some people feel that TPR is fine at the beginning of language training (perhaps the initial month or two), but then what?

Contee Seely, co-author of "Live Action English," has suggested many reasons to continue using TPR beyond the initial stages of language acquisition. For about fifteen years in San Francisco, Seely has used TPR to teach English as a second language and Spanish in a private language school. TPR, according to Seely, is valuable at any stage of language acquisition for these reasons: *First,* TPR enables learners to feel comfortable interacting with people in the new language. *Secondly,* TPR builds confidence in students to use the language outside the classroom.

Thirdly, TPR prepares students to perform role-playing with fuller emotion and to converse freely, either with a ready-made dialogue or one created by the students. The fourth *reason is* that with TPR the student can experience the meaning of a new vocabulary item. This is right brain stimulation that increases the chances for long-term retention.

Still *another reason is* that TPR-based activities at any level, can help students internalize complex structures "more effectively than any other way." Finally,—and perhaps the most important reason of all—learners at all levels enjoy TPR type activities and "are motivated to do them."

Recently, Seely and his colleagues have discovered that a marvelous follow up to the TPR experience is storytelling with the *Look, I Can Talk!* student textbook for Level 1 and *Look, I Can Talk More!* student textbook for Level 2. The series may be ordered in English, Spanish, French or German.

When should reading and writing be introduced?

When a sample of spoken directions is internalized, after 10 or 12 hours of TPR training, many instructors introduce reading. The reading content is confined to utterances students have thoroughly internalized through the imperative. For example, the instructor may write on the chalkboard, "Stand!" and gesture for a student to perform the action. The next written direction may be "Walk!" and so forth. Instructors seem to agree that students who are literate in their native language appreciate access to a printed representation of the spoken utterances. Again, reading should shadow comprehension of the spoken language.

If reading is introduced too soon, seeing the printed language may produce mispronunciations, especially if the target language is English. With Spanish, Ramiro Garcia has been successful with this reading approach applied to high school students and adults: After 12 hours of the TPR experience, he distributes a list of 30 commands (stand, sit, walk, touch, etc.) and an alphabetized list of all vocabulary items that have been used in training. Given these two lists, students can create hundreds of novel directions that are used in role reversal or writing a script for a skit that students will act out. (See Garcia's *Instructor's Notebook*, and see his sequel called *The Graphics Book*, which is available in English, Spanish, French, and German.)

For students with limited English what can the regular classroom teacher do to help these students?

I have three suggestions. The first is to transform your lessons in mathematics, geography, social studies and so forth from the declarative into the *imperative*. For example, the usual declarative approach would be to tell the students that: "The capital of Alaska is Juneau. The Hawaiian Islands are in the Pacific Ocean. Canada is north of the United States. The Atlantic and Pacific Oceans border the United States."

A more effective approach which *everyone* in your class can understand is this: "Myrna, please walk to the wall map and outline with your finger the United States. Now, outline Alaska. Touch the capital of Alaska, which is Juneau. Now, outline Canada. Touch the Pacific Ocean. Touch the Atlantic Ocean."

Even though foreign students are unfamiliar with the language of instruction, the meaning is transparent when the teacher skillfully uses the imperative to communicate.

My second suggestion is to train your teacher's aid in how to use the imperative so that the student is *not* listening for translations, but instead hears a direction in the target language, then performs an appropriate response. If the goal is to increase the student's competency in the target language, translations only delay—and perhaps even retard the student's achievement of competency. The third suggestion is to train English-speaking children in the use of the imperative to help the limited-English student. Children naturally do this during recess in game behavior. For example, children direct each other with utterances such as:

"Don't step on the line."

"Move forward three steps. Now catch the ball."

"Throw the ball to Mary."

Should we expect students to make mistakes in responding to commands?

A few mistakes, perhaps, but as Ramiro Garcia has observed in his *Instructor's Notebook,* "If a student gives an inappropriate action in response to a spoken direction, it is the instructor's fault." This means that if the directions from the instructor are logical and flow in a systematic step-by-step pattern, students will perform the appropriate action almost perfectly. Occasionally, students will make errors through inattention or when they attempt to translate. However, with skillful guidance from the instructor, errors will be rare.

Can TPR be used in the vocational training of non-English speakers?

TPR is an ideal approach to train people in understanding English while they are learning a vocational skill. For example, utter a direction (i.e., "Insert the thread in the needle here."), model the appropriate response; then utter the direction again with a gesture that the students should thread the needle in their machines. Step-by-step with one direction logically following another, you can help students develop a vocational skill and simultaneously build comprehension of English. This is an exciting way to acquire understanding of another language because the motivation is keen to assimilate the vocational skill.

CHILDREN

What can be expected for children's pronunciation?

If the children have not yet reached puberty, they have a high probability that eventually their pronunciation will shape itself in the direction of the native speaker. We do *not* rush this process; nor do we attempt to force "perfect" pronunciation for utterances the children attempt to speak. At some point in comprehension training, children will spontaneously produce utterances in the target language. With confidence, children will talk more and more. It is important not to threaten their self-confidence by insisting upon "perfect" pronunciation, especially in the initial and even the intermediate stages of acquisition.

The task is *not* to shape pronunciation so that the speaker is accent-free (which may not be possible, nor desirable, especially in the adult learner), but rather that the student is intelligible and easily understood by the native speaker. This is a delicate task to achieve since the tendency of the native-speaking instructor is to strive for perfection, meaning an accent-free pronunciation.

How does your TPR approach help children acquire a language?

First, since there is no translation, children think in the target language. Secondly, they have long-term retention. This means, for example, that when the students return from the three month summer vacation, they are responding, after a few warm-up trials, as if they had never been away from school. Even if the children's training is discontinued until high school and many years have elapsed, the comprehension skills that were internalized through the body can be rapidly retrieved. Since a language-body approach such as the *total physical response is* stress-free and fast-moving, there is a keen level of motivation.

What must be done to apply the TPR approach successfully with children?

Since the TPR approach is so fast-moving, children internalize material more rapidly than expected by the instructor. Preparation becomes extremely important. As a hint, to encourage flexible thinking in the target language, constituents should be recombined continually to produce novel directions. As an illustration, in this example, the concept of "under" is presented in the context of many different situations: "Maria, put the red book *under* the table." "Eduardo, go to the chalkboard and draw a picture of the school." After the action is completed, say: "Now *under* the school, write your name."

"Now draw a box. *Under* the box, write the name of your father." "Jeffe, sit *under* the table."

As students advance in their comprehension skill, try using the target language to present lessons in art, mathematics, social studies, civics, and so forth. Remember to transform the declarative into the imperative so that concepts are immediately transparent to students. In other words, instead of "telling," which is left brain input, demonstrate yourself or direct students in a step by step demonstration through actions, pantomime, or drawing.

In designing these lessons, transform information from *the declarative into the imperative.* As an illustration, suppose the mathematical concept is the area of a rectangle. The usual approach is to explain the concept with declarative sentences such as: *This is called a rectangle. To find the area, you measure the width of the rectangle which is 5 inches; then you measure the height which is 3 inches. Now to find the area, simply multiply the height times the width. Five times three is 15 square inches.*

A student with, let us say, limited English, will understand almost none of that explanation. But, if you transform the declarative sentences into the imperative, understanding will increase to 95%. For instance, you say: "John, please come up to the chalkboard with your ruler. Pick up a piece of chalk and use your ruler to draw a five inch vertical line like this" (GESTURE IN THE AIR). "Now draw a three inch horizontal line here" (GESTURE). "And another vertical line here" (GESTURE). "And another horizontal line here" (GESTURE). "Class, this" (POINTING TO THE RECTANGLE THAT JOHN HAS DRAWN) "is a rectangle." "Mary, please come up to the chalkboard and draw a smaller rectangle next to John's" (PAUSE). "Thank you." "Edna, come to the chalkboard and draw a rectangle that is larger than John's rectangle." "Next, I want to find the area" (GESTURE) "inside John's rectangle. John, please come up to the chalkboard again and bring your ruler." "Measure the width which is this line and write it here" (GESTURE). "Now measure the height which is this line and write it here" (GESTURE). "Now, John, find the area of the rectangle which is 5 X 3=15 square inches" (DEMONSTRATE).

Why don't our students have the self-discipline to endure the stressful left-brain instruction just as the students in European and Oriental cultures?

In other cultures, communicating in another language is often a survival skill. The need is apparent. Also, there is no alternative but to endure the stressful nature of the training. It is the only option that is available. Also, there are strong cultural differences. For example, children in rural China often follow directions that they hear on a loud speaker from an instructor who may be a hundred miles away. The concept of a teacherless classroom in which students work quietly and conscientiously is almost unthinkable in our culture.

I teach children another language. I'm intrigued with the process of TPR but I feel overwhelmed. What should I do?

Step one is to read my book, *Learning Another Language Through Actions* and Ramiro Garcia's *Instructor's Notebook.* If possible, attend a TPR workshop or view our video demonstration, *Children Learning Another Language: An Innovative Approach*.

Step two is to select starter lessons from the books I have just mentioned or use Nancy Marquez's *Learning Through Movements* which is available in English, Spanish, or French.

Nancy has experienced enormous success applying TPR in the Head Start Program. You will especially like the simple patterns in her book that make it easy for you to direct children or adults in the target language.

Be sure to try the lessons with your own children or the neighbor's children before you go into your classroom. The reason I recommend this is that I want you to feel comfortable, confident, and enjoy a smooth delivery.

Step three is a TPR "textbook" by Stephen Silvers which is chuck full of variety that keeps students excited and moving along from activity to activity. The title is, Listen & Perform which is now available in English, Spanish, or French. Another option for moving successfully from the imperative to the declarative is an effective storytelling technique developed by Blaine Ray called, L*ook, I Can Talk!* which can be ordered for each of your students in English, Spanish, French or German. Still another option is Francisco Cabello's popular book, *The Total Physical Response In The First Year*, now available in English, Spanish, or French.

For a change of pace, try my *TPR Student Kits* which are fun to use. Other playful activities that are fun and yet productive (a rare combination), I recommend these products: *Favorite Games for FL-ESL Classes, The Graphics Book,* and *TPR Bingo.* Also try *Total Physical Fun,* which can be ordered from Jo Ann Olliphant, 11004 - 111th Street, S.W., Tacoma, WA 98498.

Is it a myth that children learn a second language faster than adults?

When an immigrant family settles in another country, it is a common observation that children in the family become fluent speakers while the adults struggle to communicate. Hence, the conclusion that children are faster learners of a second language compared with adults.

I believe that the success of children is a function of frequent ***language-body conversations*** (which is the essence of TPR), while adults only occasionally have these important linguistic transactions. For example, one may hear, "Hand me that hammer" and someone picks up a hammer and puts it in the outstretched hand of the speaker. When the target language is followed by a physical action, one understands what was said.

This context of language followed by physical behavior is common for young children but not for their parents. Children experience hundreds of TPR transactions in caretaking relationships and in play. Therefore, their learning curve for the new language rises rapidly. Quickly, they make the transition from a noise-filled environment to one rich in meaning.

Since adults have fewer TPR opportunities, their learning curve will rise slowly and stressfully since they remain suspended indefinitely in a noisy speech environment. Therefore, the humane approach is first to experience several hundred hours responding to the target language in a TPR classroom where every utterance spoken by the instructor is clearly understood. Then, when this comprehension skill is well internalized, one is ready to enjoy the entry into a foreign country because one is not inflicted with the harshness of noise coming from every speaker one encounters.

Why do most people believe so strongly that speaking is the primary language skill one should acquire?

Anyone who has attempted to learn a second language in school has observed that the instructor starts with having students speak the foreign language. Naturally, if this is all students observe, then they believe that this must be the logical starting point in acquiring another language. Of course, this assumption is a myth—but a pervasive myth that is visible in ordinary conversation. For instance, you hear people say, "Do you *speak* Spanish?" or, "Do you *speak* French?" Notice the focus of attention is on speaking skill so that most people are unaware that *before* one can speak, one must acquire the skill of understanding the foreign language.

Is memorization different from internalizing information?

Yes. Definitely yes. Some birds can *memorize* and say utterances such as, "I can talk. I can fly." Children can *memorize* the Pledge Of Allegiance, but they do not know what they are saying. One child, for example, gave this recitation: "I pledge allegiance to the flag and to the Republic for which it stands. One Nation *invisible* with liberty and justice for all."

When we *internalize* information, we are able to *retrieve* and then to *use* the information appropriately. The Total Physical Response produces an *internalization* of information.

ADVANCED STUDENTS

How does your TPR concept apply to more advanced students?

One instructor received a summer fellowship from Princeton to help increase the English speaking skills of young scientists from other countries who would be working for the coming year in American universities. The instructor anxiously debated with herself whether a strategy based on commands would either be too elementary or perhaps offensive to these people who had studied English in their own schools for many years and had outstanding accomplishments in science. The safest strategy would be to use something familiar to the students such as a traditional textbook with dialogs to memorize, translations, grammar explanations, and rule memorization. Ignoring the safest approach, the instructor decided to see what would happen when a TPR approach with language-body conversations was used.

The results were spectacular. Students responded with great enthusiasm and keen interest. Even though they had many years of textbook English, their understanding of spoken English was rather rudimentary. With an instructional strategy based on TPR, English could be internalized and integrated in chunks rather than word by word as they had experienced in their own schools.

How far can you go with this TPR idea?

We believe that all grammatical features in the target language can be communicated through the skillful use of the imperative. In addition to structural features, we know that concrete vocabulary items are easily assimilated through TPR.

For example, you will discover how to TPR more than 50 grammatical features in English, Spanish, or French from these books by Eric Schessler:

English Grammar Through Actions

Spanish Grammar Through Actions

French Grammar Through Actions

Stephen Silvers demonstrates in his *Command Book* how to TPR 2,000 high frequency, vocabulary items, most of which are abstract. This is an excellent resource for making your own TPR lessons.

The latest innovation for moving children and adults effectively from the imperative into the declarative is the storytelling technique developed by Blaine Ray. Also, see Ramiro Garcia's *Graphics Book*, which shows how to use simple drawings that anyone can make, to advance students with brainswitching techniques into speaking, reading, and writing.

You emphasize variety. Can you elaborate?

Even if TPR is the major or minor format of training, ***variety*** is critical for maintaining continued student interest. The language-body conversation is a powerful facilitator of learning, but it should be used in combination with many other techniques.

The optimal combination will vary from instructor to instructor and class to class. As a rule of thumb, continually brainswitch from the right to the left and back again. If you play to the right brain too long, the left brain will kick in with sabotaging messages such as, "This again? Am I still learning? This seems too easy. I'm getting tired of moving when you utter a direction. Can't we do something else?" Hence, intersperse a left brain activity such as a short grammar lesson or a story to write or questions to answer in writing.

But no matter what you do, keep the performers moving towards short-term goals that are *attractive to students* such as: reading the headlines in a Japanese newspaper, ordering breakfast from a German menu, understanding three TV commercials from Spain, buying a bus ticket in China, giving directions to a taxi driver in France. When you arrive at a goal, mark the achievement with a colorful celebration.

How is "error detection" used as a way to increase student self-confidence?

Each teacher who tries an instructional approach based on commands, seems to invent an exciting new twist. For example, Karen Bouldin from San Diego developed a procedure of "error detection" to increase the self-confidence of her students who were learning English. It goes this way. Not in the beginning, but as the training progressed, Bouldin would periodically utter a wrong command. For instance, with a book in her hand she would say, "Shirou, take this *glass* from my hand and put it on the table!" Instantly, students would spontaneously correct her with, "It's *not* a glass! It's *not* a glass! It's a book!"

Students developed more and more confidence through "error detection." Of course, this can be over-done producing adaptation. But if applied conservatively, it could enhance student self-confidence, and encourage independence from the teacher as an authority figure. For instance, Bouldin reported that eventually her students had the courage to walk in spontaneously on administrators and start a conversation such as, "Hello. My name is Kim. What is your name? How old are you?

Are you married? No? Why not?" (Also, read Stephen Krashen's article [1978] about self-monitoring.)

Of course, when the student begins to speak, pronunciation will not be perfect; but as the assimilation through the imperative continues, the internalized "voice in the head" becomes clearer and clearer. The result is more and more skill at error detection in one's own speech and that of others. For a dramatic example of this process, notice how hesitant Randy was when he first uttered Spanish commands in role reversal as shown in my video cassette, *A Motivational Strategy for Language Learning*. Then, three weeks later with more TPR, you will see a striking improvement in his confidence to produce Spanish utterances.

Once a person acquires a second language, why is it then easier to acquire a third?

When one has acquired skill in a second language, there is positive transfer-of-learning to a third language. One explanation is that "I-can't-do-it" messages from the left brain have been quieted. Since you have already achieved skill in another language, it is difficult for the left brain to deny that you can do it again.

How does your TPR approach fit into a complete language program from zero fluency to advanced students?

I am recommending that entry level students of *any* age and in *any* language, experience instructional strategies that play to the right hemisphere of the brain. TPR is a powerful right brain approach. Students should enter the target language with stress-free right brain instruction and gradually, as training advances, left brain instructional techniques are blended.

Hence, the student begins with comprehension training, then gracefully makes the transition to production. As students progress and their confidence increases and increases, they become ready to *speak, to memorize* (idioms and grammatical fine points), and to *accept corrections* for distortions in production. The important thought is that each student becomes *ready* to speak, to memorize, and to accept corrections. This is quite different from the usual classroom where students attempt to perform these tasks *on demand from* the instructor, often before there is student readiness to perform.

CLASSROOM

What is the ideal group size?

Probably 20 to 25 students, but many instructors have successfully functioned with 60 or 70 students at a time. Instructors teaching Spanish to adults for three hours one night a week report that 60 people increases the excitement. One instructional strategy for very large groups is to utter commands in the target language and then model by responding yourself with the appropriate action. Then divide the students into small groups and give each group a cassette recorder which is used to play back a series of commands you have just modeled. Members of each group then listen to the tape and respond with actions to the spoken commands.

What is the optimal design of the classroom?

The usual classroom with students sitting in rows facing one direction is ideal for left brain instruction in which students focus upon the instructor who delivers the information. However, in TPR we have a dramatic brainswitch from the left to the right brain which means a different arrangement of the classroom furniture.

In his book, *Instructor's Notebook,* Ramiro Garcia recommends an arrangement of the chairs in which one half of the class faces the other half with the area in-between open for students to move about freely in response to directions in the target language from the instructor.

If I were to design the ideal environment for high speed, right brain language acquisition in the school of the 21st century, it would look like this: I see a large open area with many different break-away movie sets that represent different life situations such as the living room, the kitchen, the bedroom, the bathroom, a store, a train station, a hotel, etc. A model arrangement may be seen in the Concordia Language Villages, Concordia College, Moorhead, MN 56560.

Students would start in the living room with language-body conversations (i.e., the instructor gives a direction and the student makes a physical response) that quickly and easily let students internalize a huge chunk of the phonology, morphology and grammar of the target language. As a bonus, students rapidly acquire practical vocabulary associated with a living room as for example:

> "Juan, stand up and walk to the sofa."
>
> "Maria, pick up a pillow from the sofa and give it to Juan."
>
> "Juan, throw the pillow to Jeffe."
>
> "Jeffe, put the pillow on the chair and move the chair under the window."
>
> "Maria, if Jeffe moved a chair under the window, raise your hand, but if he moved the chair next to the table, make a funny face."
>
> "When I raise my left hand, Juan will run to the cabinet and take out a plate."

From the tiny sample above, you can sense the complexity of grammar that students *internalize* which includes the present, past, future and the conditional. In addition, students internalize the phonology of the target language including rhythm, pacing and stress patterns. Finally, they internalize hundreds of practical vocabulary items.

Incidentally, you may notice that I use the term *internalization* rather than *memorization* because there is a striking difference. Language-body conversations, which are the essence of TPR, are *internalized* in, the right brain while a cognitive attempt to repeat, for example, a vocabulary item, over and over, until it can be retrieved is *memorization* stored in the left brain usually for short-term memory only.

After students work (or perhaps I should say play) their way through one movie set, they move on to the next. I can't think of a more delightful way to assimilate another language, can you?

GRAMMAR

The Total Physical Response is fine for commands, but how can it be applied to other grammatical features?

You will find abundant examples in Part IV of this book showing how to nest almost all grammatical features in the imperative. Also, see the TPR books by: Eric Schessler, *English Grammar Through Actions*—which is also available in Spanish and French; Ramiro Garcia's *Instructor's Notebook: How to Apply TPR for Best Results;* Stephen Silver's *Listen and Perform* (available in English, Spanish and French) and Francisco Cabello's *Total Physical Response in First Year English* (also available in Spanish and French).

Of course, once you have a successful TPR experience with your students, you will enter an ever-expanding labyrinth of information and begin to discover TPR ideas in unlikely places.

HIGH SCHOOL STUDENTS & ADULTS

Do adult students resist obeying commands?

It depends upon their expectations and how well they understand the rationale of the approach. If the students are English speakers trying to learn a second language, maximum cooperation can be obtained by introducing the approach to students with one or more of the video demonstrations which are available. Often the rationale cannot be explained to people learning English as a second language. Students will cooperate, however, if the instructor moves firmly but gently, step by step, so that each student response is successful. The friendly manner of the instructor communicates that you are an ally interested in helping students achieve a successful learning experience.

As a hint, delay a novel command that is "non-serious" (i.e., silly or crazy) until you have solid rapport with your students.

Do adult students resent being ordered around?

Not if the approach is properly introduced through video demonstrations or a "live" exhibition. For instance, one instructor teaching Spanish to adults one night a week, tells the students at the first meeting: "Before you go home tonight, you will understand everything I'm going to say next" and then he rattles off ten commands in Spanish. The immediate student response is: "Who, me understand what you just said? In one evening? No way!" The students are curious, skeptical and keenly interested to see whether the instructor can keep his promise. By the end of the three-hour session, the students are believers.

Will adult students resent silly or crazy commands as, "Sit on the floor!" or "Stand on the ceiling!"?

Many instructors who fear that students will react with resentment are surprised when students—children and adults—respond with delight and enjoyment. Adults have an enormous capacity for playfulness, especially when it results in a successful learning experience.

My students are in high school and "control" is often a serious issue. What do you recommend?

Well, the "noise" level will be higher in a TPR classroom because the students are elated, but this is productive noise. Often administrators who know nothing about TPR, will appear in the doorway and whisper, "Settle those kids down!"

Sure, if the objective is "control," then the ideal strategy is to confine students to their seats filling in missing words and sentences in a workbook.

But, if our objective is a memorable learning experience—a learning experience that creates teacher-of-the-year awards, then the volume of noise in the classroom will be higher. No question about it.

My advise is to contain the noise level within your comfort range. This is achieved by a gradual transition to TPR from whatever you are now doing. Start with only five or ten minutes of TPR and then continue with what you have been doing such as working with a textbook.

What happens is this: First, you will develop more and more confidence in the approach which means that your tolerance for "productive noise" expands and expands, and secondly, your students will ask you for "...more of that activity we do at the beginning of each class meeting. You know, you say something in Japanese and someone acts. It sure seems to help me. Can we do more of that?"

PRONUNCIATION

You mentioned that correction *of student pronunciation is often a stressful time-waster for both the students and the instructor. What do you mean?*

Beginning students have no attention units available to hear coaching from the instructor about flaws in pronunciation. As students advance in their acquisition of language skills, more and more attention units are free to focus upon feedback from the instructor. In addition, any intrusion with pronunciation correction, although well intentioned, may be interpreted by the student as criticism which further lowers an already rickety self-confidence.

Evidence for this comes from the latest electronic brain-mapping showing that at the beginning of the skill learning curve there is maximum brain activity which diminishes as a skill is internalized. The more exquisite the level of skill one has acquired, the least amount of brain activity that flashes on the electronic screen. This suggests to me that the span of attention (for error-correction) increases as one advances in the internalization of the target language.

Do you correct mistakes that students make in production?

Yes, but since we operate on a developmental theory to explain production, our feedback is modeled after the feedback which parents give to children learning their first language. You notice that for infants, parents begin with an extremely wide tolerance for distortions. In fact, parents try to encourage any attempt at infant speech by even imitating the infant's distortions (e.g., "Does sweetheart want an 'abdung' or a 'peepunch?'"). As the child develops, a parent gradually narrows his or her tolerance for production or grammatical errors. Eventually, a tolerance which began as wide as the Grand Canyon becomes as narrow as the width of a razor's edge.

Hints as to how wide our tolerance is for production mistakes may be seen in our video demonstrations. Remember, when the student begins to speak, the individual's entire attention is directed at trying to produce, so the student cannot attend efficiently to feedback from the instructor. Thus, feedback should not interrupt a student in the middle of an attempt to express a thought. The feedback should be gentle, rather than harsh and sharp. And the feedback should be modified by a wide tolerance for errors.

The instructional goal should be uninhibited communication that is intelligible to a native speaker. We want students to talk and talk and talk. Eventually, they can be fine tuned for more perfect speech. We have observed that as the student acquires increasing skill at understanding what is heard, more and more attention units, so to speak, are freed to receive phonological corrections from the instructor.

Can production be taught?

This is a controversial issue, but we are inclined to agree with Winitz (1981, 1982), Nord (1981) and Krashen (1978) that production cannot be taught. Production can be shaped perhaps, but not directly taught. There are three reasons for the radical conclusion that production cannot be taught.

The first is the observation that in all cultures and in all of recorded history, when infants acquire their native language, production always *shadows* listening comprehension throughout childhood which suggests a developmental sequence in which the appearance of speech is contingent upon an expanding internalized map of the target language. In a child's development, speech always lags behind listening understanding.

Secondly, puberty is a critical factor which determines whether one will ever achieve a near-native pronunciation in a second language. For example, Asher and Garcia (1969, 1982, 1986) did a study of Cuban immigrants in the San Francisco Bay Area and found that if a person arrived in the USA *after* puberty, there was only a rare probability that the individual would achieve a near-native pronunciation no matter how many years the individual lived in America. While puberty seems to be a critical time in the determination of native-like pronunciation, it is not related to how fast one can acquire listening skill (Asher and Price, 1967, 1982).

There is a third reason why production may be a developmental event like the appearance of walking in the infant—and that is individual differences. Teachers of a second language often have a strong conviction that their teaching procedure produced excellent speech. This may be an illusion if the conclusion was based on selected data. That is, by Level II, according to Lawson (1971), 64 percent of all students who started in Level I have dropped out. By Level III, 85 percent of all those students who started in Level I have dropped out, and by Level IV, 96 percent of the students who started in Level I have dropped out.

In classes beyond Level I, teachers are observing a smaller and smaller group of students who are able to produce fine pronunciation, not necessarily because of instruction, but probably due to a high aptitude for languages taught by a listen-and-repeat-after-me approach. The group is so small that by Level IV, less than 5 percent of those who started language training in Level I still remain.

Our conclusion, then, is that production is a natural and spontaneous event *following far behind* the internalization of understanding. Once speech appears, it can be gently shaped—but not forced into perfection.

If you permit errors in production at the beginning, won't students learn "bad habits" which will be difficult to correct?

This depends on whether production is directly teachable or developmental. Our hypothesis is that production is primarily a developmental phenomenon. Therefore, just as a parent cannot teach an infant to walk or talk, an instructor cannot directly teach a student to speak a second language. The appearance of speech will emerge at a point of readiness in perceptual development.

The student must internalize a large portion of the language code before there is readiness to produce. Now, when speech appears in one's first or second language, there will be many, many distortions. Gradually, in time, the distortions will be reduced. However, whether the student's production will ever match a native speaker seems to be contingent on two factors: one is puberty and the other is individual differences. The data (Asher and Garcia 1969, 1982, 1986) strongly suggest that the probability is extremely slight that one will achieve a near-native pronunciation if the language training starts after puberty. Even though most post-puberty students will probably retain an accent, the individual can, in time, realistically expect to achieve speech that is understandable and acceptable to a native listener.

TRANSFER TO OTHER LINGUISTIC SKILLS

After one achieves understanding of spoken language, what is the transfer-of-learning to reading and writing?

It will be extremely high, especially if there is a good fit between the phonology and orthography of the target language. As may be seen in the video demonstration, *Children Learning Another Language: An Innovative Approach*, when students had a keen understanding for everything the teacher was saying in Spanish, they could immediately read Spanish directions printed on flash cards.

If the language sounds the way it is written as is the case

in languages such as Arabic and Spanish, then there should be a large amount of positive transfer to reading and writing from understanding achieved through language-body conversations. But, even when there is not a good fit between the sound and printed symbolization of the language as is the case in English, the transfer is remarkable, given the assumption that the students are already literate in their native language.

What about the transfer-of-learning from listening understanding to reading for people who cannot read in their native language?

The transfer will probably be zero. Apparently it is necessary to have prior skill in the orthography of one's native language before there is transfer from listening skill in the second language to reading and writing.

How do you make the transition from the imperative to other grammatical structures?

We have observed that most, if not all, grammatical features in a language can be nested in the imperative. That is, you can use the accelerative effect of the imperative to teach almost any grammatical constituent. Consider these illustrations:

Future tense "Luke, walk to the door! When Luke walks to the door, Maria *will* write Luke's name on the chalkboard."

Past tense "Abner, run to the chalkboard!" After Abner has completed the action, the instructor says, "Josephine, if Abner *ran* to the chalkboard, run after him and hit him with your book!"

Present tense "Luke, walk to the window! When Luke *walks* to the window, Mary will draw Luke's face on the chalkboard."

Richard Pugh reported that he has obtained excellent results with the imperative in shaping the production of correct grammatical forms in Spanish of "gifted" 6th graders. In the first year, the students amassed understanding of spoken Spanish through the instructor's use of the imperative in which other structural features were nested (e.g., "Give me the pencil that Shirou had in his hand!"). Then in the second year, Pugh used the imperative again, but this time to "fine tune" the students' skill in speaking grammatical Spanish. For example, the instructor said in Spanish, "Jane, walk to the chalkboard and write your name." After Jane completed the action, the instructor said in Spanish, "Jaime, explain what Jane did." Jaime would say, "Jane *walked* to the chalkboard and *wrote* her name." Since the students already had understanding of spoken Spanish, it was easy for them to focus their full attention on intensive practice designed to "fine tune" their speech to produce correct grammatical forms.

TPR LESSONS

How can I use my students as a resource in creating TPR lessons?

Llyn Brickley who teaches Spanish in Bothell, Washington asks her students to scout for props from a long list of items that she has prepared, and to suggest additional TPR activities of keen interest to the students. Her students also volunteer as artists to (a) draw pictures and (b) use tape or chalk to outline on the floor and the playground, maps of the town, the state, the USA, and the world.

With her maps, Brickley helps her students *internalize* the geography of different locations with directions in Spanish such as: "Walk north on Elm Street, then make a left-hand turn to Broadway and stand next to the fire station."

What is the ideal number of vocabulary items to introduce at a time?

Usually we attempt to introduce only three new vocabulary items at a time. These are manipulated with commands until it is clear that they are well internalized by the students. Then, another set of three vocabulary items is introduced and so on. There is nothing magical about three, but we have observed that a limited number of items at one time is more easily differentiated and assimilated. In an hour, it is possible for students to assimilate 12 to 36 new lexical items depending upon the size of the group and the stage of training.

How much time per session is optimal?

This seems to vary depending upon the age of the students. For kindergarten and elementary school children through the sixth grade, about 30 minutes of training at any one time appears to be effective.

Junior high and high school students respond well to 60-minute sessions. College students and adults in night school can handle up to 3-hour sessions. These time intervals are estimates and have not been determined rigorously from scientific data. For English as a second language, Karen Bouldin reported that Vietnamese children under 12 in an adult class with family members were attentive and responsive for 5 hours a day, 5 days a week for 11 weeks.

Is there a TPR dictionary that I can use to look up vocabulary in creating my own TPR lessons?

Yes. Professor Stephen M. Silvers has written *The Command Book* which shows how to TPR 2,000 vocabulary items used in most ESL/FL textbooks into customized lessons especially for your students no matter what age group or what language.

After how many hours of TPR training should the instructor introduce role reversal?

It roughly varies from 10 to 20 hours. The students themselves will give you many indications when they are ready to try speaking commands that will direct the instructor and their co-students. As an example of this readiness, in one experimental German course, the intent was to delay speaking for one semester, but after 12 hours of comprehension training using TPR, the students spontaneously began to utter commands and they insisted on the opportunity to try production during class time. Their insistence was a signal of readiness which we responded to with the introduction of role reversal. (See Asher, J.J. "Children's First Language As A Model For Second Language Learning," *Modern Language Journal,* 1972, 56(3), 133-139.)

How do you ask questions using the imperative?

First of all, asking questions is not introduced too soon. This is delayed until a large amount of understanding has been internalized. Then there is a sequence of a command followed by a short-answer question such as:

"Juan, put the pencil on the table! Maria, did Juan put a pencil on the table?" The *answer* expected will be "yes" or "no". Later, longer answers can be elicited in this sequence:

"Jose, write your name on the chalkboard! What is your name?" The answer can be "Jose Garcia," or "My name is Jose Garcia".

Gradually, students will develop more and more skill in expanding their spoken responses. We do not rush this process. We do not force it. With patience, responses appear and in time, they become expanded. Remember, it may be a mistake to demand behavior from students that they are not ready to produce. This only generates an experience of failure for the student and frustration for the instructor.

What are novel utterances?

Novel utterances are recombinations of constituents you have used directly in training. For instance, you directed students with "Walk to the table!" and "Sit on the chair!" These are familiar to students since they have practiced responding to them. Now, will a student understand if you surprise the individual with an unfamiliar utterance that you created by recombining familiar elements (e.g., "Sit on the table!"). This would be a novel utterance.

Why are novel utterances important?

We feel that skill in understanding novel sentences moves the student in the direction of true fluency. If students only understand the exact sentences used in training, the program would be a failure. The goal is *not* for input to equal output, but for output to be *more than* input. When students demonstrate that they comprehend novelty, they are showing that they have achieved the flexibility to reorder elements, which is crucial to fluency.

Can students learn merely from watching a model perform?

Yes, there is at least short-term memory from observing a model perform in response to commands. For long-term memory, the research (Asher 1969, 1981) suggests that each student should follow up the observation of a model by performing individually. I believe that people sitting in the audience observing a student perform in response to directions from the instructor also have long-term storage in the right brain. The problem is that the students in the audience don't believe that they personally can perform until *each individual* has a chance to demonstrate competency.

I need every lesson prepared in such fine detail that I follow the directions step-by-step. Where can I find a book that requires no preparation on my part?

Since the last edition of my book, Sky Oaks Productions has published many TPR textbooks for children, high school students and adults. See the back of this book for more details.

As students progress in role reversal, you ask them to work in pairs to create skits in the target language. In preparing the skits, what can the instructor do to shape pronunciation and grammar?

In the early days of our research we did not intervene while adult students brainstormed to prepare a skit. I would still recommend non-intervention while students are creating unless they ask for assistance. For instance, they may ask you for a vocabulary item or a grammatical detail. However, once the students have prepared a script that they will act out, the instructor should read the script and fine-tune with corrections in spelling and grammar.

Can students perform any actions at their seats?

Yes, I have developed effective TPR activities that students can perform at their seats. Each student has a kit in color such as the interior of a kitchen. Then, you say in the target language, "Put the sink in the kitchen." With your kit displayed so that it is clearly visible to the students, you place the sink in the kitchen of your kit and your students follow by performing the same action in their kits. As you move from one direction to the next, you can sense how rapidly the students are assimilating the content. As items are internalized, you can gradually discontinue the modeling. Eventually, you will utter a direction and the students will quickly respond without being shown what to do.

Each figure in the ***TPR Student Kits*** will stick to any location without glue. Just press and the figure is on. It can be peeled off instantly and placed in a different location over and over. You can create thousands of fresh sentences that give students practice in understanding hundreds of useful vocabulary items and grammatical structures. Also, students quickly acquire "function" words such as *up, down, on, off, under, over, next to, in front of,* and *behind.*

To guide you step-by-step I have written 10 complete lessons for each of the following ***Student Kits*** in your choice of English, Spanish, French, or German:

Home	Beach
Kitchen	Playground
Restaurant	Farm
Supermarket	Harbor
Town	United States Map
Gas Station	Calendar (English only)
Hospital	4-Kits-in-1, *includes Community,*
Airport	*School, Work, and Leisure Time*

The ***TPR Student Kits*** can be used with children or adults learning any language, including ESL and the sign language of the deaf. For current prices, see our TPR Catalog which will be sent upon request or order online at www.tpr-world.com

In front of a large class, if I demonstrate an action on the playboard of a TPR Student Kit, people in the back of the room sometimes have difficulty seeing. Any suggestions?

Yes, we have developed the ***TPR Teacher Kits*** to solve the problem of large classes. For example, let's say that your students in a large class have on their desks the ***TPR Student Kit: The Home.***

You use an overhead projector to flash the playboard transparency for *The Home* on a large screen. You utter a direction in the target language such as, "Put the man in the living room in front of the couch." Then your students watch you perform the appropriate action on the screen and they follow by doing the same action in their kits at their desks. Everything you need for an overhead projector is contained in the ***TPR Teacher Kits*** which are now available for the *Home, Kitchen* and *Airport.*

A new innovation is "seat commands" developed by Blaine Ray in his ***Look, I Can Talk*** series. Blaine uses gestures to supplement body movements in response to directions in the target language. See his book entitled ***Gestures for First-Year Mini-stories.*** For another effective list of seat commands, see Todd McKay's ***Teacher's Guidebook for TPR Storytelling***— written especially for children in elementary and middle school. Ads describing all these fine TPR products are located in the back of this book.

How can the TPR Student Kit called The Calendar help my students.

With the ***TPR Student Kit: The Calendar,*** you direct students each day to change the weather, the temperature, the day of the week, the date, and special events such as a birthday, a party, or a holiday. For example, you may say, "Maria, if it is raining today, please stick the appropriate picture on our calendar." *No glue is needed.* Each number, word, or picture on the TPR calendar can be peeled off instantly and replaced with a new piece of information. Once your students comprehend what you are saying in the target language, they are ready for reading and writing.

Can the TPR Student Kits be used with students of all ages, even adults?

The ***TPR Student Kits*** have been used successfully with language students of all ages, including adults. For example, the University of Delaware and the University of Texas at San Antonio have used the kits to train several hundred students in Spanish, French, German, and English as a Second Language.

TPR TEXTBOOKS

Are there any TPR textbooks that I can adopt for my classes?

Sky Oaks Productions now has published many books that will guide students step-by-step from the "golden tense" into all other grammatical features. For example, here are some exciting TPR textbook suggestions.

For elementary and middle-school students:
- ***Listen & Perform*** in English, Spanish, or French—by Stephen Silvers
- ***TPR Storytelling*** for Year 1, 2, 3—by Todd McKay

For high school, college, or adult students:
- ***The Total Physical Response in First Year*** English, Spanish, or French—by Dr. Francisco Cabello
- ***Look, I Can Talk!*** for Level 1, 2, 3—by Blaine Ray

What do you recommend to supplement the TPR textbooks?

The ***TPR Student Kits*** are fun for a change of pace. Try games from ***Favorite Games for ESL/FL Classes*** and from the book ***Total Physical Fun.*** *You* can't miss with ***TPR Bingo***. Also, create your own TPR lessons custom-made for your goals with the book entitled, ***The Command Book*** that shows you how to TPR 2,000 vocabulary items in any language.

HOMEWORK

Is any homework assigned?

Usually not, simply because retention from class to class is almost 100 percent. But this does not mean that homework is inadvisable. Through trial-and-error, each instructor discovers what mix of activities produces the best results. One French teacher, for example, who used TPR with kindergarden children was asked by parents to make cassette tapes of each lesson so that, at home, the mother could learn French by acting along with her child as a model.

Another suggestion: Ramiro Garcia has created a homework book packed with exciting TPR activities. For details, see the ad for ***Instructor's Notebook: TPR Homework Exercises*** in the back of this book.

Is there any research to support the effectiveness of TPR Storytelling?

Yes, there is. You recall that Blaine Ray developed this innovation to make a smooth transition from the imperative to other grammatical features such as the declarative. For his explanation of how this works, see his books, ***Look, I Can Talk Teacher's Guidebook*** and ***Fluency Through TPR Storytelling***. Evidence that the technique works comes from teacher testimonials.

As a follow-up, Todd McKay developed some new products called ***TPR Storytelling especially for children in elementary and middle school***. McKay furnished me with data from his students and asked me for a statistical analysis to determine the effectiveness of the storytelling approach. Here are the results when a class of 30 middle school students experiencing ***TPR Storytelling*** (TPRS) were compared with a class of 30 ALM students. Both classes were exposed to the same set of vocabulary. Then both classes listened to a story none of the students had heard before but the story contained familiar vocabulary.

On a ten item true-false test to assess student comprehension of the "novel" story (one they have never heard before) the TPRS students had significantly higher comprehension compared with the ALM students. (t = 3.69, p < .001 for 58 df.)

The effect size as measured by r squared was .19 which is, according to Cohen's Table, almost a large effect size. For further verification, a Median Test with Chi Square was also statistically significant at 11.38, p< .001 for df = 1.)

For graduate students who would like to expand upon this exciting pilot study to create a master's thesis or doctoral dissertation, here are some suggestions:

- Use multiple stories rather than only one story so that the ceiling is high enough for differences in performance to show up between the groups.
- Assess ***listening comprehension*** and ***reading skill*** by presenting every other story either aurally or in print.
- Be sure that the groups are comparable in age, aptitude, and hours of exposure to instruction in a language program.
- Assess ***writing skill***. Given a printed set of familiar vocabulary items, ask each student to write an original story (the wilder and crazier the better) in a limited time period.

  Submit the stories coded with A, B, C. (and no other names or identification) to two or more impartial language teachers. Ask the teachers independently to compare the stories two at a time (i.e., A with B, A with C, etc. and make a simple decision such as which of the two is better on spelling? Then, compare the stories again for originality. Then compare again for grammaticality, and so forth.

  Score the stories for each student and determine the reliability of the teachers' judgements.
- Assess ***speaking skill***. The procedure is similar to the one above except record on video each student telling a story that they made up. Compare two students at a time again in a "double blind." Compare first on fluency. Then view the video again and compare for originality, and so forth.

The Office of Education would be an ideal place to submit for a research grant to support this worthwhile project.

How can an instructor test to assess the students' comprehension of spoken directions?

One procedure suggested in Garcia's *Instructor's Notebook* is to write 10 or 20 lists with ten different commands on each list. For example, List A may have these directions:

1. Stand.
2. Go to the chalkboard.
3. Write your name on the chalkboard.
4. Go to the door.
5. Touch the door twice.
6. Lift your arm.
7. Sit on the floor.
8. Stand up slowly.
9. Go to the small table.
10. Return to your seat slowly.

Next, put all lists in a hat, mix them up, and ask a student to reach into the hat, select a list, then perform each action from one through ten. Then the next student selects a list and performs, and so forth. Each correct action scores one point. For example, if the direction is to "Go to the small table." but the student goes to the large table, the score is one point from a possible score of two points.

Another exciting option is Garcia's *Graphics Book* which has 300 multiple-choice items. The unique feature of each item is that the student sees a drawing and identifies the concept by selecting one of four choices in the target language of English, Spanish, French, or German.

How can I acquire a foreign language with your stress-free TPR approach when there are no instructors in my community?

One option is this: Find a local person who is a native speaker of the language you want to acquire. This person need not have formal training as a language instructor, but you do want someone with whom you feel comfortable and relaxed. This should be someone who is patient and can follow directions easily.

The *easiest way is* to ask the native speaker to start with Lesson 1 in the *TPR Student Kit: The Home.* The person reads the first direction in Lesson 1 in the target language (without a translation, of course), then as you watch, performs the appropriate action in the instructor's kit, and you follow by performing the identical action in your kit. For example, the instructor says in the *target language:* "Put the sink in the kitchen." (The instructor presses the sink in the kitchen of his or her kit and you do the same in your kit.) "Put the stove in the kitchen." (Again, you watch the instructor put the stove in his or her kit, and you do exactly the same move in your kit.) "Put a table in the kitchen"—and so forth. By the end of ten lessons, you will have assimilated an enormous understanding of the target language with many, many useful vocabulary items found in the home and also complex structures involving the present, past, and future tenses. Once you have worked through the home, try other *TPR Student Kits* such as *The Kitchen, The Town, The Restaurant,* etc. Ten lessons are included with each kit. Just start with the first direction in Lesson I and follow each direction, step-by-step.

When you have worked through all the lessons that are included with the TPR Student Kits, you will have assimilated a sophisticated understanding of the target language and you will have made a graceful, stress-free transition to speaking, reading, and writing.

My recommendation is to work with only one lesson at each session. Take your time and enjoy the process of assimilation. (For a description and picture of each *TPR Student Kit,* write, call or fax: Sky Oaks Productions, Inc. P.O. Box 1102, Los Gatos, CA 95031, Phone: (408) 395-7600/ FAX: (408) 395 8440. Also, see the TPR order form at the end of this book). The important thing to remember is that the learner is silent. You listen to a direction in the foreign language, watch the instructor act, then do exactly the same thing. There should be no English translation at any time, and do *not* attempt to pronounce the foreign words. Be silent, listen, watch, and act.

HOME SCHOOL

How about parents who have a home school? How can they help their children have a stress-free experience acquiring another language?

TPR is the ideal approach for home schoolers if a parent, neighbor, or friend is fluent in the target language. Use our TPR textbooks and *TPR Student Kits*.

LAND MINES

Where are the land mines buried in this approach so that I can carefully step around them?

One land mine we have marked with a skull and cross bones is adaptation. Adaptation is the phenomenon in which one discontinues making a response to a continual stimulus.

Adaptation has both a positive and negative side. The positive application can be demonstrated in body-building. If a muscle is extended one feels the stretch which will disappear from awareness in about ten seconds. This means that a person can move muscle "limits" further and further out using the principle of adaptation and as muscle limits disappear, one becomes more and more flexible.

Language-body conversations in the TPR procedure are powerful in helping children and adults internalize huge chunks of the target language often on the first exposure. Because the technique is so effective, instructors tend to over-use it producing adaptation.

We detect this in the following comment from instructors: "Gee, it was absolute magic for a month or so and then the students seemed to shut down and refused to perform. Their motivation went from 'I can't wait to get in this class! I can't get enough of this! Don't stop!' to 'No, please! Do I have to do what you just asked me to do?'"

What happened was adaptation. To use a cliche, "they ran the technique into the ground." No matter how effective a technique is, it will not carry the entire instructional load. It must be used judiciously with frequent change of pace and frequent change of activities. I recommend frequent brainswitching from the right to the left and reverse, from the left to the right. Exactly how does one do this?

The highest priority before we select activities is to have a series of short-term student goals that are what I call, operational. For contrast, consider how goals are determined in the current classroom.

First you notice that the textbook or the teacher usually defines one long-term goal that is non-operational, that is unmeasurable such as "fluency in a second language" or "appreciation of the culture of another people" or "able to read and write in a another language," etc. All of these goals are admirable but they are high-level abstractions that defy measurement; hence, we are never sure when we reach the goal.

Also, these goals, noble as they are, appeal to teachers, not students. Other teacher goals (that should be invisible to students) are "understanding the grammar of the target language" or "developing a native-like pronunciation."

Students (especially beginning students) are not interested (nor should they be) in pronunciation, grammar, and other technical aspects of the language code. They are keenly interested in understanding and expressing thoughts in the target language. Specifically, they want to use the language to read a classified ad, understand a television commercial, buy a train ticket, order a meal in a restaurant, find the rest rooms, and direct a taxi driver to a location.

Now, you may say, "Sure they want to read a classified ad and do the other things, but they need pronunciation, grammar and other technical details to achieve those goals." Quite true, they need the technical details, but they do not have to be directly aware of those details to use them. In fact, as Krashen has pointed out in many articles, explicit instruction in those technical details hinders rather than facilitates communication goals that motivate students.

One has only to look at the Japanese student to validate. For example, for college admission, the Japanese students know that one giant hurdle is to answer questions about English grammar. Hence, they become more skilled in understanding the technical details of English grammar than most graduates of universities in English-speaking countries, but there is little if any, transfer to communication skills in English.

Remember that our nemesis is adaptation. We select activities only after we have selected our goals. I recommend a series of short-term student goals (because they are rich in motivation for students) each of which can be attained in two weeks or less. Again, for contrast, teachers in a traditional format imagine that they have short-term goals and they do, but these are objectives such as "cover Chapter 1 in two weeks," "then in the next two weeks, cover Chapter 2..." Students follow us, but only because they trust us, not because covering a chapter is rich in intrinsic motivation. And, of course, student motivation to "cover a chapter" is nominal.

Notice that the student goals I have selected are operational meaning that at the end of two weeks, we can demonstrate to the satisfaction of students that, indeed, they can, for instance, read three classified ads in a German newspaper. Setting short-term student goals is perhaps the most powerful strategy for coping with adaptation.

Incidentally, as you get into this TPR business and your students understand how it works, ask them to brainstorm more short-term goals of keen interest to them. You will be surprised when they suggest: Let's go to a Mexican restaurant where the staff speaks only Spanish. Prepare us to (a) call up and make a reservation, (b) explain who we are when we get there, (c) order our meals, (d) ask about the location of the rest rooms, and (e) pay our checks. Let us select a feature film we like that has been dubbed in German. Prepare us to attend the movie and understand every word of the dialogue.

But how do we set those powerful short-term goals? Do we tell students what they can expect in two weeks? Perhaps so, but telling plays to the left brain and is not as convincing as playing to the right brain with a dramatic demonstration such as this: Let your students view three television commercials in Japanese (assuming, of course, that Japanese is the target language) and promise: "At the end of two weeks, I will show these commercials again and you will understand them perfectly."

We promise students a sensational goal that can be achieved in two weeks. They are excited and curious to see whether we can keep our promise.

So, how do we keep that promise? We start on the right side of the brain with instant success using language-body conversations of TPR. The short-term goal guides us in the selection of vocabulary and activities that include continual brainswitching from one side to the other. For example, TPR, storytelling by the instructor, and dramatic skits created by students are techniques that play to the right brain while speaking, reading, and writing mini-dialogues and stories plays to the left brain.

What are some other land mines that I should walk around?

I will mention three: over-modeling, under-modeling, and mindless repetition.

Over-modeling is continuing to perform with students beyond the point at which they can perform alone without you. This is tiring for ourselves as well as the students and achieves no additional gain in learning.

The guideline that will help you is, MINIMUM INPUT FOR MAXIMUM OUTPUT. Think of yourself as the director of the play and your students as the actors. Do not over-direct. You give only enough direction (i.e., modeling) to get the actors to perform on their own. This is a marvelous example of the "less is more" principle.

The instructional flaw at the other end of the continuum is *under-modeling.* Here the novice instructor rushes through a routine; then expects the students to be ready to perform.

The third land mine to walk around is mindless repetition. For example, let us say that the vocabulary you want your students to internalize is "open" and "close". Mindless repetition (that can make people crazy) would be the following directions in the target language:

Open the door.
Close the door.

Open the door.
Close the door.

Open the door.
Close the door.

Open the door.
Close the door.

Rather, include open and close in a colorful variation of sentences such as:

Open the door.
Close the door.

Open the drawer.
Close the drawer.

Open your mouth.
Close your mouth.

Open the book.
Close the book.

Why is variety so important? If TPR works, why not continue with it day after day?

First, TPR is powerful, but it is not a panacea. Secondly, no matter how effective a technique is, an unending continuation will result in adaptation. Students will experience symptoms of "burn-out" and then want to escape—to flee away from a noxious situation.

An analogy is film-making. Notice that the home movie in the hands of an amateur film-maker tends to either hold on a scene for what seems to be an eternity or move the camera so quickly that the scene is a blur—a jerky kaleidoscope of people, places, and things that causes a spontaneous outburst from viewers. "Wait! Not so fast! I didn't see that! What was that on the screen?"

In contrast, the professional film-maker presents a smooth flow of images that change imperceptibly from a long shot to a close up to a reverse angle, etc. Notice that the rapid transition from perspective to perspective in a scene is so smooth that the viewer is unaware that the camera moved at all.

Like the professional film-maker, the instructor's task is a smooth change in activity that moves the student imperceptibly from one side of the brain to the other and back again. Remember, our goal is not simply to switch back and forth from one hemisphere of the brain to the other, but like the movie-maker, each scene moves the viewer act by act to reveal more and more of the plot until we reach the climax of the story.

Our intent in language instruction is to move the student step by step in an engaging way with many unexpected and delightful surprises until they reach a destination that they express a keen interest in visiting. You know that you have been a successful linguistic tour director when your clients (the students) recommend the trip to others in enthusiastic word-of-mouth advertising.

POLICY-MAKERS

How can an instructor get the support of administrators for this rather unusual approach to language instruction?

Rarely do instructors invite administrators, parents, and board members to a special demonstration that shows the effectiveness of an innovative approach. We all complain that administrators neither understand us nor support our projects, but how can they when they are unaware of what we are trying to do? I would personally invite policy-makers to lunch and an elegant presentation with a video and a live demonstration that clearly shows the impact of the innovative approach.

There is nothing so persuasive as witnessing beginning students responding rapidly to complex directions in the target language especially when traditional approaches only produce fragmentary responses such as reciting numbers from one to ten, the colors, a few adjectives, and the letters of the alphabet. Once people understand that a project is worthwhile, they become problem solvers in helping us create conditions that will enhance the chances for a successful instructional program. (As a friendly hint, by all means invite the policy-makers to participate as students in your TPR demonstration.)

TPR MENTORS

If I run into problems, can I contact someone for help?

In every school district in North America, you will find instructors who have discovered TPR and are using this stress-free approach as the core of their language program or as an extremely effective supplement. To locate these instructors, place a call to elementary and high schools in your area and talk with FL/ESL teachers. Other places to call are your local community college or university. Specifically ask for instructors in the Department of Education who teach bilingual courses or language methodology. Then try the modern language department and applied linguistics.

Another idea for finding TPR instructors is to place a small ad in the regional newsletter of your professional language association. I find that FL/ESL teachers are generous in sharing ideas.

Consider organizing a TPR User Group similar to computer user groups who meet periodically to discuss their progress, share insights, and solve problems. I believe you will thoroughly enjoy a get together with other TPR aficionados to share tips and tricks. It will be an entertaining evening.

OTHER APPROACHES

Some people do acquire fluency in a second language with the traditional grammar-translation approach. How come?

Only about 4% of students who start second language learning with the traditional left brain approach with textbook translations, pronunciation exercises, and dialogue memorization continue with the program long enough to achieve fluency. I asked one of these successful students who now heads a foreign language department in a major university: What is your secret of success? Why did you continue when nine out of ten of your classmates gave up?

His answer was intriguing. He said, "All I can tell you is that the exercises were not drudgery for me. It was more like play. For example, I remember driving home from class and inventing a conversation with an imaginary friend. All the way home in the car, I talked in Spanish (the second language he was studying in class) with an invisible companion who sat next to me in the car and with other people I created in different scenes. I didn't perceive this as tough 'practice,' but as a playful activity that I thoroughly enjoyed.

He dissolved the usual "boundary lines" that contain the learning process within a starting and finishing point. For example, most students think: We start this activity when the bell rings and end it when the bell rings again. Most students do not continue with the activity outside the boundary lines unless it is assigned homework. Underline the "work" in homework. Activity at home is perceived along with the activity within the boundary lines as work, work, work. My colleague, by comparison, perceived the activity inside the boundary lines as play, play, play and continued the play outside with invented conversations. I call this *self-talk,* which is intrinsically pleasurable.

Incidentally, for details on how to convert any activity from work into play see Chapter 4 entitled, "Work and Play" in my book, *Brainswitching*.

How does your TPR approach compare with the Silent Way?

There are similarities in that both use commands to manipulate the behavior of students. For instance, in the Silent Way, students are directed to "Pick up the longer rod!" "Take the red rod!" and so forth. One difference is the point in training when students produce the spoken language. In the Silent Way, an attempt is made to "fine tune" pronunciation immediately. In our approach, there is ***delay in production*** until students indicate a readiness to speak. Another difference is that the content of our material tends to manipulate the total body movements of students. In the Silent Way, students sit and are directed to handle abstract materials such as rods of different shapes, sizes, and colors.

How does your TPR approach compare with the Berlitz method?

As we understand Berlitz, there is a one-to-one interaction between instructor and student. Immediately, from the beginning the student is pressed to speak, and commands from the instructor are only used occasionally. In our approach, commands are the dominant feature with other techniques as "questions and answers" integrated later as supplemental features. Also, in TPR there is a delay in speech until there is evidence that students are ready.

How is your TPR approach similar to Lozanov's Suggestopœdia?

I believe that Suggestopœdia also plays to the right hemisphere of the brain. Students are encouraged to regress to childhood in which they recite nursery rhymes, sing songs, and dance. Students are furnished with a new identity including a name, occupation, family, and background. They perform as an actor playing a role in a theatrical production. All of those features are designed to relax the critical faculties of the left brain which permits the right brain to assimilate the target language in chunks. For more information on the application of Suggestopœdia to instruction, write S.A.L.T., P.O. Box 1216, Welch Station, Ames, lowa USA 50010. (S.A.L.T. publishes a newsletter, a journal, and books about educational applications of Suggestopœdia.)

How is TPR similar to Winitz's comprehension training with The Learnables?

In the Winitz approach, the student listens to a native speaker on tape and responds by *looking* at a picture. The voice, without translating, directs the student's attention from picture to picture as the individual internalizes an expanding cognitive map of how the language works. The "total physical response" in the Winitz model is the behavior of *listening* and *looking*.

How does TPR compare with the Natural Approach?

To get an authentic answer, I asked Stephen Krashen who worked with the late Tracy Terrill to develop the Natural Approach (NA). He said in a letter to me dated September 15, 1992 that the main features of the Natural Approach are:

> *"A focus on acquisition, not learning. This means that the emphasis in NA classes is on providing comprehensible input."*

We are in complete agreement with only a difference in terminology. To him, *learning* would be conscious intake of information while *acquisition* would be unconscious, using a model proposed by Freud. For me, I conceptualize learning as a function of the left brain which involves concepts such as "multiple exposures before intake occurs," "studying," "stress," "short-term retention," and "work." Acquisition to me is a brainswitch to the right hemisphere with concepts such as "intake of information in the first exposure", "stress-free," "long-term retention," and "play."

> *"No grammatical syllabus. NA classes are organized, but not around grammar."*

Again, we are in agreement for beginning and even intermediate classes. This means that although students intake grammar through right brain activities, they are not aware that the process is occurring. There is no need to focus student attention on linguistic relationships between words that imprint without study. In fact, study may hinder the intake of grammar until students are ready for a brainswitch from the right to the left hemisphere. This readiness appears after about 60 hours of TPR experience. At this time, students actually request the opportunity to memorize grammatical fine points and other subtleties in phonology and syntax so that they are better able to "polish" their production in the target language.

> *"Speech is allowed to emerge. It is recognized that speech/output is a result of acquisition, not its cause."*

Of course, this was another pioneering thought that I introduced 30 years ago to a skeptical generation of language teachers who initially received the concept as heresy, since they believed that "everyone knows that comprehension follows production."

I am delighted that the Terrill/Krashen Natural Approach synchronizes with my Total Physical Response. I feel that we are guiding people into the promised linguistic land of milk and honey.

How does TPR fit in with an approach developed in Canada circa 1950 called Tan-Gau?

Tan-Gau is a contraction for the names of the people who developed the approach, Dr. Tan-Gwan Leong and

Dr. Robert Gauthier. There are no empirical studies of the effectiveness of Tan-Gau, but many people tell me that it worked. The concept behind Tan-Gau is this: The instructor comes into the class and begins to talk in French with individual students (who of course, know no French). The transaction goes like this: "My name is Andre. What is your name?" The student looks puzzled, so the instructor repeats in French, "My name," and he points to himself, "is Andre. What is your name?" Puzzlement disappears into a smile and the student replies in English, "Robert." "Ah, your name is Robert." "And," turning to the next student, "What is your name?" The student replies in English, "Susan." "Ah, your name is Susan and your name," turning to the boy, "is Robert." "You," pointing to the girl, "are Susan;" and then pointing at the boy, "You are Robert; and I," pointing to himself, "am Andre."

"Well, how do you do, Robert" and he shakes Robert's hand. The boy smiles, and says in English, "How do you do?" "Robert, I want to introduce you to a friend of mine," and the instructor pulls a turtle out of his pocket. "My friend's name is Sam and Sam is my turtle." "Do you like turtles, Robert?" "Yes." "Then, Robert, take this turtle from my hand." Robert giggles as he accepts the turtle. "Now, Robert, give the turtle to Susan." He hands the turtle to Susan. "Susan, please give the turtle to me. Thank you." Notice that the approach is laced with TPR-type activities, but the twist is that the instructor initiates a conversation immediately in French with students responding in their native language which is English. In theory, as the Tan-Gau training progresses and students become more and more comfortable understanding and responding to the target language, there is a spontaneous and graceful transition when the students begin *responding in French.*

In viewing Tan-Gau on film, my personal opinion is that the instructor works too hard—unnecessarily hard for the results that are obtained. For example, students are engaged in a guessing game to decipher the meaning of the "noises" coming from the instructor's mouth. If the instruction was limited *only* to TPR, students would experience immediate success and *every utterance* from the instructor would be understood and believed. There would be no wasted energy by the instructor and no puzzlement from the students. We are privileged at Sky Oaks Productions to have the only remaining motion picture print in existence showing an application of Tan-Gau in a Canadian classroom.

How does TPR relate to an approach developed in France in 1894 by Francois Gouin?

I think there is an intimate connection. In Gouin's book, *The Art of Teaching and Studying Languages,* the author confesses his utter sense of failure in trying to acquire German from famous professors who used conversation, translation, and grammatical analysis. Gouin observed that when he left France for Germany, his 2 1/2-year-old nephew could run about but was not yet talking. After ten months in Germany struggling unsuccessfully to master German, Gouin returned home to discover that the child was chattering in French about all sorts of things. Why did this happen? "Why is it that I (Gouin)... versed in the sciences, versed in literature, versed in philosophy—armed with a powerful will, gifted with a trained memory, guided by an enlightened reason, and furnished besides with books and all the aids of science (had) arrived at nothing or practically nothing!" (p. 34) while the child in the same period of time was fluent in French?

"How happy should I be," continued Gouin, "if I could talk German as this little child can talk French; if I could express in German the simple facts which come to his tongue so spontaneously and this without seeking either words or rules to construct his sentences." (p. 35). Gouin became angry that linguistic science has "deceived me, has misguided me, has led me completely astray." He concluded, "The classical method, with its grammar, its dictionary, and its translations, is a delusion—nothing but a delusion." (p. 35)—to which I add, Amen.

Gouin's book is beautifully written and his thoughts are almost in complete harmony with the Total Physical Response except that—and this is not clear from his writing—whether one *silently* acts out a series of movements in a scenario or *speaks* sentences immediately in the target language that *link* one action to the next as, for example:

The alarm clock rings. I shut off the alarm. I open my eyes. I see that it is still dark outside. I pull back the covers. I sit up in bed. I swing my feet to the floor. I stand up. I walk to the door. I open the door.

I searched his book carefully to find the answer, which I believe is this: A "listen-and-repeat-after-me" strategy was used. Students started with the target language and a translation as, "Marche, Marche... Walk, Walk... "as they observed the instructor walking. Then each action was *linked* to the next action with students speaking the French after the instructor:

I walk toward the door. I draw near the door. I draw nearer and nearer. I get to the door. I stop at the door. I stretch out my hand. I take hold of the handle. I open the door. I pull the door.

If we *link* one thought to the next in a logical sequence, can people immediately produce sentence-after-sentence in the target language with long-term retention, zero stress, and the flexibility to recombine constituents—all features demonstrated in studies of TPR?

A comparison of Gouin's speaking-immediately-approach and TPR's silent period of comprehension through body movements is an exciting contrast for a future research project by some enterprising master's or doctoral candidate.

As another clue concerning the concept of *linking* one thought to the next, Blaine Ray has demonstrated in his everyday classroom experience that linking one thought to another in storytelling is a powerful agent for helping students *internalize* the skill of speaking, reading, and writing the target language. To see how storytelling "piggybacks" on TPR, see Ray's series of books for Level 1 and Level 2 students.

Can TPR be applied to learning sign language?

Professor Paul M. Culton, who was the head of the Hearing Impaired Program at Golden West College in Huntington Beach, California, suggested this idea. There should be an instructor and an aide, both of whom know sign language. The instructor makes, for example, a sign for "stand up" and the aide, sitting in between two students, stands up and gestures for the students to stand. Next, the sign for "sit down" and the aide, together with the students, sits down. Then, the procedure continues to develop in the same manner as when the target language was spoken. That is, basic commands are expanded into more and more complex linguistic patterns. It is important that one person—the instructor—gives commands in signs, while a different person—the aide—responds with the physical action. If the instructor gives the sign, then makes the action response, there is often confusion in the student's mind as to where the sign ends and action begins. The action is mistaken as being part of the sign.

Just as in FL instruction, when students are *ready* they begin production by spontaneously "babbling with their fingers." That is, they playfully make signs to express ideas.

What do you think of Krashen's concept of "comprehensible input"?

It is catchy, but should not be taken too literally. For example, *translation is* "comprehensible input" that tends to have a low index of believability. If I point to a chair and tell you that this is a *kursi,* you comprehend momentarily but you do not believe; hence, a short time later, the meaning of *kursi* is erased from memory. You had comprehensible input—but this does not necessarily mean that you have *intake,* to use another of Krashen's attractive terms. As I mentioned, to *translate* or *assert* the validity of an utterance may be comprehensible input *without intake.* This seems to be especially true of beginning and even intermediate students. Advanced students may accept *translation* as believable and therefore, intake the information into long-term memory. (This, of course, is an issue to be resolved in future research.

My hypothesis is that comprehensible input with *high believability* will produce long-term memory compared with short-term memory for low *believability* input. The Total Physical Response works because it is *comprehensible input with high believability* since we create intimate, personal experiences for the students. Hence, there is intake by the students.)

I'm confused. I hear the terms TPR, Natural Approach, and the Comprehension Approach. Why so many different labels for what seems to be the same process of learning?

The famous entertainer, Jimmy Durante, explained it best with his classic expression, *"Everyone wants to get in on the act!"*

It is only human nature for people to want to possess something that works. Success has many fathers but failure is an orphan.

Thirty years ago I opened up the right brain movement in language acquisition with my heretical concept that comprehension was more than the millisecond delay between asking a question of a student and receiving an answer. I pulled comprehension out of the chorus line and made it the star of the show. It was such a hit that many people wanted it in their own show.

TPR UPDATES

How can I be updated on TPR publications?

When you write, call, or fax Sky Oaks Productions, Inc. for a current TPR catalog, your name and address will be on the mailing list for future updates.

HOW TO PUBLISH YOUR WORK

I have developed new TPR materials that are effective with my students. How can I get my material published?

I recommend that you submit the following: a title, a preface, the table of contents, and one or two sample chapters. The preface should communicate your *goals,* the *age group* to whom the book is directed, the *level* intended (i.e. I, II, III, etc.), why your book is unique, and the advantages to the people who will use your book. Also report the effectiveness of your material when you pretested it with your students.

As Executive Editor of Sky Oaks Productions, Inc., I am keenly interested in publishing new TPR materials. *TPR is our specialty* and we are the TPR World Headquarters for the last 21 years with a market that is expanding. Teachers have discovered that TPR works—so they want more and more ideas to *expand the* application of TPR for their students.

By all means, send me your proposal in the form I have suggested and I will respond promptly. You can mail or fax your proposal to me c/o Sky Oaks Productions, Inc., P.O. Box 1102, Los Gatos, CA 95031. Phone: (408) 395-7600/ FAX: (408) 395-8440. Incidentally, we not only publish books, but we will consider games, videos, films, and software that are TPR—compatible.

APPLICATIONS TO MUSIC, SCIENCE, MATHEMATICS

Can your TPR approach help students acquire mathematics?

Yes, definitely. For stress-free acquisition of mathematical concepts, start with instruction that *plays to the right hemisphere of the brain.* Once students have stored a right brain experience, they are ready to scan the experience with the left brain. They are ready to transform the experience into language. In a study (Blakeslee, 1980) done in the forties, of eminent mathematicians, the surprising finding was that these people did *not* think in sharp symbols such as algebraic signs or even words. Outstanding mathematicians solved problems by thinking in visual images or tactile experiences. This suggests to me that people we think are "gifted" in mathematics or have an aptitude for mathematics may simply be able to receive the verbal explanation in the left brain and transfer it to the right brain where they find or invent an experience to make sense from the words they are hearing. The "low aptitude" student may receive the verbal explanation in the left hemisphere but does not have the "talent" or skill to create an imaginary experience to match the words. If so, then the answer is to provide visual and tactile experiences no matter what the age of the student.

For examples of instructional materials that play to the right brain, see my book, *Brainswitching*, and my new book entitled, *The Super-School of the 21st Century* published by Sky Oaks Productions.

How is your TPR approach related to Montessori mathematics training and the Suzuki technique of music instruction?

All three approaches play to the right brain since communication with students is through body movements. Students demonstrate competency through performance rather than talking or writing paper-and-pencil tests. Primary school teachers, especially K through the 3rd grade, understand the power of right brain instruction. Information is continually translated into experiences in which children touch, look, feel, explore, and manipulate. After the third grade, there is more and more of a shift to left brain instruction in which communication is verbal through talking, reading, and writing. While verbal skills of talking, reading, and writing are obviously important, understanding of language, mathematics, science, and music can be stress-free and assimilated rapidly through right brain instruction.

WHAT'S NEW

What is a language-body conversation? This is a new expression that I have not seen in your earlier writing.

When I use the term, conversation, we tend to think of two or more people talking to each other. Conversation means talking back and forth. Notice that we can have a conversation with ourselves which is called, "talking to yourself." Often we are admonished not to talk to ourselves because "people will think we are crazy."

While it is true that people confined to mental institutions often talk to themselves, self-talk in normal people can be extremely helpful in problem solving because the conversation is between both sides of our brain. You will notice that in many popular game shows, a contestant is often urged by the host to "talk it out" meaning to talk out loud so that the other side of the brain, the right hemisphere, can hear you and respond by flashing information on your cognitive screen.

A language-body conversation is the only format of communication for the infant. It is our left brain communicating with the baby's right brain. To the newborn, we say, "Look at me!" "Look, at me!" and the infant turns its face in the direction of the voice. "She's looking at me and she's smiling."

Language-body conversations are the first and the primary means of communication with the infant in continual day after day transactions that number in the thousands. Examples: "Stand up... Sit down... Come here... Walk to daddy... Don't spit up on your shirt... Let's go for a ride in the car..."

In acquiring another language in the TPR experience, the language-body conversation is the primary technique for instant communication of messages in a strange language along with effortless understanding of the language code (that is, the phonology, morphology and syntax). The essence of the Total Physical Response is the *language-body conversation.*

My students were successful with Blaine Ray's TPR storytelling student book, Look, I Can Talk! *Is there a follow-up book for my advanced students?*

Yes, we have published a sequel entitled, *Look, I Can Talk More!* This may be ordered in English, Spanish, French, or German. Overhead Transparencies for the ten main stories are also available.

Ray definitely recommends that the sequence for student success is to start with his first student book, *Look, I Can Talk!* followed by the second (perhaps more demanding) student book, *Look, I Can Talk More!*

What new projects are you working on?

I am working on a new book with the working title, *The Super-School of the 21st Century: We Can Have It Now!* After you have read this book, you will want to register your children and grandchildren so that they are the first to get in!

TPR WORKSHOP PRESENTERS

Dr. James J. Asher
Originator of TPR
P.O. Box 1102
Los Gatos, CA 95031 USA
Phone: (408) 395-7600
Fax: (408) 395-8440
tprworld@aol.com

Dr. Francisco Luis Cabello
Author: TPR in First Year-English, Spanish or French
Almutamid, 39
41005 Sevilla Spain
Phone: (95) 463-3215
flcabello53@hotmail.com

Joan Eling Christopherson
Organizes and Conducts 4–Day TPR Workshops
c/o Arla Crosier
9463 Mieras Raod
Yakima, WA 98901 USA
on_the_roaders@yahoo.com

Mark Chung
CEO of a Private Language School in Seoul, Korea
chungmc@cyberdude.com

Berty Segal Cook
ESL/FL Teacher Trainer
1749 E. Eucalyptus Street
Brea, CA 92821 USA
Phone: (714) 529-5359
Fax: (714) 529-3882
bertysegal@aol.com

Elizabeth Cunniff
Language Laboratory
Indiana Univ. at South Bend
1700 Mishawaka Avenue
South Bend, IN 46634 USA

Dr. James C. Davidheiser
Professor of German
German Department
University of the South
735 University Ave
Sewannee, TN 37383-1000 USA
Phone: (931) 598-1544
Fax: (931) 598-1145
jdavidhe@sewanee.edu

William Denevan
Foreign Language Teacher Trainer at Stanford University
105 Lance Court
Santa Cruz, CA 95065 USA
Phone: (813) 459-6894
diniquit@cruzio.com

Ramiro Garcia
Author: Instructor's Notebook
110 Valley Oaks Drive
Santa Rosa,CA 95409 USA
Phone: (707) 537-9105
cogarcia@compuserve.com

Bina Guerrieri
How best to learn Hebrew with TPR
1989 Kent Drive
Los Altos, CA 94024
Phone: (650) 961-8678
Fax: (650) 961-1175
eshel-guerrieri@worldnet.att.net

Mary J. G. Harris
Author: *"Withdrawal from grammar-translation to TPR"*
Associate Professor of Spanish
Iowa Wesleyan College
601 N. Main
Mt. Pleasant, IA USA 52641
Phone: (319) 385-6334
Fax: (319) 385-6296
mharris@iwc.edu

Gretchen L. Klein
Initiated TPR in four level of a foreign language curriculum
Pella High School
212 E. University Street
Pella, IA 50219 USA
Phone: (515) 628-3870
Fax: (515) 628-9319
pchsglk@pella.k12.ia.us

Joay Klopp
Author: Actionlogues
713 Rockhollow Road
Edmond, OK 73034 USA
Phone: (405) 330-1318
kloppjr@aol.com

Jenni Kotarski
Teacher of Spanish
1680 Karen Drive
Dorr, MI 49323 USA
Phone: (616) 681-2035
jkotarsk@aol.com

Elizabeth Kuizenga (Romijn)
Co-Author: Live Action books
City College of San Francisco
1047-63rd Street
Oakland, CA 94608 USA
Phone: (510) 658-6095
Fax: (510) 658-6095
elizabethk@pacbell.net

Dr. Gen Lennon
Gen Lennon and Associates
Language & Culture Consultants
8420 Cornell Ave
St. Louis, MO 63132-4905 USA
Phone: (314) 997-0845

Gene Lynch
Teacher of Excellence Award
1317 E. Oak
Lompoc, CA 93436-4228 USA
Phone: (805) 736-8889
grlynch@sbceo.org

Dr. E. Jules Mandel
FL Consultant, LA Unified School District, UCLA, and CAL State University at Los Angeles
20918 Calimali Road
Woodland Hills, CA 91364 USA
Phone: (818) 884-0923
Fax: (818) 887-5937
jmandel70@ aol.com

Marcio Lunardelli, Principal
Top School
Av. Paraná, 945 - Centro
Foz do Iguassu
Cep: 85.852-170
Paraná, Brasil
Phone: (55) 45-5236536
Fax: (55) 45-5237326
top.school@foznet.com.br

TPR WORKSHOP PRESENTERS

Todd McKay
TPR Storytelling for Children
1306 Kerwood Lane
Downingtown, PA 19335 USA
Phone: (610) 873-7774
Fax: (610) 566-8665
thmckay1@aol.com

Joe Moore
High School Teacher of Spanish
44 Morningside Drive
Tiffin, OH 44883 USA
Phone: (419) 447-2756
joe_moore@tiffin.k12.oh.us

Joe Neilson
Co-Author: Look, I Can Talk *More!* and Look, I'm *Still* Talking!
5418 E. 9th Street
Tucson, AZ 85711 USA
Phone: (520) 745-5140
jmombligo@aol.com

Jo Ann Olliphant
Author: Total Physical Fun
11004 111th Street S.W.
Tacoma, WA 98498 USA
Phone: (206) 584-7473

Doreen Rabbit, M.ED.
Application of TPR to the preservation of Native Indian Languages
Box 28
Standoff, Alberta
Canada T0L 1Y0
Phone: (403) 653-4660
Fax: (403) 653-1023

Blaine Ray
Originator of TPR Storytelling
3820 Amur Maple Drive
Bakersfield, CA 93311 USA
Phone: (661) 665-9523
Fax: (661) 665-8071
blaineray@aol.com

Contee Seely
TPR is More Than Commands-at All Levels
1755 Hopkins Street
Berkeley, CA 94707-2714 USA
Phone: (510) 524-1191
Fax: (510) 524-5150
contee@aol.com

Professor Steven M. Silvers
Author: Listen and Perform
University do Amazonas
Departamento de Linguas Estrangeiras
Campus Universitario-ICHL
69077-000Manaus-Amazonas
Brazil
Phone: (092) 644-2244 Ext. 2155
Fax: (092) 644-2451
gil@fua.br

Carol Spady
Memorial Middle School
S. Portland School Department
130 Westcott Road
S. Portland, ME 04106 USA
Phone: (207) 761-8330

Dr. Sam L. Slick
President, Command Spanish, Inc.
The Application of TPR in Training Police, Firefighters, Paramedics, Nurses, Doctors & other personnel
Box 1091
Pedal, MS 39465 USA
Phone: (601) 582-8378
Fax: (601) 582-5177

Tadashi Takahashi
Associate Professor of English
Kansai University of Social Welfare
1165-2 Shikata, Kakogawa
Japan
Hyogo 675-0321
Phone: 07-94-52-2424
Fax: 07-94-52-2424
tadtak@wt.ask.ne.jp

Sandy Terrill
How to Apply TPR for Best Results with Private School Students
Faith Christian School
122 Dante Street
Roseto, PA 18013
Phone: (570) 421-2975
terrill@epix.net

Patricia Verano
Professor of English
Graduate of the Universidad del Salvador
Medrano 179
(1722) Merlo-Buenos Aires
Argentina
Phone/Fax: 54-220-483-2090
vyvastor@infovia.com.ar

Dr. David Wolfe
French and Spanish Instructor
FL Supervisor in Moorestown, NJ
7021 Chew Ave
Philadelphia, PA 19119 USA
Phone: (215) 248-2462
Fax: (215) 248-2462
dwolfe70@aol.com

Dr. Margaret S. Woodruff-Wieding
Prize-winning author: Comprehension Based Language Lessons & Favorite Games for FL/ESL Classes
115 West 32nd Street
Austin, TX 78705 USA
Phone: (512) 474-1396
Fax: (830) 372-8096
wieding@sierra.onr.com *or*
mwieding@txlutheran.edu

Laura Zink de Diaz
Migrant and Bilingual Specialist
Mount Vernon School District
124 E. Lawrence Street
Mount Vernon, WA 98273 USA
Phone: (360) 428-6118
Fax: (360) 428-6118
profecita@yahoo.com

How does it feel to create an entire industry of books and workshops that focus upon comprehension rather than production as the first linguistic skill a student should acquire?

It is satisfying to realize that if one patiently transmits a message long enough, it is finally received. In my case it has taken 25 years, but it was certainly worth staying "on-task" when I meet so many friends, supporters and fans of TPR everywhere I go.

What was your experience as a student in the Arabic program of the Defense Language Institute in Monterey, California?

On a sabbatical leave in 1964 from San Jose State University and just after completing my first film demonstrating in Japanese the effectiveness of TPR, I was offered the opportunity to enroll as a student in the Arabic program at DLI. At that time, DLI used a combination of the audio-lingual and translation (almost exclusively left brain) for language instruction.

The fine faculty worked heroically 6 hours a day five days a week to apply dialogue memorization, pattern drill, and "repeat-after-me" exercises. But, of course, since the input was playing to the left rather than the right side of the brain, student achievement was in slow-motion, with high stress, and short-term memory. The faculty would have been thrilled if *input equalled output*—which *is* impossible for almost all students when instruction plays to the left brain. There was no expectation that students would recombine constituents in memorized dialogues in any substantial way to express thoughts.

Privately, using Japanese, I did demonstrate TPR for one of my instructors who tried it with his children and was delighted with the results. Immediately, the next day, he assembled on the parade ground, the students who were all, except for myself, military personnel, and gave commands in Arabic to move the students in close order drill. It was an amazing experience because the students in a few trials understood exactly what the instructor was saying in Arabic and they executed intricate movements almost perfectly.

Did you try to persuade the policy-makers at the Defense Language Institute to try TPR?

I sure did. My proposal was this: Military personnel often sit around the barracks for a few weeks waiting for the cycle to start with a new class. Give me a native speaker of the target language which the students will study. Let me work with the people for two weeks in pre-training exercises with TPR using the content they will encounter in DLI lessons. My objective: The students will understand everything spoken in the target language for the initial six to twelve weeks of DLI instruction. Then we will compare the achievement of my pre-trained group and those who did not have the TPR experience. I believe we can show a dramatic reduction in stress, a significant acceleration of all skills, long-term retention, and flexibility in recombining constituents to understand and express novel thoughts. The response was, "Yes, I'm sure that would work with children but certainly not with adults. Besides, our instructors are too old to be jumping and running."

Is TPR being used to instruct students in the Foreign Language Department of San Jose State University where you teach?

Individual instructors do incorporate TPR activities into their teaching, but there is no systematic application throughout the department. There are several reasons: First, it is difficult for the FL faculty to believe that a breakthrough was achieved one block away. Secondly, it is difficult to solicit or accept suggestions for running one's shop from an "outsider" who is not a member of the Foreign Language faculty. Thirdly, it may not have occurred to you, but there is no reward in state college teaching for expanding the demand for one's services. For example, if you enhance your teaching skill which then attracts more students, you will be punished with larger class sizes and an increase in your work load (i.e., paperwork, student counseling, etc.), with no increase in income. Furthermore, the increase in class size will substantially reduce the time you have available for scholarly research and writing which is highly prized in colleges and universities. Strangely, the reward system is designed to encourage a performance in the classroom that is satisfactory but not outstanding. Hence, there is no motivation at the college level to attract new students or to reduce the attrition of students now in the program.

Examples of outstanding college teaching, which you may have seen, are the result of the individual's pride in their work and talent. I have never tried to proselytize my colleagues in foreign languages. When people are ready, they will seek out the information. However, I might add that if they had been ready, and if teaching as well as scholarship was rewarded, then frankly, there would be a waiting list for every foreign language class at San Jose State University. Also, we would be a world-wide model for teaching and research in language acquisition.

How many languages do you speak?

English and enough Arabic so that if we visited a Middle Eastern country, I could get you something to eat, a hotel room, find the rest rooms, and arrange for a tour of the city. Also, since I volunteer to be the first "guinea pig" in any research project that I conduct, I have internalized through the TPR experience a sample of Japanese, Russian, and Spanish.

Did your children take a foreign language in school?

No, I advised them not to since the instruction was a traditional left-brain approach. I feel that a principle from medical school training applies, which is: "If you can't help the patient; *don't harm the person.*" I knew that the probability was only 5 chances in 100 that my children would be successful in the slow-motion, high-stress audio-lingual classes. The chances were overwhelming that they would experience failure and even worse, they would walk away with a self-image of, "I'm-no-good at learning foreign languages. I-can't-do-it."

I notice that you create a safe *environment in this workshop so that people feel comfortable expressing themselves. How important is this in a second language class?*

I think it is crucial. It sets the stage for a successful learning experience. If students feel safe, that is, anything they say is not only O.K. but appreciated by the instructor, then all channels of communication open up.

I picture communication, trust, and affinity as three corners of a triangle. If one of them increases, the other two automatically increase. Of course, if one of them is decreased, the others also decrease.

Do you have some epigrams — you know, philosophical bits of wisdom that you consider to be personally inspirational?

Yes. Let me share three that I personally like very much. The first is that, "One father is worth ten schoolmasters." The second, I think would be, "Trouble is the tool by which God fashions us for better things." The third, from the Christophers is this: "It is better to light one candle than to curse the darkness."

What are your comments on the storytelling craze?

The technique has a huge following. My thoughts are:

- This is effective because storytelling is another input to the right brain.
- The best selling book in the world is the Bible and the Bible is a book of stories. A story seems to transcend time, language barriers, and different cultures. A story is understood by literate and pre-literate people. A story is "brain compatible."
- Storytelling is a powerful tool but not a panacea. To use one tool for all tasks in language acquisition is like using a hammer to cut, drill and weld. A hammer is a whiz at pounding but not for cutting, drilling or welding.
- To me, the most effective application is to stabilize a set of vocabulary with TPR, then use those words to tell a short story of perhaps three or four sentences. An excellent resource for the TPR part of the equation is Steven M. Silver's book: ***The Command Book: How to TPR 2,000 vocabulary items in any language.***
- When you create your short story, keep in mind a recommendation you will find in every memory book ever written. As an illustration, if you want to remember a list of items to buy from the hardware store, integrate the list into a colorful mental picture. For example, let's say this is the list: a drill bit, sandpaper, paint thinner, and a three-way light bulb. Create a picture in your mind of a huge can of paint thinner. See yourself sitting cross-legged on the face of the can with a three-way light bulb over your head. You have a sheet of sandpaper in one hand and a drill bit in the other. The more bizarre and crazy the image, the easier it is to recall.
- Storytelling is a novelty. The danger with any novelty is adaptation. You know that students have "adapted" to the novelty when you hear asides such as, "No. No, please. Not another story!" or "If I have to listen to another story, I will wretch in the wastebasket."

You hypothesize that comprehension is critical in tracing a blueprint for the appearance of speech. Does "comprehension" have a different location in the brain compared with speech?

The answer is, yes. Brain scans (Ivry and Robertson, 1998) show that patients with extensive damage to Broca's Area in the left hemisphere where speech is located, can still comprehend oral lan-

---

Ivry, Richard B. ***The Two Sides of Perception.*** The MIT Press, Cambridge, MA., 1998.

guage. The area in the right brain called Wernicke's Area is correlated with comprehension of speech.

Curiously, when deaf people communicate with sign language, both Broca's Area in the left brain and Wernicke's Area in the right brain, "light up" in brain-images (Begley and Hayden, 1999). This suggests to me that TPR's use of language-body conversations is playing to both sides of the brain.

What is new in teaching chimps to communicate with sign language?

The latest hypothesis is that humans may have developed sign language before speech. Chimps learn hundreds of signs used by the deaf and can combine them into simple but novel sentences they have never seen before. Examples: "tickle me" or "give banana." Chimps can match a two year old human in novel sentence construction, but progress no further in complexity.

Deaf people throughout the world and throughout time have invented sign languages with fully developed grammars. This suggests that "gestural communication" may be as natural as speech (Begley and Hayden, 1999).

People use hand gestures, studies have suggested, to communicate words that have spacial connotations such as giving directions to a location. Electrodes on the arms signal more muscle activity when people try to define a word as "castanets" which connote movement. Donna Frick-Horbury in the *American Journal of Psychology* discovered that when volunteers held onto a bar to keep their hands still and listened to the definition of "abacus," they took longer to think up the word than when they could move their hands freely. Often, when their hands were "still," they failed to think of the word (Begley, 1998).

These studies suggest to me that hand movement when we speak, is an attempt by the right brain (which is mute) to convey vital information to the left brain. The right brain knows things that are unknown to the left brain. There is a "desperate" attempt to communicate answers with body movements.

How is the right brain related to the "unconscious" brain?

Freud coined the term "unconscious" or "subconscious." We now think that Freud was referring to the right brain which is always conscious but is mute. Since the right brain cannot talk (except perhaps to whisper) , it is easy to see how it has the illusion of being

---

Begley, S., and Hayden, T. *Talking from hand to mouth.* Science & Technology, Newsweek, March 15, 1999.

Begley, S. *Living hand to mouth.* Newsweek, November 2, 1998.

"unconscious" or "subconscious." The right brain can communicate vital information if it has a synthetic voice box such as gestures, drawing, acting, body movement, singing, etc.

Some learning theorists believe that learning can be explained with the simple repetition of a stimulus and a response until the student makes a connection. Do you agree?

No, I don't. Let me explain why. On the surface, it looks as if repetition imprints something in the brain like a rubber stamp. On the first trial, there is little ink on the pad, so the imprint is faint, almost indelible. So, continue to stamp until the image is bold print.

I don't believe that each trial is a duplication in the brain of each previous trial. I think the Right Brain monitors the first trial and then processes the information to find (or create) a pattern that matches the model. We are not aware of this process because the Right Brain is mute. It cannot tell us what it is doing (except perhaps in a faint whisper which we don't hear unless the talkative Left Brain is silent). Often we can hear the whisper when our hands are busy with an automatic task such as shaving or mowing the lawn or driving the car. We suddenly hear ourselves exclaim, "Wow! I just got a great idea!"

On each trial, the Right Brain makes a subtle alteration of the intake (and sometimes it is not so subtle) until there is a satisfactory match between the input and the intake. How do we know when there is a satisfactory match? This comes from "feedback" or "knowledge of results" as when the instructor says, "Great! You got it! Perfect!" Notice that the Right Brain is working by shaping the intake even when we are not "on task." The right brain is working even when we have switched to other tasks, even when we are resting, and even when we are sleeping. This explains why hundreds of learning studies recommend that "distributive practice" produces better results compared with "massed practice."

In one of your books, either ***Brainswitching*** *or* ***The Super School of the 21st Century,*** *you mentioned that teachers become disconnected from students. Can you discuss this.*

I think this disconnection is a by-product of acquiring any skill. When one achieves a skill, there is amnesia for the learning process. We no longer have a memory for our perceptions of the learning task as we struggled from one plateau to the next. This is true of any skill from typing to calculus, from auto repair to fluency in a second language. You can see this phenomenon in technical manuals. If you already understand how something works, then every word in the manual is understandable. Otherwise, the manual reads like hieroglyphics. Almost always, there are missing steps in the explanation. The writer does not intend to baffle the reader by leaving out vital details. It is just that the writer no longer remembers many details or assumes that the missing details are obvious. The teacher has achieved an exquisite master of whatever it is the person is now "teaching." Automatically, the teacher is disconnected from the perceptions of students. Amnesia has erased our memories of the learning process.

How can we reconnect with student perceptions?

I recommend teaching yourself an "alien" skill. For example, I recently started the process of teaching myself computer programming. Wow! What a revelation! For three weeks, I read and reread passages from computer books that "explain" how to program. These books had enticing titles such as: " QBasic for Rookies" or "QBasic 101" or "QBasic by Example." For three weeks, it was like wandering around a huge mansion that was in complete darkness, trying to feel the walls to locate a light switch. As I groped, I cursed every time I stumbled over some heavy furniture. Suddenly, I found a light switch that lit up one room. Then it was easier to find the light switch in the next room. Now, most of the mansion is lit up, but there are still some dark rooms yet to explore.

I realized that once I understood a procedure, the explanation in those books had a kindergarten simplicity. If you know how to do it, there is nothing to it. What kept me from giving up during the three week struggle, was the experience of one of the greatest mathematical minds of all time, Sir Isaac Newton. Newton, the Englishman, was the contemporary of another mathematical giant, the Frenchman, René Descartes. Descartes was searching for a "lost city of Atlantis" in mathematics, the invisible connection between geometry and algebra. For hundreds of years, mathematicians believed that such a connection did not exist. Descartes believed they were wrong. As Descartes, a devout Catholic, reported in his personal papers, "One night while I was asleep, the Angel of Truth appeared to me and whispered the secret connection between geometry and algebra. Immediately, I awoke and scribbled down the exciting revelation." *(paraphrased)* That connection is now known as "Analytic Geometry" without which all the engineering marvels of the 20th and 21st centuries would disappear.

Newton needed to understand Descartes' discovery as a stepping stone to his own marvelous discovery, the Calculus. But Descartes was not a generous man. His book describing Analytic Geometry was "difficult" to read. Descartes' attitude was, "If you don't understand it, that's too bad!" Even the great Sir Isaac Newton, who discovered the Laws of Gravity, could not follow what Descartes had written. Newton said, "I would read a paragraph, become so utterly exhausted trying to decipher it that I had to go to bed. I would awake and read the passage again and again and again until finally, I understood..."

My personal message from Sir Isaac Newton is this: "If Sir Isaac can be perplexed to the point of exhaustion and still persist until he understood, then I certainly can endure a little stress until I understand."

Do you think that the right-left brain model explains great discoveries such as Newton's laws of gravity?

Yes, I do. When people asked Newton how he made his astonishing discovery, he replied, "By thinking about it all the time." I believe that once we pose a question, the right brain will continue to search for an answer until we respond with, "Ah, that's it!" or "I give up. There is no answer." Most people expect an immediate answer which prompts them to switch off the right brain's search too soon. Newton kept his right brain continually searching.

Before Newton, René Descartes offered the theory that planets move like a tornado with the tail whipping around to produce the movement of the planet. Newton reasoned: "No, I don't think so. If that were true then objects falling to the ground such as an apple from its tree would fall at a slant. They don't. They fall straight down. So planets must move around with no sudden changes in velocity."

Another famous example of how the right brain works comes from the Father of Astronomy, Johannes Kepler who was a contemporary of René Descartes. Kepler played with hundreds of equations in an attempt to predict the movement of the planets which he assumed were orbiting in a circle. None of the equations worked until, in a flash of insight, he heard his right brain whisper, "The planets are moving in an elliptical pattern, not a circle."

A friend is studying to be an English teacher in Austria where they have very rigid teaching methods. Any suggestions on how she can overcome these traditional methods would be appreciated.

My recommendation is to "go with the flow" by conforming to the demands of the system, but gradually opening it up with a five minute TPR episode at the beginning of each class. Use this opportunity to TPR vocabulary that the students will encounter in the next chapter of the textbook. For cues as to how to accomplish this, see Stephen Silver's ***The Command Book*** which shows how to TPR 2,000 vocabulary items. If you are successful in easing the load on your students, slowly expand the amount of time you dedicate to TPR activities.

What is the optimal size for the effective application of TPR?

Joan Christopherson says this: "I have used TPR in classes as small as 3 and as large as 40. I have used it with kids as young as 3 and adults with equal success... but understand that those in the larger classes will get less individual attention. I have also used it with an exchange student I had in my home a couple of years ago... It helped him a lot. Joan's e-mail is: garyc@wolfenet.com

Any new ideas for handling grammar?

Joan Christopherson recommends a technique called "roll call" which she uses successfully in her high school classes. She says, " I ask a volunteer to do different things such as, "Please stand up, walk to the chalkboard and write your name." Then I call the name of a student and say, "Luke, ask Maria what she is doing." or "Luke, ask Maria what she did."

Another variation: "Luke, ask Ellen what Maria is doing?" The entire class gets a chance to ask a question using the same basic structure and hear a response over and over except with enough variation to be interesting. If you would like a copy of the "roll call" handout that Joan uses in her workshops, send your name and complete address by e-mail to Joan at garyc@wolfenet.com.

Any new twists on your TPR student kits?

Yes. Jim Baird in Georgia reports this: "I have kind of enlarged on your student kit idea. My classroom has a wall-to-wall white board and I have used it to create complete communities and an entire country with cut-outs and markers (wish I had stick-on cities).

"Students are required to drive, walk (with their fingers), fly, hop, run etc. between buildings or cities, pick up things or people and deliver them to other places. They can fly into an airport and rent a car and drive it to another city where they can catch a flight or a boat, all kinds of possibilities. Sure is fun!"

Want to ask Jim more about this neat innovation? His e-mail is: ghc@ocsonline.com

Are there any people who meet regularly on the net to discuss classroom strategies using the Total Physical Response?

To develop a circle of teachers around the world who are also interested in a discussion group, my suggestion is to post a note on various bulletin boards of FL/ESL newsgroups such as FLTalk. You will get many responses and some excellent suggestions to any question you may ask. You will find leads to these newsgroups on our web site (www.tpr-world.com). Look under "TPR Experts" at the bottom of the page or ask your reference librarian for help.

Any new findings on right-left brain research since the 5th edition of your book?

Yes. Robert Ornstein's book, ***The Right Mind*** and Michael S. Gazzaniga's book, ***The Mind's Past*** did give some interesting new bits and pieces about the hemispheres of the brain.

I discovered that since Roger Sperry's Nobel-prize winning experiment with cats, more than 4,000 experiments have been conducted exploring the right and left brain. Gazzaniga, for example, reveals that "The mind is the last to know things. After the brain computes an event, the illusory "we" (that is, the mind) becomes aware of it. The brain, particularly the left hemisphere, is built to interpret data the brain has already processed..." (p1). He thinks there is a special device in the left brain which he calls the interpreter. After the brain executes a googleplex of automatic brain processes, the interpreter makes one more review to reconstruct our perceptions, memory and judgment.

The implication for second language instruction—or instruction in any subject, for that matter, seems clear to me. That is, every instructor is playing (whether they know it or not) to a student's brain that is independent of the student. The brain is processing information that is hidden from the student but appears in conclusions printed out obliquely in student thoughts such as: "Is there really a language like this or is this guy making it up as he goes along? After all, he claims that this is a *kursi*, that is a *taala* and that over there is a *suburra*. However, he is the only person in this room, in this school, in this nation, who believes everything he is saying is true. The rest of us know he is pointing to a chair, a table and a chalkboard. This is a pack of lies..." It is not puzzling, therefore, that the brain refuses to store the "information" into long-term memory. Why waste storage space on false data?

Another interesting conclusion from Gazzaniga is that "Brains were not built to read" (p6). He feels that reading is rather recent in human development. The brain has a place to regulate breathing and a million other activities, but there is no definite place for reading. Modern brain imaging studies show that the brain lights up in slightly different locations when people read.

A third conclusion from Gazzaniga verifies my hypothesis that the right brain can operate on parallel tracks while the left brain moves in a serial order on one track. Hundreds of studies with verbal material show that memorizing task A followed by task B, will interfere with the recall of task A. This is the left brain moving a train down a track. If it must stop to let another train enter the track at some juncture, it gets confused as to where the first train is located. It can only manage one train at a time.

Douglas Medin at Northwestern University showed, for example, that information in the right brain such as tasks involving spacial memory, can move along almost simultaneously on multiple tracks with no interference. The right brain does not get confused as to where the different tasks are located.

How can I adapt TPR to block scheduling of 90 minute classes for high school students (especially in the pre-speaking stage)?

Professor Stephen Mark Silvers from the University of Amazonas in Manaus, Brazil has this suggestion: "I think the best guide is to have lots of variety. One possibility would be to use the whole 90 minutes for several classes until the students are ready for role reversal and are beginning to give the commands.

"During these 90 minute periods, along with the active physical commands, you will also need to use some quieter commands in which the students are working at their seats. For these quieter commands you can use Dr. Asher's TPR Student Kits. They cover all of the key vocabulary areas and are visually very stimulating. They are easy to use with the students at their seats, and offer a nice change of pace from the more active commands.

"Another idea for the quieter commands would be to use the Visual Practice Exercises and the drawing exercises from my book ***Listen and Perform***. After the students are into role reversal and can easily give and follow commands, you can then divide your 90 minute period into active TPR activities, a continuation of the student kits, and language games. The best little book I know for language games is ***Favorite Games for FL-ESL Classes*** by Dr. Margaret S. Woodruff-Wieding and Laura J. Ayala." You can explore this further with Professor Silvers at his e-mail address of: gil@fua.br

How can we reduce the attrition in our school program for second languages?

The answer comes from the Top School, a private language school in South America. The principal told me that when they used a traditional textbook approach, their attrition was about 80%. After the introduction of TPR, the attrition has dropped to 2%. To contact the Top School, e-mail: top.school@foznet.com.br

What guidelines can I use to select vocabulary for beginning students?

My suggestion is, first of all, "less is more." Instead of a long, ambitious list, limit yourself to a short list of three or four items. Be sure they are "stabilized,"—that is, internalized by your students and then try three more items.

Secondly, select vocabulary items that are "brain compatible" and not "brain antagonistic." For example, I demonstrated TPR for university students at San Jose State University in a language methods class. After a successful TPR lesson in Arabic with several students, I invited the instructor to try her hand at TPR in her native language of Vietnamese. I wanted to show that TPR is brain compatible meaning it plays to the pattern-seeking right brain.

One of the valuable features of pattern-seeking is that the right brain can process information on parallel tracks. The left brain, for contrast, processes information in serial order on one track. This means that the right brain can internalize several incoming languages without interference—without static. I wanted to show that using TPR, the students could internalize both Arabic and Vietnamese without confusion.

The instructor started with "Stand, sit, walk, turn" which worked. Then she expanded into, "Point to the chalkboard, point to the chair, and point to the table." At this point, the lesson was shattered because she used two words in Vietnamese that sounded almost identical to the non-native speaker. Now the lesson dissolved into an involved discussion of the subtleties between the two vocabulary items. This was a mistake, in my judgment, because the lesson shifted suddenly from the right brain to the critical left brain and we were now deep into the zone of "brain antagonistic" instruction.

The instructor was explaining sound characteristics of Vietnamese with linguistic doodles on the chalkboard. The student's brain was listening to this and concluding, "I knew it! This language is impossible to learn! I can't hear the difference no matter how many times she repeats it!"

The mistake was including two similar sounding vocabulary items in the same lesson. This does not mean that students will never hear the difference. They will, but not in the early stages of language acquisition. Select items that are easy to differentiate. We want success, success, success for the students. Why create unnecessary brain antagonistic instruction which is non-productive?

Selecting vocabulary items can be difficult for a native speaker. This sounds ridiculous, but it isn't. I realized this one evening helping one of my grandsons with his spelling. He is nine and in the third grade. To a native adult speaker, the list he was supposed to

learn looked simple and easy. And the items were simple and easy *for an adult.*

As I read the words and listened to my grandson respond to the drill with hesitation and confusion, I realized that the list of spelling words was a classic example of brain antagonistic instruction. When you read the list below, ask yourself, "Why would a child have any difficulty learning the spelling?"

The list		*Bonus words*
wreck	wrench	homonym
wrong	write	synonym
wrist	know	antonym
knee	knew	exclamation
knife	knock	
knot	knob	

There are several problems with selecting this list of vocabulary items. The first is similar to the Vietnamese lesson. To the native speaker, the tone differences were obvious, but the learner is "functionally deaf" to the differences. To a third grader, knee and knew and knife are subtle sound differences, especially when the words are ***out of context***. Why set up pairs that are not easily differentiated? This only convinces the child that, "I don't know these words! This is difficult! The more I try, the more confused I am! I will never know how to spell these words!" Remember, the more trials to internalize anything, the lower the probability that one can retrieve the information later. Trials to learning is inversely related to long-term retention. The more trials the lower the chances for recall later.

For comparison, let's create a list that dramatically increases the probability of success for the child. Let's create a list that is brain compatible.

The list	
wreck	deck
know	blow
hand	band

In another lesson,

The list	
wreck	twist
knock	rock
hike	bike

In another lesson,

The list

wrong	right
knew	new
light	sight

All of these pairs are subject to sampling with students. If a pair is confusing, substitute a different set until there is first-trial learning which is the essence of brain compatible instruction.

Are there teachers in the New York City area who know how to do TPR? I would like to find someone to help my children acquire French.

Dr. David Wolfe (dwolfe70@aol.com) recommends that one call the foreign language division of the schools in your area and inquire. Also, place an ad in the paper.

When Dr. Wolfe teaches French in Philadelphia using TPR, he prefers a group of students to enroll for private lessons rather than one-to-one. "It is too demanding to interact using TPR one-to-one for an hour or so a day, especially for young children."

What about the effectiveness of the Canadian model of immersion?

Dr. David Wolfe (dwolfe70@aol.com) makes these observations: "For best results, children should have immersion one hundred percent daily. Children in the Canadian model are usually 'bilingual' by the sixth grade. This means they can take standardized tests in both languages and do equally well. Their speech is OK but will have Anglicisms because the language (French) is rarely used outside of school.

"The model used most often is this: children are immersed one hundred percent in kindergarten through the third grade. After that there is a gradual transition until the mix is fifty-fifty by the sixth grade."

How does "suggestion" fit into the right-left brain model?

I think that suggestion by-passes the critical left brain. How does it do this? It does it with a message that automatically opens or closes the gate to the right brain. Remember that the left brain is verbal and critical while the right brain is a mute, uncritical pattern-seeker. Anything is possible to the right brain. Like a heat-seeking missile, the right brain is only looking for patterns.

Classic examples of suggestion that shunt messages directly into the right brain would be propaganda techniques such as "glittering generalities." In the movie, *A Few Good Men,* Jack Nicholson said, "The Marines use words like honor, loyalty, country..." The left brain responds with, "Who can argue with those words? Those are great words! I see no flaws in those words! For any message associated with those words, the gate to the right brain automatically swings open."

Another example of suggestion (which is also a powerful propaganda technique) is "name calling." Notice that calling a message a name such as, "This is propaganda," automatically closes the gate to the right brain. That message does not pass through. A name that will automatically open the gate for Americans is, "This is an official announcement from the President of the United States."

Still another example of suggestion is the "testimonial." Thirty years ago, ads in magazines, newspapers and television showed a man in a white lab coat with his name and M.D. on the pocket. He is enjoying a cigarette. The left brain evaluates this image with, "If this medical person whom I respect as a health authority is smoking, it is something that will not harm me. In fact, smoking must be good for me."

In mathematics, what is right brain and what is left brain?

Geometry and trigonometry play to the right brain. Arithmetic and algebra play to the left brain.

Euclid, who lived in 300 AD, organized everything known about points, lines, circles, triangles, squares, etc. into the second best-selling book of all time, ***Elements of Geometry***. This was a stunning feat by a rather mysterious Greek mathematician. It is interesting that all of Euclid's geometrical "proofs" were right brain pictures.

When arithmetic and algebra were discovered, mathematicians believed for hundreds of years that these languages had no connection with geometry. René Descartes in the 17th century was the first to show that the right brain pictures of geometry can be translated into the left brain language of algebra. Without this connection, the scientific discoveries and technological marvels of the 20th and 21st centuries would never have occurred.

How do children acquire number concepts? Is there a connection between understanding math patterns and understanding language patterns?

Excellent question. I just finished a fascinating book by Reuben Hersh entitled, "What is mathematics, really?" (Oxford

University Press, 1997). He comments that Jean Piaget, the famous child psychologist, believed that children learn about natural numbers not by talking, but by real physical activity. The child abstracts number patterns from physical movements such as picking up, putting down, moving, and using objects.

For contrast, Aristotle was an ALM type person. He believed, for example, that children acquire the number concept of "three" by seeing three apples, three coins and three pebbles. Learning comes from passive observation just as when a teacher in an FL class holds up a picture of three coins and says in the target language, "These are three coins. These are three coins."

Piaget would say that observation is not enough. A cat observes also but does not discover concepts—does not abstract because the cat does not handle, play with, pick up and put down objects. A child does. This is a terrific testimonial for TPR.

"Crazy English" is the latest frenzied approach to learning another language. What do you think?

The originator of "Crazy English" is 29-year old Li Yang in Beijing, China who describes himself as a "real loser" in school. After taking English classes for 14 years, he still could not speak it. He hit upon a strategy of overcoming inhibitions to speak English by shouting it. According to an account from Renee Schoof of the Associated Press (6/15/99), "Li mimics how not to say it 'I have-a-heard-a so much-a about-a you.' Then naturally, with pauses and dramatic punch: 'I...have heard...SOOOO much...abowwwt-choo.'"

Along with ***whispering,*** I think that ***shouting*** is another interesting brainswitch from the left to the right brain. Therefore, we have a useful tool. It certainly is worth further exploration in experimental research.

How does meditation—and prayer fit into a right-left brain model?

I think there is an intimate connection. Remember that each hemisphere of the brain can operate independently. Each has information that is concealed from the other because each side is a different information processor. The left is a loud talker and the right is a quiet pattern-seeker. The left offers edited information while the right has unedited information.

During waking hours, almost all we hear is the talkative left brain. We cannot hear messages from the right brain because it is whispering so faintly that the signal is almost undetectable. We can hear the faint messages if we can quiet the incessant talking from the left brain. I believe some ways of silencing the left brain, at least for a short interval, is meditation and prayer.

PART IV

CLASSROOM LESSONS

The First Class

Motivation of students. One powerful way to motivate student interest is to show one or more of the documentary films (see pages 5-12 to 5-18) which demonstrates what will be done and the language skills achieved by other students. Another excellent approach devised by Ramiro García of San José, California is to tell students attending their first class in Spanish: "When you leave here you will understand perfectly everything I am going to say next." Then García would rapidly utter about ten commands in Spanish. The immediate reaction of students is keen interest and skepticism. Many say, "Who, me understand everything you just said? After one session? Never!" Still a third way is to simply demonstrate the approach with a few students.

For English as a second language, Carol Adamski has found that at least a brief explanation of the theory, goal and instructional format is most helpful in setting students at ease and quickly involving them in the action. Since a variety of languages are spoken in a beginning ESL class, an explanation is not always possible. However, beginning students often come to class with a relative or friend who speaks some English and can translate. And, often there is one student in the school who can act as a translator.

Orientation of students. If you would like to further orient your students with a detailed explanation of the theory behind this approach, the following rationale may be helpful:

The first step in learning another language is to internalize the code of that language. You will internalize the code in the same way you assimilated your native language which was through commands. Like most of us, you probably have amnesia for your infancy but research suggests that many, many of the utterances directed to you when you were a baby—perhaps half of what you heard—was in the form of commands such as: "Don't spit up on your blouse!," "Give mommy a big kiss!," "Hold daddy's hand!," or "Look at the bird on the branch of that oak tree!" So what I am saying is that, as an infant, you probably deciphered and internalized the code of your first language in a chain of situations in which people manipulated and directed your behavior through commands.

For hundreds of hours you were silent except for babbling, but during that time you were deciphering that important code. You were sorting out the patterns that would transform the noise coming from people's faces into information. It was only after many months of decoding that you began to speak and even then your understanding was far in advance of your speaking skill and it remained that way for years. Well, that's the way you will enter this new language—through commands. I will utter a command and act along with you for several times. Then each of you will act alone when I give you a command. Gradually, the entire code of the new language will be visible to you and spontaneously your tongue will produce utterances in the new language. Let's begin. I need four volunteers.

Let's begin. Using hand signals, motion four students to come up to the front of the classroom. Then gesture for two students to sit on either side of you facing the class. Other students in the class are often seated in a semi-circle so that there is a rather large space for the action.

Then say, "Stand up!" and immediately stand up as you motion the students seated on either side of you to stand up. Next say, "Sit down!" and immediately sit down along with the four students. If any student tries to repeat what you have said, signal silence by touching your lips with your index finger. Then say, "Stand up!" and the group, including the instructor, should stand up; and then "Sit down!" and all sit down. Repeat the utterance "Stand up!" and "Sit down!" each followed by the appropriate action until all respond confidently, without hesitation.

Then the command is "Walk!" and all walk forward. The next commands are "Stop!" "Turn!" "Walk!" "Stop!" "Turn!" "Walk!" "Stop!" "Jump!" "Turn!" "Walk!" "Stop!" "Jump!" "Turn!" "Sit down!"

By observing the hesitation or non-hesitation of students, you can make decisions as to how many more times you should model with the students. For cues about student readiness to try it alone, after uttering a command, delay your own response slightly to give the students a chance to show they understand and to decrease their dependency on you.

When you think the students are ready to try it themselves, sit down and utter commands which the students as a group act out. As you progress in a routine, it is important to vary the order of commands so that students do not memorize a fixed sequence.

By observing the group, you can decide when individuals are ready to try it alone. Certain students seem more confident and ready than others, so begin with those people. One by one, use gestures to invite each student to try it alone. Next, invite students from the audience to try. If you can memorize each student's first name in the beginning of the class while you take roll, you can then call out individuals from the audience with, "Juan, stand up!" "Walk!" and so forth.

Of course, the concept of a command implies an authoritarian harshness, but this is not what is being advocated. The commands are given firmly but with gentleness and pleasantness. The kindness, compassion, and consideration of the instructor will be signaled in the tone of voice, posture and facial expressions. You are the student's ally and they will sense this in the way you direct their behavior.

Another hint is this: Students will be quite literal in their interpretation of what an utterance means. You must be careful to make "clean" responses that are uncluttered with extraneous movements or gestures. For example, one instructor would say "Turn!" then unconsciously move his head in either direction and then turn. Whenever the students heard "Turn!" they would swivel their heads from side to side and then turn. Remember, the students are watching every move you make and if you add irrelevant cues, they will internalize them as a false part of the meaning.

When the students can individually respond quickly and accurately to "Stand up!" "Sit down!" "Turn around!" "Walk!" "Stop!" and "Jump!" they are ready for an expansion of utterances that will move students to different locations in the room. With a few students, begin the expansion with:

Point to the door. ***(You and the students point to the door.)***

Point to the chair. ***(You and the students point to the chair.)***

Point to the table. ***(You and the students point to the table.)***

After you have uttered the commands and pointed with the students, say:

Point to the door. Walk to the door. ***(You and the students point to the door; then you all walk to the door.)***

Touch the door. ***(You all touch the door.)***

Now try:

Point to the chair. Walk to the chair. ***(You all point to the chair; then walk to the chair.)***

Touch the chair. ***(You all touch the chair.)***

Next try:

Point to the table. Walk to the table. ***(You all point to the table and then walk to the table.)***

Touch the table. ***(You all touch the table.)***

At this point, say:

Point to a chair. ***(Each student points to a chair.)***

Walk to a chair. ***(The students walk to their chairs.)***

Sit down. ***(The students sit down.)***

You sit down also and direct *individual* students with commands as:

Maria, stand up. ***(Maria, who is sitting next to you, stands up.)***

Walk to the table. ***(Maria walks to the table.)***

Point to the door. ***(Maria points to the door.)***

Walk to the door and touch the door. ***(Maria walks to the door and touches the door.)***

Novelty

Maria, point to a chair. ***(Maria points to a chair.)***

Jump to the chair. ***(You have now uttered a novel command—one Maria has not heard before.)***

She has heard "Jump" and "Walk to the chair," but *not* "Jump to the chair." Usually, Maria will delight you and the other students by responding correctly. If not, you demonstrate by uttering:

Jump to the table. ***(Then you jump to the table.)***

Or perhaps you say,

Juan, stand up. ***(Juan stands up.)***

Then you say,

Juan, jump to the door. ***(Usually Juan will respond correctly by jumping to the door.)***

Then return to Maria with,

Maria, jump to the chair.

Now try:

Eduardo, stand up. ***(Eduardo, who was in the audience, stands up.)***

Eduardo, walk to the table. ***(He walks to the table.)***

Now point to the table. ***(He point to the table.)***

Now touch the table. ***(He touches the table.)***

Eduardo, point to a chair. ***(He points to a chair.)***

Walk to the chair and sit down. ***(He walks to a chair and sits down.)***

Now try a novel command with Eduardo. He has been responding quickly and confidently to utterances he has heard you use to direct other students. Try a recombination of familiar constituents (i.e., a novel command). Try this:

Eduardo, stand up. ***(He stands up.)***

Walk to the table. ***(He walks to the table.)***

Now sit on the table.

Usually Eduardo will not disappoint you, but if he does not respond, do *not* press him by repeating the novel command. Rather, say:

Walk to the table ***(and you walk to the table).***

Sit on the table ***(and you sit on the table).***

Or, illustrate with another student by saying:

Maria, sit on the chair. ***(Maria sits on the chair.)***

Maria, stand up. ***(She stands up.)***

Maria, sit on the chair. ***(She sits down on the chair.)***

Maria, stand up and walk to the table. ***(She walks to the table.)***

Maria, sit on the table.

With practice you will become extremely skilled at recombining utterances to produce novel commands which students respond to correctly. Novelty is *not* meant to *trick* the student. We expect a successful response to each novel utterance. The intent is first to encourage flexibility in understanding the target language in the richness of recombinations. Secondly, novelty is a keen motivator. The surprises will delight both you and the students. And thirdly, student self-confidence is enhanced because they are aware that they instantly understood an unfamiliar utterance—one they had never heard before in training.

Introduce more vocabulary. After individual students are responding rapidly and confidently, add new vocabulary such as window, light, ceiling, floor, clock, wall, and chalkboard. As a rule of thumb, be sure students are responding confidently to three new items before you try the next set of three. Too many items at one time is confusing and merely slows down the learning process. Since there is continual interaction with the students, you will have abundant cues from their behavior that will tell you when they are ready to continue with something new.

You are constantly monitoring their progress. You are able to "read" where each student is at all times. Relax! Don't be too ambitious and rush ahead so fast that the students experience failure. Each move—familiar or novel—should be a success for the student.

Enjoy the adventure with them. Keep the action moving briskly. As a hint, the pace is fast-moving because students assimilate the target language through their bodies very rapidly. Therefore, have an outline or script because the movement of the learning experience tends to be faster than the instructor is able to think spontaneously.

NOTE

The content to be presented in the next 53 classroom lessons is based on a training log used by one instructor to teach English as a second language. Each class was a three-hour session with adults from ages 18 to 69. The nationalities of the students were Japanese, Chinese, Greek, Russian, Korean, and Latin American.

The class size was approximately 25 students, which varied from day to day as new students continued to join the group throughout the year. The daily three-hour classes were held five days a week.

The material you will read next is for 159 hours of classroom instruction. The content is flexible and can be shifted around without negative consequences. The criterion for including a vocabulary item or grammatical feature at a particular point in training is ease of assimilation by students. If an item is not learned rapidly, this means the students are not ready for that item. Withdraw it and try again at a future time in the training program. The guideline for inclusion is this: If students do not assimilate an item in a few trials—preferably the first trial—they are not ready. Delay the introduction of that item until a future time.

The Second Class

Review. The instructor selected a *small group* from the audience and spoke English to move them, beginning with:

Stand up.	Stop.
Sit down.	Turn.
Stand up.	Jump.
Walk.	Sit down.

Then she expanded to:

Walk to the window.
Touch the window.
Walk to the table.
Touch the table.
Walk to the door.
Touch the door.
Walk to the chair.
Touch the chair.

After a small group performed, the instructor manipulated the behavior of *individual students* selected at random. She said:

Juan, stand up and walk to the door.

Maria, stand up and walk to the window.

Jaime, walk to the table and sit on the table.

Notice that the instructor is the director of a stage play in which the students are the actors. You can "feel" the pace that is optimal for your students. The objective is to move students as rapidly as they are able to respond successfully. Remember, your intent is not to trick the students with complexity beyond their development. Your goal is continuous student success. Therefore, you should move students in a logical progression.

New commands. In the semi-circle, the instructor had a table on which were pencils, books, and papers. She said, "Juan, stand up and walk to the table!" When he had responded, she led him around the table so that both the instructor and the student faced the class with the table in front of them. Then she said:

Touch the pencil. ***(She and the student touched a pencil.)***

Pick up the pencil. ***(She picked up a pencil and gestured for Juan to pick up a pencil, which he did.)***

Put down the pencil. ***(They both put their pencils on the desk.)***

Touch the book. ***(They both touched a book.)***

Pick up the book. ***(They both pick up a book.)***

Put down the book. ***(Juan put down the book before the instructor could move, which indicated that assimilation was occurring.)***

Touch the paper. ***(Now she delayed her response slightly to let Juan demonstrate his understanding.)***

Pick up the paper. ***(Again she delayed a moment or so to let Juan make the correct action, which he did.)***

Put down the paper. ***(Immediately Juan put the paper on the desk.)***

Once Juan was responding quickly and accurately, the instructor called two other students to the table and moved them through the routine of:

Touch the book.

Touch the paper.

Touch the pencil.

Pick up the book.

Pick up the paper.

Pick up the pencil.

Put down the paper.

Put down the book.

Put down the pencil.

Then the series was varied with commands as:

Pick up the paper and the pencil.
Put down the paper only.
Now, put down the pencil.
Pick up the pencil and the book.
Put down the book but do *not* put down the pencil.
Pick up the paper.
Do *not* put down the paper.
Now, put down the paper.

Notice that "small" words as "now," "only," and "not" were presented in context and seemed to be assimilated easily.

Next, two other students were moved rapidly with the routine which was expanded to include:

Open the book. ***(The instructor did it with the students the first time.)***
Close the book. ***(She closed the book and the students closed their books.)***

Novel commands. When students selected at random were able to perform quickly and confidently, familiar utterances were recombined to produce commands the students had never heard before but could instantly understand. Examples would be:

Jaime, stand up. Walk to the table. Pick up the pencil and paper. Walk to the window and *put the pencil on the floor. Put the paper on your chair.*
Maria, stand up. *Pick up the pencil from Jaime's chair* and put the pencil on the table.
Eduardo, pick up the book and *put it on Juan.*

To maintain the pace, it is wise to have a long list of novel commands (i.e., recombinations of familiar utterances) which you have prepared ahead of time. If a student is baffled, do not press; but simply try the same command with another student or act it out yourself.

New material. At this point in the three-hour class, the instructor introduced the following lexical items:

Name	I will write my name on the board. Juan, run to the chalkboard and write your name Jaime, go to the chalkboard and write your name. Everyone, write your name on your paper.

Address

I will write my address on the board.
Delores, write your name and your address on the chalkboard.
Write your address on your paper.

On

Maria, pick up the book. ***(The instructor and Maria pick up a book)*** and put it on the chair. ***(They put their books on the chair.)***
Maria, put the book *on* the table.
Put the book *on* your head.

Under

Jaime, pick up the pencil. ***(The instructor and Jaime pick up a pencil)*** and put the pencil *under* a chair. ***(They put their pencils under a chair.)***
Jaime, pick up your pencil and put it *under* the table.
Now, put the pencil *under* the book.

Numbers from 1 to 10

I will write the number 1 on the board.
I will write number 2.
I will write 3. ***(This continued through the number 10.)***
Rita, write the numbers 1 and 2 on the board.
Miako, write 3.
Jeffe, write 4 and 5.

Head

Pablo, touch your head ***(and the instructor touched her head while Pablo touched his).***
Everyone, touch your head.
Wing, touch Ramiro's head.

Mouth

Carlos, touch your mouth ***(and the instructor touched her mouth while Carlos touched his).***
Everyone, touch your mouth.
Lauro, touch your head. Touch your mouth.

Ear(s)

José, touch your ears. ***(The instructor touched her ears while José touched his.)***
Wing, touch one ear. Now touch both your ears.

	Miguel, touch Ana's ears.
Eye(s)	Eduardo, touch your eyes ***(The instructor touched her eyes while Eduardo touched his.)***
	Everyone, touch your eyes.
	Elaine, touch just one of your eyes. Now touch both eyes.
Hand(s)	I will touch Ramiro's hands.
	Juan, touch my hands.
	Delores, touch one of my hands.
	Rita, put your hand on the table.
	Pablo, put your hands on Ana's head.
Arm(s)	I will touch Rita on the arm.
	I will touch Jeffe on both arms.
	Ramiro, touch both of Antonio's arms.
	Elaine, Touch one of my arms.
Leg(s)	I will touch my legs.
	I will touch one leg.
	Carlos, touch your legs.
	Everyone, touch one leg.
	Touch both legs.

Remember not to introduce too much new material at one time. As a hint, try working with only three new items. When students are responding confidently to those items, try three more.

Review of new material. The instructor uttered one command at a time, then two in a row to move people all over the room. The object always was maximum involvement which can be achieved by continual activity from each student. Do not work with one student too long. Keep an interesting pace by continually calling upon different students. Keep them moving and they will be happy and learning. Incidentally, at this point, the instructor reported that she felt her students were ready to respond to four or five commands in a row.

A final note on novelty. You probably noticed that novelty was integrated into both the review and introduction of new material. Now, you have an abundant content to generate fascinating recombinations that will delight your students and at the same time increase their linguistic flexibility which is critical for the achievement of listening fluency.

Again, as a hint, it is wise to write out the exact utterances you will be using and especially the novel commands because the action is so fast-moving, there is usually no time for you to create spontaneously. Here are more examples of novel utterances used in this unit:

Pick up number three and number seven (each of which was printed on large flash cards) and put "three" on your head.

Put number ten under your chair.

Pick up the book, put the number five in the book and put the book under your arm.

Touch your nose with the pencil.

The Third Class

Review. This was a fast-moving review with individuals, small groups and the entire class. Some of the commands were "Stand up!" "Jump!" "Turn Around!" "Pick up the chair and put the chair on the table!" The instructor used two, three and even four commands in rapid succession.

New commands. Notice that new vocabulary was integrated with familiar material.

Hit	your arm. the table. Juan me on the hand
Throw	the paper on the floor the pencil to me. the book to Maria.
Give	the book to me. the pencil to me. the paper to Delores.
Take	the book from me. the pencil from me. the paper from Delores.
Turn on	the light.
Turn off	the light.

Note: "Turn on" and "turn off" were not optimal at this point in training because the expansion is limited to one possibility which was "Turn on the light!" or "Turn off the light!"

In addition to verbs, the following nouns were introduced through the imperative:

Flower(s)	Pick up the flower and put it under the book. Throw the flower to me. Hit Jaime with the flower.
Magazine(s)	Take the magazine from Maria and give it to me. Put the magazine on the flower. Give Shirou the magazine. Pick up the magazines from the floor and give them to Rita.
Chalk	Walk to the chalkboard, pick up the chalk, and give it to Pablo. Pablo, put the chalk on your head. Maria, take the chalk from Pablo's head and write your name on the chalkboard.
Colors	Jaime, touch the red book. Maria, pick up the blue pencil and Juan, give me the pink paper and the yellow chalk.

Numbers (Each number from 1 through 15 was on a large flash card which students manipulated.)

Rita, pick up 11 and 12 and throw them to Jaime.
Juan, put 12 and 15 on your chair.
Shirou, point to 14.

Hint: As a reminder, the pace is usually so fast-moving that you will not have time to "think on your feet." It is most helpful to write up the network of commands you intend to use, especially the recombinations. Again, we encourage novel commands that are playful, silly, crazy, bizarre, and zany. The element of surprise is exciting for the instructor and the students.

The Fourth Class

Review. All the commands in this review were novel since they were recombinations of familiar constituents. The students usually understood even though they had never heard the exact utterances spoken by the instructor. Examples would be:

Consuelo, pick up the book from the table and put it on Ramiro's nose.

Ramiro, throw the book to me, hit Consuelo on the arm, and draw a funny picture of Consuelo on the chalkboard.

Jaime, walk with Juan to the table. Now, put Juan on the table.

Most students could respond immediately with the appropriate action. If someone did not, the instructor would repeat the utterance and call upon another student to perform it, or she would carry out the action herself.

New commands. Notice that there was no drill in the sense of tedious repetition of the *same* sentence over and over and over. Rather, new items were constantly recombined with familiar elements so that students heard "fresh" sentences—ones they had never heard before, but the novel sentences were so thoughtfully recombined that almost every new command was perfectly understood by the students.

Here are the new verbs:

Draw	a circle around your name. a funny face on the chalkboard and write Miguel's name under it. a table on your paper.
Laugh	at the funny face on the chalkboard. at Juan who is on the table. when I call out your name.
Cut	the paper on the table. around the table which you drew on your paper. your paper in half.
Run	to the window. to the door. to the chalkboard.
Show	Juan your hands. your paper to José. the book to Maria.
Push	the table. the chair. Jaime into his chair.

Pull	the chair back from the table. the door open. my arm.
Scream	when you look at the funny picture Shirou drew on the chalkboard. when Carlos hits you on the arm. when I call your name.

The verbs were combined with these lexical items:

Straight line	Run to the chalkboard and draw a straight line. Use your finger to draw a straight line in the air. José, Jaime, and Carlos—walk to the table in a straight line.
Crooked line	Maria, run to the chalkboard and draw a crooked line next to the straight line. Miguel, walk to the table in a crooked line. Delores, use your finger to draw a crooked line in the air.
Circle	Write the number 13 on the chalkboard and draw a circle around it. Shirou, run to the chalkboard and draw a circle. Then write your name in the circle. Draw a circle on your paper.
Square	Write the number 11 on the chalkboard and then draw a square around it. Maria, write your name on the board, then draw a square around it. On your paper, draw a square. In the square, draw a circle.
Cat	Pick up the cat and give it to Wing. Wing, give the cat to Miako. Eduardo, run to the board and draw a picture of the cat.

Shoulder(s)	Touch Miako's shoulders Miako, scream and hit Jaime on the shoulder. Touch your shoulders.
Knee(s)	Touch your knees with a pencil. Miguel, run to the table and put your knee on the table. Put your hands on your knees and laugh.
Foot (Feet)	Put the book on your foot. Drop the chalk on José's foot. On your paper, write the number of feet that Jaime has.
Hair	If Jaime has black hair, laugh at him. If Miako has blond hair, hit her on the arm. Pull your hair and scream.
Wrist	Put the chalk on your wrist. Touch your wrist with two fingers. Touch the book with your wrist.
Wrist watch	Give me your wrist watch. Put your wrist watch to your ear. Put your wrist watch under your chair.
Between	Draw a straight line between the numbers 11 and 12. Wing, walk between Delores and José. Maria, put your chair between the table and me.
Next to	Write the number 15 next to the circle. Juan, stand next to Wing. Elaine, put your book next to Ramiro's shoulder.
Around	Draw a circle around your name. Walk around the table and scream. With your finger, draw a circle around your ear.

Reading. After the first week of training (12 classroom hours), the instructor distributed the first handout (Exhibit 1) which had all the vocabulary and grammatical structures which the students now understood when they were uttered by the instructor.

It took 15 minutes for the instructor to read and act out each item on the page. The students did not read aloud nor repeat each utterance.

EXHIBIT I

VERBS	VOCABULARY		
1. stand	table	head	my
2. sit	chair	mouth	your
3. turn around	window	eye(s)	on
4. walk	door	nose	under
5. stop	light	ear(s)	in
6. jump	ceiling	arm(s)	between
7. point to	floor	leg(s)	next to
8. touch	clock	shoulder(s)	around
9. pick up	wall	knee(s)	
10. put down	chalkboard	foot-feet	
11. write	paper	hair	
12. open	pencil	wrist	
13. close	address	hand(s)	
14. hit	name	red	
15. throw	flower	pink	
16. turn on	magazine	yellow	
17. turn off	chalk	green	
18. give	cat	blue	
19. take	book	straight line	
20. draw	wrist watch	crooked line	
21. laugh		circle	
22. cut		square	
23. run			
24. show			
25. push			
26. scream			

SENTENCE STRUCTURES

1. Touch the table.
2. Write your name.
3. Turn on the light.
4. Pick up the pink flower.
5. Point to the floor.
6. Draw a circle on the chalkboard.

The Fifth Class

Review. This was a quick, fast-moving review in which a command was given and, as the individual moved into action, another command was uttered to move another student and then still another command. The effect was that many students were in motion almost simultaneously performing different actions. As you practice moving students with commands in the target language you increase your sense of timing so that there is an optimal pace which keeps students continually moving, but not so fast that they experience failure. Every move by a student should be successful.

New commands. These new verbs were introduced:

Eat	the orange. the apple. the pear.
Drink	the water. the milk. the coffee.
Raise	the cup from the table. the cup to your mouth. your arm above your head.
Count	three pencils and give them to me. five students and touch each on the head. the six papers on the desk and give them to Wing.
Drive	your car (a toy car) to the chalkboard. your car around your chair. your car to Jaime.
Honk	the horn in your car. your horn when you drive past Maria. your horn three times.

The verbs were combined with: orange, apple, pear, water, milk, coffee, spoon, knife, fork, cup, sandwich, car, and horn.

Novelty. New material was recombined with familiar constituents for another quick review. Examples were:

Pick up the fork, knife, and spoon and put them on Shirou's chair.

Take the sandwich from Delores, hit her on the arm, and eat the sandwich yourself.
Take a drink of water, pour some on Juan's head, and laugh.
Stand on your chair and jump.
Pick up the red flower and the green chalk. Put the chalk in the cup and put the flower in your ear.

Role reversal. This was an important moment. The students had about 15 hours of training and the instructor felt that many were ready to speak some English. She invited people to give her commands and she had no difficulty getting volunteers. The first student to speak surprised the instructor by uttering a combination that had never been used in training. The student said, "Jump around the square table!"

As a hint, if you have closed-circuit video equipment, record a sample of each student uttering commands. Video samples of comprehension and speech taken periodically during training are valuable. In future class sessions, you can playback students' earlier performances to help them become more aware of their progress. The contrast between what they did in the 5th class and what they did in the 10th class is an exciting realization.

The Sixth Class

Review. This was a fast-moving warm-up in which individual students were moved with commands as:
Pablo, drive your car around Miako and honk your horn.
Jeffe, throw the red flower to Maria.
Maria, scream.
Rita, pick up the knife and spoon and put them in the cup.
Eduardo, take a drink of water and give the cup to Elaine.

New commands. These verbs were introduced:

Wash	your hands.
	your face.
	your hair.
	the cup.
Look for	a towel.
	the soap.
	a comb.

Hold	the book. the cup. the soap.
Comb	your hair. Maria's hair. Shirou's hair.
Brush	your teeth. your pants. the table.

Other items introduced were:

Rectangle	Draw a rectangle on the chalkboard. Pick up a rectangle from the table and give it to me. Put the rectangle next to the square.
Triangle	Pick up the triangle from the table and give it to me. Catch the triangle and put it next to the rectangle. Pick up the triangle and the square and put them on Jeffe's head.
Quickly	Walk quickly to the door and hit it. Quickly, run to the table and touch the square. Sit down quickly and laugh.
Slowly	Walk slowly to the window and jump. Slowly, stand up. Slowly walk to me and hit me on the arm.
Toothpaste	Look for the toothpaste. Throw the toothpaste to Wing. Wing, unscrew the top of the toothpaste.
Toothbrush	Take out your toothbrush. Brush your teeth. Put your toothbrush in your book.

Teeth	Touch your teeth Show your teeth to Delores. Delores, point to Eduardo's teeth.
Soap	Look for the soap. Give the soap to Elaine. Elaine, put the soap in Ramiro's car.
Towel	Put the towel on Juan's arm. Juan, put the towel on your head and laugh. Maria, wipe your hands on the towel.

Next, the instructor asked simple questions which the student could answer with a gesture such as pointing. Examples would be:

Where is the towel? (Eduardo, point to the towel!)
Where is the toothbrush? (Miako, point to the toothbrush!)
Where is Delores?

Role reversal. Student readily volunteered to utter commands that manipulated the behavior of the instructor and other students.

As a hint, at this point, do not interrupt the students to correct mistakes in pronunciation. Remember, their entire attention is directed to the monumental task of production. They do not have attention units available to process feedback from you. Any early demand for perfection in speech will tend to inhibit production. Let them talk and talk and talk. Eventually, they can be fine tuned for more perfect production. And as the training progresses, each student will develop more and more sensitivity in error-detection. This process of developing acuity in error-detection may be seen if, on video tape, you periodically capture samples of student production throughout training.

Reading and writing. The instructor wrote on the chalkboard each new vocabulary item and a sentence to illustrate the item. Then she spoke each item and acted out the sentence. The students listened as she read the material. Some copied the information in their notebooks.

Note: Four new students who entered the class for the first time seemed to be "catching on" quickly.

The Seventh Class

Review. This was a quick review to warm up the students.

New commands. The following verbs were introduced:

Sleep	Juan, close your eyes and sleep. Eduardo, when I count to three, go to sleep. Jeffe, Eduardo is sleeping. Wake him up.
Snore	Shirou, close your eyes, sleep, and snore. Pablo, put your head on your desk, sleep, and snore. Ramiro, did Pablo snore?
Wake up	Juan, wake up, stand up, and wash your face. Pablo, wake up and scream. Shirou, wake up and laugh.
Shake	Maria, wake up, stand up, and shake your hands. Elaine, shake hands with Wing. Miako, shake your foot.
Pinch	Delores, pinch yourself on the arm. Rita, pinch José's nose. José, hit Rita on the arm and pinch her nose.

Other vocabulary introduced were:

Hands	Raise your hands. Show me your hands.
In half	Cut your paper in half. Cut the triangle in half. Cut the square in half.
In back of	Put your hands in back of your head. Put the paper in back of Jeffe. Look in back of Maria for the book and give the book to me.
Behind	Put your hands behind you. Put Juan behind Carlos and put Wing behind Juan. Quickly, look behind me for the number 17.

In front of	Quickly, put the number 13 in front of the number 7. Put Maria in front of Delores. Put Rita in front of Maria.
With	Shake hands with me. Walk with Shirou to the chalkboard. Run with Miako to the door and jump.

Note: In introducing new items at this point, it was only necessary for the instructor to utter a command and illustrate with herself as a model for a few times; then she began using the new item to direct student behavior.

For the manipulation of numbers, each student had a set of flash cards which they could manipulate at their desks in response to commands such as:

On your desk, put the numbers 1 through 10 in a row.
Now, put 1 under 5.
Put 12 behind 10.
Put 21 in front of 3.
Put 25 in back of 1.
Put 20 beside 12.

The richness of language which can be practiced in the student manipulation of numbers may be seen in a scene from the documentary film called, "Children Learning Another Language: An Innovative Approach" (see page 5-13).

Contrasts. Students learned to differentiate contrasts such as "long" and "short" by responding to them when they were inserted in commands. For instance, "Lauro, put the *long* pencil in your right hand and the *short* pencil on your head." Then questions calling for a brief answer were interspersed among commands (e.g., "Lauro, where is the long pencil?" Lauro's answer, ". . . in my hand.").

Here are other contrasts that were used:

Happy-sad. The instructor invited two students to come to the front of the class. She gave one a picture of a sad face and the other held a picture of a happy face. Then other students were given these commands:

Shake hands with the sad student.
Give the yellow pencil to the happy student.
Stand in back of the happy student.
Give $5.00 to the sad student.
Ask the happy student to dance.
Walk around the sad student and sing.
Hug the sad student.

Tall-short. Next, a tall and short student were invited to the front. The instructor said, "Juan is tall" and raised her hand up to the top of Juan's head. Then she said, "In comparison to Juan, Shirou is short" and she illustrated by bringing her hand down to Shirou's head. "Juan is tall and Shirou is short." Then other students were moved with these commands:

Stand next to the tall student.
Sit in front of the short student.
Give a knife, spoon, and fork to the short student.
What is the name of the tall student?

Wet-dry

Put water in the white cup.
Now, throw the cup at the window near the table.
Point to the wet window.
Point to the dry window.
Walk to the wet window and touch it.
Run to the dry window and open it.
Jaime, pour water on one of your hands.
Wing, quickly run to Jaime and touch his wet hand.
Delores, touch Jaime's dry hand.

Role-Reversal. When an English-speaking aide came in the class for 20 minutes, the students gave her commands. The aide understood and responded accurately to almost all the student utterances. This produced keen excitement in the students. They were visibly astonished at their achievement.

Reading and writing. The instructor wrote the new items on the chalkboard, pronounced each, and acted out. Students listened and some copied in their notebooks.

The Eighth Class

Quick review. This was a fast-moving warm-up in which the students were performing different actions almost simultaneously. The scene was like a stage play in which the cast performed many different actions almost at the same time.

New material. These verbs were introduced:

Drop

the book on the floor.
the cup on the table.
the paper on José's head.

Catch	the book which I will throw. the spoon that Maria will throw to you. this ball.
Cry	Juan, hit Maria. Maria, cry. Look at me and cry. Carlos, when Miako pinches your hand, cry.
Angry	Jeffe, hit me on the arm. Look — I'm angry. Shirou, when Eduardo hits you, be angry. Get the picture of the angry man and give it to me.
Smile	In this picture, the woman is smiling. In this picture, she is not smiling. Quickly, Ramiro, throw the smiling woman to Pablo. Pablo, smile. Look at me and smile. Everyone, smile.

Other lexical items introduced were:

Umbrella	Catch the umbrella. Miguel, give the umbrella to Lauro. Lauro, hit Wing with the umbrella.
Basketball	Catch the basketball. Bounce the basketball twice. Throw the basketball to José after you have bounced it five times.
Frisbee	Throw the frisbee to me. Catch the frisbee. Throw the frisbee to the tallest man in the room.

Introduction of the present continuous (e.g., I/he/she/ + be + base form + ing). Notice how the grammatical feature of the present continuous was imbedded in the imperative.

Rita, touch the table. (PAUSE) Shirou, touch the table that Rita is touching.

Juan, touch the chalkboard. (PAUSE) Maria, touch the chalkboard that Juan is touching.

Miguel, draw a square on the chalkboard. (PAUSE) Jaime, draw a circle around the square that Miguel is drawing.
Maria, write your name on the chalkboard (PAUSE) Juan, erase the name that Maria is writing.

Practice of numbers. The instructor said, "Pick up your pencil and write the numbers as I say them. Ready!" Then, she would say a number, pause for the students to write, and then the instructor wrote the number on the chalkboard for immediate feedback. The numbers began with regular intervals as 10, 20, 30, 40, and so forth, and then irregular intervals as 22, 138, 67, etc.

Role reversal. Each student uttered English commands to manipulate the behavior of other students.

Introduction of a question such as, "How many fingers do you have?" which required a short answer of one or two words. Here are some examples:

Touch your nose. How many noses do you have? ***Answer:*** "One."
Close your eyes. How many eyes do you have? ***Answer:*** "Two."
Count the flowers. How many flowers do you have? ***Answer:*** "Six."

The Ninth Class

New commands. The intent was to prepare the students for an actual visit to a department store. The instructor brought the following articles to clothing to class: jacket, sweater, blouse, shirt, pants, skirt and a raincoat. These items were used with verbs such as:

Try on	the raincoat. the jacket. the pants.
Put on	the shirt. the blouse. the sweater.
Take off	the raincoat. the jacket. the sweater.
Button	the blouse. the shirt. the jacket.
Unbutton	the blouse. the shirt. the jacket.

Zip	up the pants. up the sweater. up the skirt.
Unzip	the pants. the sweater. the skirt.

Other vocabulary items were: customer, salesman, and saleswoman which were represented by pictures of clerks and customers interacting in a department store. The pictures* were pasted on cardboard so that they would be handled easily by the students when the instructor uttered commands as:

Miguel, touch the customer.
Juan, point to the salesman.
Maria, with your finger draw a circle around the saleswoman.
Jaime, put a spoon on the customer.

More on the present progressive. As usual, the grammatical feature was imbedded in the imperative as illustrated in these examples:

Miako, push the table. **(PAUSE)** Jaime, push the table that Miako is pushing.

Pablo, push the chalkboard. **(PAUSE)** Jeffe, wash the chalkboard that Pablo is pushing.

Ernest, write your name on the chalkboard. **(PAUSE)** Maria, write the name that Ernest is writing.

I am holding a book. **(PAUSE)** Miguel, point to the book that I am holding.

Introduction of "Who is . . .?" Since the students knew each other's names, this was an optimal time to work with this construction:

Juan, pull Jaime to the table. **(PAUSE)** Delores, who did Juan pull to the table? ***Answer:*** "Jaime."

Wing, who is standing near the chalkboard? ***Answer:*** "Rita."

Miako, who is sitting on the table? ***Answer:*** "Maria."

Shirou, who is wearing a red sweater? ***Answer:*** "José."

Reading. The instructor passed out Exhibit 2 to each student, then read and demonstrated each item on the sheet.

*To practice department store vocabulary *at their seats* in the classroom, try the **TPR Student Kit: The Department Store** (See page 5-11).

Introduction of the construction "Where is . . .?" The expected response from individual students was a short utterance. Examples are as follows:

Juan, put the yellow book under the orange chair. **(PAUSE)** Maria, where is the yellow book? ***Answer:*** "Under the orange chair."

Jaime, put the yellow chair next to the orange chair. **(PAUSE)** Miguel, where is the yellow chair? ***Answer:*** "Next to the orange chair."

Delores, put the spoon on the table. **(PAUSE)** Maria, where is the spoon? ***Answer:*** "On the table."

EXHIBIT 2

VERBS	VOCABULARY	
27. eat	white	toothbrush
28. drink	orange	tooth-teeth
29. raise	right	soap
30. count	left	towel
31. drive	spoon	quickly
32. honk	knife	slowly
33. run	fork	where
34. sleep	cup	jacket
35. snore	water	sweater
36. wake up	coffee	blouse
37. shake	sandwich	shirt
38. pinch	car horn	skirt
39. drop	hands	pants
40. catch	umbrella	raincoat
41. cry	basketball	customer
42. cross	frisbee	salesman
43. smile	rectangle	saleswoman
44. try on	triangle	in back of
45. put on	toothpaste	in front of
46. take off		behind
47. wash		with
48. look for		in half
49. hold		
50. comb		
51. brush		

1. Shake hands with Miguel.
2. Raise your left hand.
3. Cross your eyes.
4. Put the cup of water in front of Ramiro.
5. Turn right and honk the horn.

More practice of the present continuous. Notice that two grammatical features are imbedded in the imperative utterances. One is the relative pronoun and the other grammatical cue is the present continuous. Here are examples in which the grammatical features are in italics:

Bernardo, touch the table. **(PAUSE)** Rosa, touch the table *that* Bernardo *is touching.*

Maria, wash the window. **(PAUSE)** Miguel, wash the window *that* Maria *is washing.*

There was no attempt to explain the grammatical characteristics to the students. This was presented as another series in which the complexity of English was expanded.

A slide presentation. The instructor projected color slides that were taken of interior scenes in a local clothing store.† The students seemed to understand clearly the instructor's narration about each slide as indicated by student answers to periodic questions such as:

Which of the two people on the screen is the salesperson?
Please tell us what the customer is wearing.
What do you think the customer is asking the salesman?
What do you see in the right of the picture?

Practice with personal data. In these examples, listening, speaking, reading, and writing were all operating.

Everyone, write your first name.
Now write your last name.
Antonio, write Mr. in front of your first name. **(PAUSE)** What is your first name?

Introduction to possessive pronouns. The instructor began working with "my" and "your" as follows:

Touch your shoulder.
Touch my shoulder.
Point to your head.
Point to my head.

The Tenth Class

Touch your nose.
Touch your book.
Point to my book.
Touch my nose.

Then she continued with "my" and "your" but added "his" and "her."

Shake your hand.
Shake his hand.
Shake my head.
Point to her head.

Reading. The instructor distributed a copy of Exhibit 3 which had all the clothing store vocabulary the students had assimilated through the imperative. The instructor read each item twice and used each in a familiar sentence.

†Another way to present this is to use the **TPR Student Kit: The Department Store.** (See page 5-11).

EXHIBIT 3

1. try on **2. fit** **3. wear**

VERBS:	**VOCABULARY**	
dress	customer	cash or charge
skirt	salesman	check
shirt	saleswoman	hanger
blouse	nylons	umbrella
sports coat	socks	buttons
rain coat	knee socks	long sleeves
jacket	shoes	short sleeves
tie	slippers	striped
belt	boots	too big
bra	tennis shoes	too small
t-shirt	nightgown	too long
undershirt	bathrobe	too short
jockey shorts	pajamas	receipt
boxer shorts		
full slip		
half slip		

The Eleventh Class

Asking questions of students. Even the procedure of asking questions was imbedded in the imperative. And, as part of the activity, students had practice with the present continuous as shown in these examples:

Miguel, touch the table. **(PAUSE)** Miguel, what are you doing?
Answer: "I'm touching the table."

Maria, what is Miguel doing? ***Answer:*** He is touching the table."

The instructor observed that the students were ready to respond to her questions and they had no difficulty in applying the verb form of the present continuous to all verbs learned previously through commands.

Demonstrating the present continuous with other personal pronouns as: *we, they,* and *you.* Here are samples:

Luis and Rita, walk with me. *We* are walking.

Maria and Juan, write on the chalkboard. *They* are writing on the chalkboard.

Jaime, hit Pedro. You are hitting Pedro.

Introduction of days of the week. † The instructor had large flashcards on which was printed each day of the week and a number. The card with Sunday printed on it had a one, Monday had a two, and so forth with a seven on the Saturday card. The instructor said:

Today is Monday. It is the second day of the week. Wing, catch Monday and give it to Delores. Delores, what is today?

Yesterday was Sunday. On Sunday many people go to church ***(and the instructor held up a picture of people entering a church).***

Eduardo, quickly, get Sunday and put it in Jeffe's hand. Jeffe, what day of the week are you holding?

Elaine, what day was yesterday?

Pablo, what day is today?

Today is Monday. Delores, show the class what day today is. Tomorrow will be Tuesday. José, run to me, take Tuesday and give it to Shirou. Shirou, what day is tomorrow? Ramiro, what will you do tomorrow? Lauro, what will you do on Tuesday, which is tomorrow?

Rita, what is the first day of the week? Maria, what is the second day of the week?

The day after Tuesday is Wednesday.

On each day following this introduction, the instructor would hold up a flashcard with the day of the week and say, for example: "Today is Thursday." Then the students would be directed to manipulate today, yesterday and tomorrow. For instance:

If today is Thursday, what day is tomorrow? Carlos, get Friday and throw it to Luis.

More with the question word, "Who."
Touch the person who is sitting next to you.
Pinch the person who is standing in front of Miguel.
Who is touching the brown table?
Who is standing behind Alfred?

†Also try this exercise with the **TPR Student Kit: The Calendar.** (See page 5-11).

The Twelfth Class

Continued practice manipulating days of the week.
Maria, count the days of the week.
Juan, how many days in the week?
Luis, give Saturday to Ana.
Rita, point to Monday.
Miako, put Wednesday next to Monday.
Is this card Monday or Saturday, Wing?
Is this card Saturday or Sunday, Delores?
What day is today, Jaime?
What does this card say, Antonio?

New commands. The instructor communicated meaning by acting or gesturing, then used each item as follows:

Read	the newspaper.
	this card.
	the sign on the chalkboard.
	what I wrote on the board.
Hug	Maria.
	yourself.
	the table.
Sneeze	Juan, and take out your handkerchief.
	José, and say "Pardon me."
	Luis, and turn your head.
Look at	the picture of San Francisco.
	Miguel making a funny face.
	my hand.
Look out	the window, Antonio.
	the door, Eduardo, and scream.

Review the present continuous with I/she/he/it/you/we/they.

Everyone, look out the window. Rita, what are we doing? ***Answer:*** "We are looking out the window."

Alfredo, read each day of the week. What is Alfredo doing, Maria? ***Answer:*** "He is reading." or "He is reading each day of the week."

Rita, hug Shirou. What is Rita doing, Jaime? ***Answer:*** "She is hugging." or "She is hugging Shirou."

Elaine, Miako, and Luis, dance around the table. What are they doing, Wing? ***Answer:*** "They are dancing." or "They are dancing around the table."

More on possessive pronouns. The instructor began with these utterances:

Miguel, touch *your* shoulder.

Shirou, touch *his* shoulder.

Maria, touch *my* shoulder.

Later, the series was expanded as shown in these examples:

Luis, touch *her* shoulder. Luis, what are you doing? ***Answer:*** "I'm touching her shoulder."

Rita, cut my hair. Rita, what are you doing? ***Answer:*** "I'm cutting your hair."

Ana, laugh. Ana, what are you doing? ***Answer:*** "I'm laughing."

Reading stories. A story as seen in Exhibit 4 was read twice by the instructor while the students listened without looking at a copy of the story. When the story was read a third time, volunteer students acted it out as it was read. The actors wore large name cards of the character they were playing.

EXHIBIT 4

Mr. Smith was sleeping. It was time to wake up. He took off his pajamas and put on his clothes.

He looked out the window and saw that it was raining.

He said to Mrs. Smith, "Where is my umbrella?" Mrs. Smith said, "Look under the table!"

Mr. Smith said, "It is not there." Mrs. Smith said, "Look on the chair!" Now Mr. Smith was angry. He screamed, jumped up and down three times, and ran out the door.

QUESTIONS

1. Was Mr. Smith in a clothing store?
2. Was Mrs. Smith shopping for clothes?

3. Was it raining?
4. What was Mr. Smith looking for?
5. Where did Mrs. Smith say to look for the umbrella?
6. Was Mr. Smith happy, sad, or angry?
7. Why was Mr. Smith angry?
8. What did he do that showed anger?

After the enactment, individual students were asked questions about the story that called for a "yes" or "no" answer. An example would be, "Was Mr. Smith looking out the window?" Sometimes the instructor asked for the response to be written on the chalkboard.

Next, individual students were asked questions that required a longer response than "yes" or "no." An example would be, "What's Mr. Smith doing?" After this, Exhibit 4 was given to each student and it was examined silently.

Students together read the story aloud and they read each question twice. The instructor wrote the answer to each question on the chalkboard and students copied on their papers.

The Thirteenth Class

Slide presentation of clothing store. The color slides of activity in a clothing store were used to communicate the meaning of these verbs:

Pay	The customer is paying for the pants. When you pay for clothes, you give the clerk money. The customer is giving the clerk money. The customer is paying for the shirt.
Buy	The customer is buying a shirt This customer is buying pants. When you go to the supermarket, you buy food. Maria, what are some foods that you buy at the supermarket?
Sell	The store sells clothes such as pants, shirts, and jackets. This store sells food. This business sells cars.

Look at	Jaime, look at this jacket. Do you want to buy this jacket? Elaine, look at these boots. Do you like the color? Do you want to buy these boots? Look at this purse, Delores. It is very large. Do you want to buy it?
Steal	Sometimes customers steal items from a store. Is this customer stealing or buying the pants? If this man put the socks in his pocket without paying, that is called stealing.

The verbs were used with these vocabulary items: sleeve, cuff, pocket, button, boots, socks, nylons, size, purse, long, short, big, small, large, and medium. The students were now able to understand, with ease, descriptive speech.

Review of the present continuous. The instructor began with questions that required a short positive or a short negative response; for example:

Rita, stand up. Luis, is Rita standing? ***Answer:*** "Yes," or "Yes, she is standing."

Miguel, cry. Maria, is Miguel crying? ***Answer:*** "Yes," or "Yes, he is crying."

Later the instructor's questioning required a long answer, as illustrated with the following:

Jaime, walk around the room; Shirou, write on the chalkboard; and Lona, sing. Miguel, what is Jaime doing? Rita, what is Lona doing? Maria, what is Shirou doing?

General review. The commands integrated prior constituents in a fast-moving review which the students responded to with confidence, quickness, and ease. The important word is "integration." Constituents including lexical items and grammatical features were continually recombined to produce novel commands that increased the flexibility of comprehension.

The Fourteenth Class

Field trip to a clothing store. The students were organized into five groups consisting of five students per group. The instructor accompanied one group and there was an aide with each of the other groups. Once inside the clothing store, the interaction was as follows:

Pick up the blue, long-sleeved shirt. What size is it? Is it your size? Is it too big or too small?
Try on the cap.
Go into the fitting room.
Is that woman a salesclerk or a customer?
Ask the salesclerk how much this shirt is.
Let's walk up to the men's department.
Maria, what color coat would look good on Juan?
Jaime, help Eduardo on with the coat.

Wing, does Jaime look handsome in that coat or ugly?
Point to the shirts.
Point to the pants.
Point to the ties.
Point to the coats.
Jaime, what size shirt do you wear?
Eduardo, help Jaime find his size in the shirt section.

The Fifteenth Class

Review of the clothing store experience. The instructor read each clothing store vocabulary item in Exhibit 3 and wrote on the chalkboard representative sentences that students responded to in the clothing store such as: "Try on the cape. Pick up the blue, long-sleeved shirt. What size is it?" Students copied the sentences in their notebooks.

Review of (a) *the present continuous,* (b) *short answers,* and (c) *long answers.* Very quickly, a chain of responses were elicited from individual students.

Maria:

Who is sitting on your right?
What are you doing?
Are you studying Spanish?
Is Juan standing on the chair?
Write your name on the table.
What are you writing?
Where are you writing your name?
Who are you sitting next to?
Are you thinking?
What are you thinking about?
Where are Elena and Young standing?

Alberto: Are you listening?
Is Tom sleeping?
Where is Maria standing?
What are Tom and Rita doing?
Where are they standing?
Are they reading?
Are you jumping?
Is Tom writing my name?

Note: At this point, the students have experienced 45 hours of TPR instruction. Notice that *flexibility of thinking* is continually encouraged by recombining constituents.

The Sixteenth Class

Review contrasts through commands.
Stand between a tall and a short person.
Give the wet towel to Alfredo and the dry towel to me.
Put the (picture of the) handsome man on the chalkboard and put the ugly man on Ana's head.
Put Jeffe in the large box and Ramiro in the small box.

Review contrasts through short answers.
Is the string short or long?
Is the towel wet or dry?

Then into "yes" or "no" answers.
Is the floor wet? ***Answer:*** "Yes, it is."
Is the table wet? ***Answer:*** "No, it isn't."

Students act out emotional or affective states of being such as angry, sad, happy, nervous, tired, and afraid. First, the instructor would either demonstrate an emotional response or show a picture. As usual, the new vocabulary was introduced through the imperative. She would say:

I am angry. The man in this picture is angry. José, turn the picture of the angry man toward the wall. Maria, be angry. Hit Lauro on the arm.

For *sadness,* the instructor said:

The woman in this picture is sad because she lost her purse. She looks like this. ***(The instructor put a sad expression on her face.)*** Look at my face. I am sad.

Elaine, take Maria's purse. Maria, look sad. Now cry.

A typical treatment of *happy* was this:

Wing, run to the table, get ten dollars and give it to me. Now I am happy.

Carlos, find a picture of a happy face and put it next to the sad face.

Delores, draw a happy face on the chalkboard.

Rita, tell Luis that he is handsome. Luis, when she tells you you are handsome, look happy.

The emotion of *nervous* was handled like this:

This boy is about to take a test in school. He is nervous. When I am nervous, I tap my foot.

Pablo, show us what you do when you are nervous.

This woman is nervous because she is late for work. Eduardo, what do you do when you are nervous? Show us.

The state of being *tired* was communicated in this fashion:

This man has walked many miles. He is tired.

After I work all day, I feel tired.

Carlos, jump ten times. Carlos, do you feel tired? Delores, do you think Carlos looks tired?

For the emotion of *afraid,* the instructor said:

This girl has just seen this horror movie which has monsters that look like this. The girl is afraid.

José, I am going to hit you. Look afraid. José, scream.

Shirou, hit me with your book. Look at my face. I am afraid of Shirou.

General review. Everything from the beginning was rapidly reviewed. This included all verbs, parts of the body, colors, numbers, clothing, opposites, prepositions, possessive pronouns, the present progressive, and so forth. A sample of the review was as follows:

Put the long string around Juan's neck.

Put the full glass of water into the empty box.

Pick up the light blue paper and cut it into three pieces.

Draw a happy face.

What are you doing?

What are you drawing?

Where are you drawing the face?

Draw ears on the sad face.

Count the happy faces in the room.

Write number 86 on the pink paper and give it to Maria.

Who is sitting next to Alicia?

Point to a student with long hair.

Sit on the basketball.

Where is Angelo sitting?

Take off your shoes.

New commands. The new material included verbs as dance, play, sing, act, and speak, and other vocabulary as volleyball, guitar, Spanish, Chinese, English, piano, and violin. These items were presented as follows:

Dance	with me.
	with Juan and Carlos.
	around the table.
Play	the guitar.
	the piano.
	volleyball.
Sing	a song.
	as you dance around the table.
	loudly.
	softly.
Act	crazy.
	as if you were drunk.
	as if you were happy.
	as if you were sad.
Speak	to Luis in Chinese.
	to Ana in Spanish.
	to me in English.

Review opposites and state-of-being words.

Run to the tall man who is standing in the center of the room, touch his arm; then touch the nose of the short man who is standing next to the tall man.

Throw the long pencil to Miako and the short pencil to Shirou.

Give the dark sweater to Antonio and the light sweater to Pablo.

Put the pretty girl on Elaine's chair and put the ugly girl in Ramiro's book.

Carlos, be happy. Sing a song and laugh.

Jeffe, hit Wing on the leg. Wing, be angry and cry.

Delores, give Maria a dollar and look sad. Cry.

Introduction of "can." The instructor said, "I can jump over this box. Juan, tell me to jump over the box." Juan said, "Jump over the box," and the instructor acted by jumping over the box.

Maria, can you jump over this box? ***Answer:*** "Yes."

David, can Maria jump over this box? ***Answer:*** "Yes."

Shirou, ask Maria to jump over the box.

The students caught on quickly, so the concept was extended with these questions to which students responded with "yes" or "no":

Can you touch the ceiling?
Can you stand on the ceiling?
Can you play the guitar? (If the student said "Yes," then the instructor said, "Then play the guitar," and the student would strum an imaginary guitar.)
Can you draw a cat? ("O.K., draw a cat," and the student would draw a cat in the air with his finger.)

Since the concept of "can" was rapidly understood, the instructor asked for an expanded response to "can" type questions. For example:

Can I sit in the filing cabinet? ***Answer:*** "No, you can't."
Can Maria sit in the filing cabinet? ***Answer:*** "No, she can't."
Can Maria stand on the filing cabinet? ***Answer:*** "Yes, she can."

As a hint, each expansion is a step-by-step process that should be gradual. The students should demonstrate that they have assimilated the previous step before you move to the next step. For instance, it would be too demanding and counter-productive to say at the beginning, "Can Maria walk on the ceiling?" and expect a response as "No, she can't." You should gradually and patiently lead the students in small steps. They should experience success, success, success. So, don't be over-ambitious. Take your time. Move gingerly but logically with no gaps that leave your students puzzled and unable to respond.

Role reversal. Now the students were given a chance to ask "can" questions. The instructor was amazed that they had no problem reversing roles and uttering the appropriate English.

The Eighteenth Class

Review. The instructor selected one student at a time and very quickly fired five to ten commands and questions such as:

Juan, touch your nose.
What are you doing?
What is Mary doing?
Is the floor wet or dry?
Is the window clean?
Pick up the chalk and break it.
What's your last name?
Maria, walk to the chalkboard and write your first name.
Draw a flower under your name.

Where is the flower?
Can you touch the ceiling?
Are you a student?
What are you studying?
How old are you?
Pick up the flowers and count them.
How many flowers do you have?
Shake your head.

Role reversal. Each student asked the instructor one question and gave her one or two commands.

Pancho Carrancho. The students enjoyed this game created by Ramiro Garcia in which the instructor began with, "Pancho Carrancho packed his bag and bought a coat." A student would say, "No, Pancho Carrancho did not buy a coat; he cooked a meal." The next student might say, "Pancho Carrancho† did not cook a meal; he hit the salesclerk on the head."

As a suggestion, if you use Pancho Carrancho periodically throughout training, this may be an excellent exercise to record on video tape. Students can appreciate their progress by seeing how their language skills have progressed at different stages of training. This could be a powerful motivator to sustain a keen level of interest.

†For fascinating variations of Pancho Carrancho, see Ramiro Garcia's book, "Instructor's Notebook: How to Apply TPR for Best Results." (See page 5-10.)

The Nineteenth Class

Reading. The following story was read aloud twice by the instructor.

STORY 2

The students are in their classroom. They're early and they're waiting for the teacher, Miss Jan Englebrecht. She is usually on time.

The classroom is large. The lights are on and the door is open. The windows are closed. The chalkboard is dirty and John Petrik is erasing it. Maria Jiminez is sitting at the table. She's reading her English book. Tomoko Ito is sitting next to Maria and she is studying a grammar lesson.

Alberto Vera and Juan Medina are talking and laughing. Roberto is tired and doing nothing.

Then, as the instructor read the story a third time, volunteer students acted it out. The actors wore large name cards of the character they were playing.

Next, the instructor asked oral questions about the story as:

Where were the students?

Is the teacher usually late or on time?

Was someone erasing the chalkboard?

Notice that the questions required a variety of either short or long responses. Incidentally, for further variety, the instructor asked the students to write in their notebooks their answers to some of the questions.

At this point, a copy of the story was distributed to each student to be read silently. In addition to reading the story, the students also read each question that was asked about the story.

New material. The verb "wear" was introduced with commands such as:

Point to the student who is wearing the brown jacket.

Look at the student who is wearing the light green shirt.

Hug the student who is wearing the red sweater.

Shake hands with the person who is wearing the long skirt.

Then, after students had internalized the verb through the imperative, the instructor used the verb to ask these questions:

Who's wearing the blue, long sleeve shirt?

What is José wearing?

What's Carlos wearing?

Review with question words—what, who, and where.

What's he holding?

What's she looking at?

Who's sitting next to Ana?

Where is your purse?

The Twentieth Class

Review. Using commands, the instructor moved individual students rapidly with utterances that contained each verb or verb tense previously used in any class session.

New material (the past tense). The past tense was introduced by imbedding it in the imperative. First, the instructor directed an individual to perform an action such as, "Juan, throw your pencil on the floor." This was followed by a command to a different student—a command which contained the past tense as a constituent. For instance, the instructor said, "Maria, pick up the pencil that Juan *threw* on the floor. Other examples were: "Sal, write the number six on the chalkboard. Point to the number you *wrote.* Eduardo, point to the number that Sal *wrote.* José, close the window! Maria, open the window that Juan *closed.* Eva, write the number 83 and Şilvia, write the number 64. José, erase the number that Silvia *wrote."*

New material (occupational vocabulary items). The instructor used the Michigan Cue Cards to teach the names of occupational roles through the imperative. Each card was manipulated as follows:

Luke, show the *mechanic* to Miguel. Miguel, take the *mechanic* from Luke and put it on Maria's head.

Juan, throw the *doctor* to Alicia. Alicia, put the *doctor* under your chair.

Everyone look at the *nurse.* Jaime, run to the front of the room, take the *nurse* and throw her out the window.

The Twenty-First Class

More with the past tense.

Sit on the orange chair. Eduardo, go to the student who *sat* on the orange chair.

Throw the paper on the floor. Jaime, pick up the paper that he *threw* on the floor.

After a review of the past tense imbedded as usual in the imperative, the instructor presented the past tense again but with a twist. For example, she said, "Juan, stand up." Then she said to the class, "He *stood* up." Other examples were as follows:

Maria and Rosa, stand up. **(PAUSE)** They *stood* up.

Alicia, stand up, go to the chalkboard, write your name, and sit down. **(PAUSE)** Alicia *stood* up, *went* to the chalkboard, *wrote* her name, *went* to her chair, and *sat* down.

The exercise continued with ten verbs that were varied as to person (i.e., I, you, he, she, they, etc.), but emphasizing the change in the verb associated with past actions.

Review of occupations. Again with the Michigan Cue Cards, the instructor directed individual students. For instance, "Put the *teacher* next to the *engineer."* Then individual students were invited to continue with the cards by reversing roles and giving directions to the instructor and other students.

Reading. Exhibit 5 was distributed to each student. The instructor read each item and then used it in a sentence such as:

Monday	Today is Monday. Luis, are you happy on Monday?

Tuesday	Tomorrow is Tuesday. Antonio, will you come to class on Tuesday?
Doctor	Is Jaime a doctor? ***Answer:*** "No, he isn't."
Fire fighter	Is Maria a fire fighter? ***Answer:*** "No."

EXHIBIT 5

DAYS OF THE WEEK	OCCUPATIONS
Sunday	student
Monday	teacher
Tuesday	doctor
Wednesday	dentist
Thursday	mechanic
Friday	housewife
Saturday	waiter
	waitress
	nurse
	cashier
	lawyer
	police officer
	fire fighter
	secretary
	farmer
	laborer
	truck driver
	beautician

SENTENCES

What do you do? ***Answer:*** "I'm a student."
Is Delores a dentist? ***Answer:*** "No, she isn't."

The Twenty-Second Class

More with the past tense. Familiar commands containing the past tense were used such as, "Luke, put the picture on the floor and jump on it." **(PAUSE)** "Maria, pick up the picture that Luke *jumped* on."Then there was a series in which a command was followed by a declarative sentence which had a sharp focus of attention on the change in the sound of the verb when the action happened in the past. For instance, "Carlos, Maria, and Jaime, stand up." **(PAUSE)** "They *stood* up." "All sit down." **(PAUSE)** "They *sat* down."

A further twist in presenting the past tense was to utter a command followed by a question. As an illustration:

Eva, walk to the window. **(PAUSE)** Eva, what did you do?
Answer: "I *walked* to the window."
Juan, what did Eva do? ***Answer:*** "She *walked* to the window."

Review occupations. The class was divided into three teams. One student from each team was given an occupation to act out. The team that guessed the occupation first got the point.

Reading and writing. Before Exhibit 6 was distributed to the students, the instructor uttered each command or question on the handout and elicited an appropriate response. Then the students silently read each item on the sheet and wrote a response.

EXHIBIT 6

1. Write your last name.
2. Write the date.
3. Draw a circle.
4. Write your address.
5. Write your telephone number.
6. Write number 7 in the upper right hand corner of this paper.
7. Fold this paper in half.
8. Write your age and draw a line under it.
9. Are you a student?
10. What are you studying?
11. How old are you?
12. Is the ash tray dirty?
13. Is the door open?
14. What are you wearing?
15. Are you married or single?

The Twenty-Third Class

Review of the past tense. In the review, most of the sentences used in the initial learning were not repeated. For flexibility, sentences were varied so that the student heard and physically responded to a grammatical feature such as the past tense, but always in a fresh context. The sentences were continually changing, but during this review the grammatical cue under study remained constant. Here are a few illustrations:

Edna, do to the window, wash it, then turn off the light and sit down. ***(Pause until the actions have been completed.)*** Edna, what did you do? ***Answer:*** "I *went* to the window; I *washed* it; then *turned* off the light and *sat* down."

Jaime, what did Edna do? ***Answer:*** "She *went* to the window; she *washed* it; then *turned* off the light and *sat* down."

Introduction of negation combined with the past tense.

Juan, walk to the door but don't close it. **(PAUSE)** Maria, close the door that Juan didn't close.

Miguel, fold the first chair that is leaning on the chalkboard, but do not fold the chair next to it. **(PAUSE)** Sara, fold the chair that Miguel didn't fold.

Reading and writing personal information. Exhibit 7 was distributed to each student. First the instructor read each item aloud and wrote on the chalkboard her own personal data to illustrate the procedure. Next she said, "Miguel, what is your last name?" **(PAUSE)** "Write your last name on the sheet here!"

EXHIBIT 7

Date: ____________

1. Mr. / Mrs. / Miss ______________________________
(Last) (First)

2. ______________________________
(Street Address)

____
(City) (State)

3. Telephone No. ______________________________

4. Age ____________ 5. Female Male

6. Single Married Divorced Widowed

7. Place of Birth ______________________________

8. Date of Birth ______________________________
(Month/Day/Year)

Systematically, each space on the personal data sheet was filled in by the students.

Review of the past tense. This was a rapid review.

Continue with the past tense that required short answer responses. Examples would be to ask questions about actual events that happened to the students as:

Jaime, did Felipe break the chair? ***Answer:*** "No, he didn't."

Maria, did Felipe break his leg? ***Answer:*** "Yes, he did."

Juan, did Ignacio read the newspaper this morning? ***Answer:*** "Yes, he did."

Miguel, did Delores and Martha push Eva? ***Answer:*** "Yes, they did."

Reading. After Exhibit 8 was distributed, the instructor read each item aloud twice. An individual student read aloud a command which other students acted out; then the student who had read the command told what had been done. Notice that all items had been internalized previously through the imperative.

EXHIBIT 8

Antonio, walk to the table.	Antonio walked to the table.
Luis, scream.	Luis screamed.
Maria, raise your hand.	Maria raised her hand.
Alfredo, throw your pencil to me.	Alfredo threw his pencil to me.
Rita, pick up the red paper from the table.	Rita picked up the red paper from the table.
Miako, open and close the door.	Miako opened and closed the door.
Wing, hit Pablo on the arm.	Wing hit Pablo on the arm.
Ramiro, draw a funny face.	Ramiro drew a funny face.

Making clocks.† The instructor directed each student in numbering a paper plate to make a clock. Then each student made the hands of the clock from construction paper. This took about ten minutes.

With the clock as a prop, the instructor then had students practice time by giving a direction and then each student simultaneously set the hands for the correct time. Examples would be:

Set your clocks at 6:30.

Now, it's 9 o'clock.

Set your clock at 7:30. Maria, what time is it? ***Answer:*** "7:30."

Set your clock at 12 o'clock. Delores, what time is it? ***Answer:*** "12 o'clock."

†For another prop to practice telling time, try the **TPR Student Kit: The Clock.** (See page 5-11.)

The Twenty-fifth Class

Continue with clocks. Each student set their clock, then asked the next student, "What time is it?"

Introduction of fine detail in telling time. The instructor had flash cards each with a picture of a clock at the quarter hour. Using the imperative, the students internalized this detail in telling time as illustrated with these examples:

Eduardo, give 1:15 to José.

Delores, pick up 8:45 and put it under your chair.

Eva, put 3:45 on top of the chalkboard.

Notice that telling time began the previous class with examples of the clock at the hour (6 o'clock) or half hour (6:30), and then fine tuned with smaller detail as the quarter hour (6:15, 6:45, etc.).

More with the past tense. The instructor directed an individual to act, then asked another student a question requiring either a short or long answer in the past tense. Examples would be:

Jaime, close the door and sit in your seat. **(PAUSE)** Maria, what did Jaime do? ***Answer:*** "He *closed* the door and *sat* in his seat."

Miguel, did Jaime close his eyes when he sat in his chair? ***Answer:*** "No, he didn't."

The Twenty-Sixth Class

Writing. After each student received a copy of Exhibit 9, the instructor read each question twice. Then the students were directed to write responses in the space provided. As further practice in reading, individual students read the question followed by the answer they had written.

EXHIBIT 9

1. What day is it?
2. What time is it?
3. What's your last name?
4. How old are you?
5. Are you married?
6. Write your first name.
7. Are you a student?
8. What are you studying?
9. Is Jeffe a student?
10. Is Elaine a doctor?
11. Is the window clean?
12. Are you angry?
13. Did you eat breakfast?
14. Is Maria tall or short?
15. Is Luis a mechanic?

Review of all content. This was a fast-moving review beginning with the first day of class. Of course, this was a sampling of vocabulary and structure which the students experienced in the previous 75 hours of training.

Pancho Carrancho. In this parlor game, the instructor begins with a declarative sentence about Pancho and a student must negate the sentence followed by a new declarative sentence. For instance, ***(Instructor)*** "Pancho Carrancho kicked the door." ***(Student)*** "Pancho Carrancho didn't kick the door; he jumped over the table."

This game had many valuable learning properties. First, it was an amusing diversion from the usual classroom format. Secondly, it is an excellent exercise in expanding English content; and thirdly, the students have a chance to be creative.

Here are samples of typical sentences you can expect from students at this point in training:

(Instructor) "Pancho Carrancho ate a sandwich." ***(Second student)*** "Pancho Carrancho didn't eat a sandwich; he wrote a letter." ***(Third student)*** "Pancho Carrancho didn't write a letter; he read a newspaper." ***(Fourth student)*** "Pancho Carrancho didn't read a newspaper; he cut the flowers."

The Twenty-Seventh Class

Consumer behavior. The instructor brought a bag of groceries to class which was used (a) to role play buyer-seller transactions, (b) to practice reading dollars and cents, and (c) as enrichment of the student's experience in shopping.†

The props in the bag were items as a can of peas, a jar of pickles, a bottle of catsup, a loaf of bread and a carton of milk. Examples of the interactions would be:

Maria, pick up the box of rice and hand it to Miguel and ask Miguel to read the price.

Jaime, how much was the rice?

Eduardo, play the role of clerk.

Juan, walk over to Eduardo and buy the bag of candy. (LATER) Eduardo, how much did you pay for the candy?

Contrast this, that, these, and those. This routine was designed to contrast sharply demonstrative pronouns. Commands were as follows:

Eva, pick up *this* loaf of bread, but give *that* loaf of bread to Maria.

Luke, put *that* jar of pickles on your chair and put *this* jar of pickles under the table.

†Another excellent tool to practice the experience of shopping is the **TPR Student Kit: The Supermarket.** (See page 5-11.)

The Twenty-Eighth Class

Slides of a supermarket. Shopping in a grocery store was continued with colored slides of a supermarket. New verbs as "compare" and "weigh" were introduced through commands as:

Look at the shopper *comparing* the price of two different brands of peas. Now she is *comparing* the price of two different brands of catsup.

The clerk is *weighing* tangerines in this picture and in the next picture he is *weighing* apples.

In addition to verbs, more food vocabulary was introduced such as fruits, frozen vegetables, chicken, fish, and meat.

After the slide presentation, the instructor had students act with plastic foods and pictures from magazines that were glued to stiff cardboard. Examples of the commands would be:

Delores, take the picture of the clerk *weighing* bananas and give it to Juan. Jaime, put the picture of the shopper *comparing* prices on top of the window. Miguel, throw the banana to Eva.

Role playing. The students were ready to role play situations in a supermarket. The instructor played one role in each situation and a student played the other. Examples of the dialogue would be:

Edna, what would you like for dinner? Would you like some fish? ***Answer:*** "Yes, I would like fish for dinner."

Fine, select the fish you would like and put it in the basket.

What kind of vegetable do you prefer? ***Answer:*** "I like cauliflower and peas."

Introduction of places. On stiff cardboard, the instructor had glued pictures of places as a hospital, post office, bank, clothing store, bakery, drug store and so forth. The pictures were arranged at different locations around the room. The students were directed as follows:

Eduardo, take Shirou to the hospital and sit down.

Rita, go to the post office and buy a stamp.

Jaime, put the bakery where the drug store is and put the drug store where the bakery was.

The Twenty-Ninth Class

More on places.† This time the cards were handed out to the students and the following questions were asked:

Maria, where are you? ***Answer:*** "I'm in the hospital."

What are you doing in the hospital? ***Answer:*** "I'm sleeping."

José, where are you? ***Answer:*** "I'm in the park."

What are you doing? ***Answer:*** "I'm playing ball."

Miguel, where is Juan? ***Answer:*** "He's in church."

What's he doing? ***Answer:*** "He's sleeping."

This was continued until each student had a dialogue with the instructor about the place card the individual was holding. Then there was a round in which the response expected was a short answer. Examples would be:

Eva, is Juan in the post office? ***Answer:*** "Yes, he is."

Are Rachel and Eva in the store? ***Answer:*** "Yes, they are."

In still another round the verbal transaction required either a long or short response from the student. Notice that each series was designed to increase the student's *flexibility* in understanding and producing the target language.

Reading sentences created by students. Each student created a sentence which the individual wrote on paper then dictated to the instructor who wrote the sentence on the chalkboard. The value of this exercise was to encourage the construction, writing, and reading of English. There was immediate feedback since the students could compare what they wrote on paper with what the instructor wrote on the chalkboard.

†For additional practice with places, use the **TPR Student Kit: The Town.** (See page 5-11.)

The Thirtieth Class

Review of constructed sentences. When the sentences created by the students were each shown on cue cards, the students easily read them. Then the students were asked to write a new sentence in their notebooks and dictate it to the instructor, who wrote it on the chalkboard.

EXHIBIT 10

SENTENCES CONSTRUCTED BY THE STUDENTS

1. He dropped his English book on the floor.
2. She showed a picture of her family to her friend.
3. He broke his father's chair.
4. He threw the yellow paper on the floor.
5. Yesterday she read the San Jose Mercury News.
6. He drank a glass of hot milk.
7. I ate too much yesterday.
8. He went to San Francisco with David yesterday.
9. José put the glass on the round table.
10. She cut the chocolate birthday cake.
11. Alicia gave the glass of hot milk to John.
12. Yesterday Miguel wrote a letter to his family in Cuba.

Review of the past tense. This was a quick review in which the students produced short and long responses as the following examples illustrate:

Did Maria go to the hospital yesterday? ***Answer:*** "Yes, she did."
Where did Juan go? ***Answer:*** He went to the post office to buy a stamp."

After this exercise, the students were given a copy of familiar verbs written in the past tense and illustrated in a sentence. For example:

Walked	Juan *walked* to the post office yesterday.
Ran	A few minutes ago I *ran* to the chalk-board.
Went	Yesterday Maria *went* to the hospital.

Pancho Carrancho with vegetables. (Instructor) "Pancho Carrancho ate the tomato." ***(First student)*** "Pancho Carrancho didn't eat the tomato; he ate the beet." ***(Second student)*** Pancho Carrancho didn't eat the beet; he ate the carrot."

Introduction of the past form of the verb "to be." The place cards were distributed to the students exactly as yesterday. Maria had the hospital, Juan had the post office, José had the park and so forth. Then the instructor only spoke as follows:

Maria was in the hospital yesterday. Was Maria in the hospital

Note: The students have now experienced 90 hours of TPR instruction

The Thirty-First Class

Review. The instructor quickly moved students with commands followed by role reversal in which students gave commands and asked questions. This was a fast-moving series of interactions.

The past form of the verb "to be" with new verbs. The instructor used this pattern:

Angela, were you hungry last night? ***Answer:*** "Yes, I was."

Why were you hungry? ***Answer:*** "I was hungry because I had not eaten."

Eva, were you nervous when I put the snake in your hand? ***Answer:*** "Yes, I was."

Why were you nervous? ***Answer:*** "Because I do not like snakes."

Miguel, when you were a boy, were you afraid to be in a dark room? ***Answer:*** "Yes, I was."

Note that answers were optional. The student could produce any response that was appropriate and grammatical.

More with place cards. This was a quick review; then students

were manipulated with fresh sentences and manipulated others in role reversals.

Short answer questions. Very quickly the instructor fired questions at individual students. Examples would be:

Were you here yesterday?
Did Juan go to work yesterday?
Are you tired?
Is Maria sitting?

Practice with ordinal numbers.

Open your book to the *first* page.
Close the *first* and *second* windows.
Give the card to the *third* person on your left.
Draw a circle in the air with the *first* finger of your right hand.

The Thirty-Second Class

Reading. Each student was given a copy of Exhibit 11. First the instructor read each item through twice and then each student in turn read a sentence from the sheet. Note that all items on the sheet had been thoroughly internalized through listening comprehension before the students saw the content in print.

EXHIBIT 11

PAST TIME (EAT - ATE)

I ate.	We ate.
You ate.	You ate.
He ate.	They ate.
She ate.	
It ate.	

. . . .

I didn't eat.	We didn't eat.
You didn't eat.	You didn't eat.
He didn't eat.	They didn't eat.
She didn't eat.	
It didn't eat.	

. . . .

What did I eat?	What did we eat?
What did you eat?	What did you eat?
What did he eat?	What did they eat?
What did she eat?	
What did it eat?	

. . . .

Yes, I did.	No, I didn't.
Yes, you did.	No you didn't.
Yes, he did.	No, he didn't.
Yes, she did.	No, she didn't.
Yes, it did.	No, it didn't
Yes, we did.	No, we didn't.
Yes, you did.	No, you didn't.
Yes, they did.	No, they didn't.

Review of the past tense. This was a fast-moving review in which the instructor moved one or more students in a transaction, then asked an individual, "What did they do?" This was followed by role reversal in which students uttered commands to produce an interaction, then asked someone, "What did he do?" or "Tell us what they did."

More with demonstrative pronouns. The instructor used the appropriate props to practice demonstrative pronouns of "this, that, these, and those." Sample utterances were as follows:

Are *these* books? ***Answer:*** "Yes, they are."
Are *those* books? ***Answer:*** "No, they aren't."
Are *these* pencils? ***Answer:*** "Yes, they are."
Are *these* pencils or books? ***Answer:*** "Books."
What are *these?* ***Answer:*** "They're pencils."

As a hint, be prepared with many, many different objects since this will move along rapidly.

The Thirty-Third Class

Slides of the supermarket. This was review in which the instructor asked questions about transactions and about familiar vocabulary items. Examples would be:

Maria, what is the man doing? ***Answer:*** "He is buying food."
Eva, what is the clerk doing? ***Answer:*** "He is making change."
Jaime, play the customer and I'll be the clerk. Ask me a question.
Answer: "How much is the cabbage?"
Juan, what is that product? ***Answer:*** "That is hamburger."

New supermarket slides. These were colored slides of other products and situations the students had not experienced before. For instance, they saw a delivery man bring in a tray of bread, a courtesy clerk carrying a bag of groceries to a customer's car, the store manager examining a customer's personal check, and the butcher chopping meat on a block. In addition, there were many new products as cheese, tuna fish, mushrooms, cake mix and so forth.

Role playing. The students role played transactions and situations in a supermarket. Often the instructor was an actor in each situation.

The Thirty-Fourth Class

Reality testing. When visitors came into the room today, the instructor first warmed up the students with a fast-moving network of commands in which all students were in motion—interacting and transacting almost simultaneously.

Then the instructor invited role reversal in which individual students moved the visitors into intricate patterns of interaction through commands and questions. The visitors were impressed with the students' facility with English and the students were delighted that strangers understood what they were saying. This encounter increased the students' confidence in their ability to produce English.

Discussion groups. The students were divided into small conversational groups for the discussion of pictures from magazines. The instructor moved from group to group to participate in the conversations. Also, each visitor was invited to join a group.

The Thirty-Fifth Class

Review of the verb "to be." Commands and questions were mixed to practice both the present and past forms of the verb "to be." Examples would be:

Where is Delores? ***Answer:*** "Delores is at the chalkboard."
Where is Luke? ***Answer:*** "Luke is near the door."
Where are the pencils? ***Answer:*** "The pencils are on the floor."
Eva, walk to the center of the room and sing! **(PAUSE)** Jaime, what did Eva do? ***Answer:*** "She walked to the center of the room and sang."

Reading. Exhibit 12 was passed out to each student. All the material on the handout was familiar and internalized previously through the imperative.

The instructor read each item twice; then individual students read from the sheet.

Pancho Carrancho with place cards. The Michigan Cue Cards were integrated into the Pancho Carrancho game. Each student had a place card which was referred to when the student's turn came to speak. For instance, the instructor began by holding up a picture of the park and saying, "Pancho Carrancho was in the park yesterday." The first student held up a picture of the school and said, "Pancho Carrancho wasn't in the park; he was in school." Then the second student held up a picture of an auto shop and said, "Pancho Carrancho wasn't in school yesterday; he was in the auto shop."

After a round or two, the instructor illustrated how to create a story using a place card. She said, "Maria is in the hospital. She is eating her lunch. Alfredo is sitting next to Maria's bed. He is eating his lunch too." Then each student created a story using the place card the individual was holding.

EXHIBIT 12
SUPERMARKET

Verbs: 1. Compare 2. Weigh

Measures:
- gallon
- ½ gallon
- quart
- pint
- pound
- dozen
- ½ dozen
- each

Miscellaneous:
- dishes
- clothes
- scale
- plastic bags
- shopping cart
- cash register
- cashier

Dairy Products:
- milk
- cottage cheese
- cheese
- cream (half & half)
- eggs
- butter

. . . .

Baby Food

Frozen Foods

Soaps & Cleansers
- Dish Soap

Fruits
- melon
- orange
- pineapple
- watermelon
- apple
- grapes

Cake Mixes

Canned Fruit

Canned Vegetables

Lunch Meats
- hot dogs
- ham
- baloney

Poultry
- chicken
- turkey

Fish

Liquor Department
- beer
- wine
- whiskey
- vodka
- gin
- pretzels
- potato chops

. . . .

ager examining a customer's personal check, and the butcher chopping meat on a block. In addition, there were many new products as cheese, tuna fish, mushrooms, cake mix and so forth.

Role playing. The students role played transactions and situations in a supermarket. Often the instructor was an actor in each situation.

The Thirty-Fourth Class

Reality testing. When visitors came into the room today, the instructor first warmed up the students with a fast-moving network of commands in which all students were in motion—interacting and transacting almost simultaneously.

Then the instructor invited role reversal in which individual students moved the visitors into intricate patterns of interaction through commands and questions. The visitors were impressed with the students' facility with English and the students were delighted that strangers understood what they were saying. This encounter increased the students' confidence in their ability to produce English.

Discussion groups. The students were divided into small conversational groups for the discussion of pictures from magazines. The instructor moved from group to group to participate in the conversations. Also, each visitor was invited to join a group.

The Thirty-Fifth Class

Review of the verb "to be." Commands and questions were mixed to practice both the present and past forms of the verb "to be." Examples would be:

Where is Delores? ***Answer:*** "Delores is at the chalkboard."
Where is Luke? ***Answer:*** "Luke is near the door."
Where are the pencils? ***Answer:*** "The pencils are on the floor."
Eva, walk to the center of the room and sing! **(PAUSE)** Jaime, what did Eva do? ***Answer:*** "She walked to the center of the room and sang."

Reading. Exhibit 12 was passed out to each student. All the material on the handout was familiar and internalized previously through the imperative.

The instructor read each item twice; then individual students read from the sheet.

Pancho Carrancho with place cards. The Michigan Cue Cards were integrated into the Pancho Carrancho game. Each student had a place card which was referred to when the student's turn came to speak. For instance, the instructor began by holding up a picture of the park and saying, "Pancho Carrancho was in the park yesterday." The first student held up a picture of the school and said, "Pancho Carrancho wasn't in the park; he was in school." Then the second student held up a picture of an auto shop and said, "Pancho Carrancho wasn't in school yesterday; he was in the auto shop."

After a round or two, the instructor illustrated how to create a story using a place card. She said, "Maria is in the hospital. She is eating her lunch. Alfredo is sitting next to Maria's bed. He is eating his lunch too." Then each student created a story using the place card the individual was holding.

EXHIBIT 12
SUPERMARKET

Verbs: 1. Compare 2. Weigh

Measures:	*Miscellaneous:*	*Dairy Products:*
gallon	dishes	milk
½ gallon	clothes	cottage cheese
quart	scale	cheese
pint	plastic bags	cream (half & half)
pound	shopping cart	eggs
dozen	cash register	butter
½ dozen	cashier	
each		

. . . .

Baby Food

Frozen Foods

Soaps & Cleansers
- Dish Soap

Fruits
- melon
- orange
- pineapple
- watermelon
- apple
- grapes

Cake Mixes

Canned Fruit

Canned Vegetables

Lunch Meats
- hot dogs
- ham
- baloney

Poultry
- chicken
- turkey

Fish

Liquor Department
- beer
- wine
- whiskey
- vodka
- gin
- pretzels
- potato chops

. . . .

Vegetables
- lettuce
- radishes
- green onions
- tomatoes
- celery
- carrots
- peas
- string beans

Meat
- ground beef
- hamburger meat
- ground chuck
- liver
- steak
- pork chops

- can of peas
- jar of pickles
- bottle of catsup
- loaf of bread
- carton of eggs
- carton of milk
- bag of candy
- bar of chocolate

STRUCTURES:

1. She's comparing prices.
2. She's weighing the grapes.
3. Oranges are 12¢ a pound.
4. Pineapples are 69¢ each.
5. She is putting the carton of eggs in the shopping cart.

The Thirty-Sixth Class

Reading. Students read aloud the items from yesterday's handout. Then the instructor had flashcards with sentences that used each vocabulary item. Rapidly, individual students read a sentence aloud.

Introduction of restaurant vocabulary. † Even though the students now had more than 100 hours of training, new vocabulary was still introduced through the imperative. Commands were created to use verbs such as "set, pass, spill, order, pour and cough" with nouns such as "knife, spoon, fork, plate, dish, saucer, napkin and salt."

Each was given a set of props to match the nouns. Then student behavior was manipulated with commands as:

Put your knife on the right of your plate. Put the spoon next to your knife and put the fork on the left of your plate.

Jaime, pass the salt and pepper to Eva.

Delores, pass a napkin to each person in the room.

Juan, pour water from this pitcher into each student's glass.

Role playing. The scene was a hamburger establishment. Some students played the customers who stood in line to place their order. Other students were employees who wrote down each order, then ran about rapidly filling the order. Food items were represented by pictures pasted on stiff cardboard. These items included cheese burgers, large and small shakes, french fries, and so forth.

†Another suggestion is to use the **TPR Student Kit: The Restaurant.** (See page 5-11.)

The Thirty-Seventh Class

Review. This was a quick review of vocabulary items introduced for the restaurant role playing. Very rapidly the instructor moved students with utterances as:

Jaime, give Luke a knife, fork and spoon. Maria, tuck a napkin into Luke's shirt under his chin. Juan, bring Luke the yellow plate and the blue cup. Eva, pour some water into Luke's cup. Delores, take Luke's order and call it out to Eduardo who will bring the order to Luke.

More restaurant role playing. This time the players had menus with pictures of entrees, beverages, salads, vegetables, and desserts. Students sat at tables playing the customers while other students played waiters, waitresses, and cashiers.

Ordinal numbers. These commands were created to internalize ordinal numbers such as:

Wash the *first* window.
Stand in front of the *second* window.
Tape this paper to the *third* chair and sit on the *fourth* chair.

The Thirty-Eighth Class

More with ordinal numbers. This was a review and expansion of ordinal numbers. Notice that utterances in a review will have a mix of utterances heard before and novel utterances which have never been experienced before but are understandable because they are recombinations of familiar constituents. It is important to avoid drills in which identical sentences are used monotonously over and over. A better strategy is to recombine familiar constituents to produce surprises. Of course, these novel sentences are not designed to trick students. The intent is to practice familiar vocabulary and structure in the context of fresh sentences. Students should still experience, with each novel utterance, the delight of immediately understanding what the instructor said.

Note the novelty in these commands and questions created for practice with ordinal numbers:

Write the *second* number that I write.
Every *second* person sneeze.
What color is the *first* book?

Is the *last* book blue?

Is January or February the *first* month of the year?

On the large calendar, point to November *tenth.*

Everyday dialogues. This was role playing in which the instructor interacted with individual students in a "small talk" conversation such as:

Hello, Juan. We missed you. Good to see you again. Where were you yesterday?

The Thirty-Ninth Class

Role play restaurant situations. Individual students role played situations such as a waiter who spills food in the lap of a customer, a person who explores with the manager the possibility of buying the restaurant, and a banquet in which someone receives a gold watch for 30 years of service and must make an acceptance speech.

Practice with the relative clause. The instructor used a mix of commands and questions to fine tune features of the relative clause. Examples would be:

Jaime, walk to the person who is sitting near the door and bring that person to the center of the room.

Eva, what is the name of the person who was brought to the center of the room?

Maria, what is the name of the person who is sitting next to you?

Eduardo, shake the hand of the person who is standing next to the chalkboard.

Review of everyday dialogues. For typical social transactions, consult any text written for students learning another language. Usually, those books begin with dialogues in which there is small talk as, "Hello, how are you? It's a beautiful day, isn't it? What's your name? My name is Jaime."

Notice that everyday dialogues were delayed until about 120 hours of language internalization that was achieved primarily through the imperative. The reason for the delay is that the content of "small talk" in everyday encounters is extremely abstract, as is the dialogue between actors in television and film dramas.

The native speaker tends to perceive everyday verbal exchanges as extremely concrete and rather elementary; therefore, a logical entry point into the target language one is trying to learn. We find that the opposite seems to be true.

Everyday conversations are highly abstract and disconnected; therefore to understand them requires a rather advanced internalization of the target language. Hence, the delay until now to begin everyday dialogues.

The Fortieth Class

Travelogue. The instructor narrated as she projected colored slides of her trip to Mexico. As she spoke she would sample the effectiveness of communication by asking questions such as:

Maria, did you live in Guadalajara? Can you describe what other shops are on this street?

Alfredo, what is this scene? Will you please describe it for the class?

Some follow-up geography. A large map was displayed in the front of the room and the instructor directed students in a geographic exploration with utterances:

Point to North America. Point to South America. Where are you from? Show us on the map where you lived. Where is California?

A tactile experience. One at a time, each student was blindfolded, given an object, and asked to describe the object. For instance, Shirou was given a lemon and he said, "It's a fruit. It's a lemon and it's yellow." The instructor would interject with, "Is it round or square? Is it smooth or rough? Is it larger than your hand?"

When Miguel was blindfolded and handed a can, he said, "It's a can. It's full. It's hard."

The Forty-First Class

Review. This was a fast-moving review which sampled vocabulary and structures beginning with the first class.

Object description. Each student described a different object in the room. For example, Eva said: "The chalkboard is on the front wall. It is large and it is a rectangle. The color is green and there is writing on the board in chalk."

Family vocabulary. Exhibit 13 was on a large piece of stiff cardboard. The instructor referred to the pictures with utterances as:

Mary and John are married. Mary is married to John and John is married to Mary. John is Mary's husband. Mary is John's wife.

After this information, the instructor directed with commands as:

Delores, point to Mary's husband. Who is Mary's husband?
After a few minutes, it was obvious that this exercise was not effective. Student tension increased with the frequency of incorrect responses.

Why didn't it work? It may be that it was too difficult to identify the relationships of people in the picture. Perhaps familial relationships as mother, father, sister, brother, and so forth should have been used rather than proper names. Also the picture could have been drawn for a clear-cut identification of mother, father, grandmother, grandfather and so forth. The instructor decided to try this again at a later time, except to have the students bring in pictures of relatives in their own families.

As a hint, if certain vocabulary or structures are not internalized rapidly, it is best to withdraw the material. Often the stimuli used to represent the vocabulary are ambiguous. If so, find other referents. And often, certain vocabulary is too abstract for a particular point in training. If you try again further along in the program, the students may be ready for rapid assimilation.

The selection of material is a trial-and-error procedure in which student behavior will influence the decision to continue or discontinue with certain materials at a particular point in time.

The Forty-Second Class

Family vocabulary. Each student brought in two family pictures which were used as referents. The conversation was as follows:

Who is this? Is this your son? Please point to your daughter. Your husband. Your mother.

Then the students were instructed to point out family members and give a description of each person to another student in the class.

Introduction of the future tense. The strategy was to tell what action would occur and then the students would see the event happen.

I'm going to write on the chalkboard. ***(The instructor wrote on the chalkboard.)***

Tom, you're going to count your fingers and then you're going to point to Juana with your first finger. ***(Tom then executed the chain of behavior.)***

I will open my book. ***(The instructor opened her book.)*** I will read a sentence from the book. ***(A sentence was read from the book.)***

Role reversal. After students were responding confidently and rapidly, they were invited to try saying what they would do; then do it.

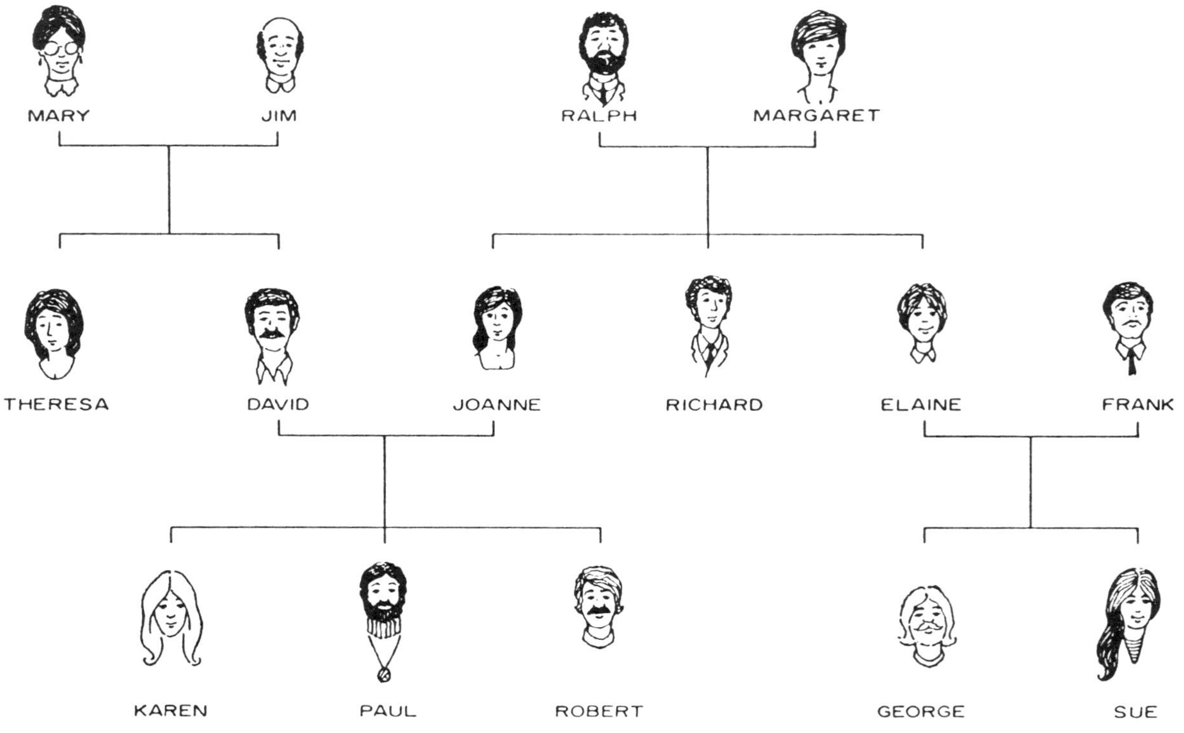

FAMILY TREE

Exhibit 13

Review of family vocabulary. Students had now internalized vocabulary as mother, father, sister, brother, grandmother, grandfather, son, and daughter. Each student was given a copy of Exhibit 14. The instructor read each item twice, then individual students read a vocabulary item and used it in a sentence.

More with the future tense. The instructor said. "Martha, in one minute you're going to turn off the light and then you're going to hit the wall three times. Martha, what are you going to do?" ***Answer:*** "I'm going to turn off the light and hit the wall three times."

After Martha completed the action, the instructor asked, "Jaime, what did Martha do?" ***Answer:*** "She turned off the light and hit the wall three times."

Sometimes as an action was in progress, the instructor would ask, "Delores, what are you doing?" ***Answer:*** "I'm walking to the table to get the picture of my grandmother."

Although the future was emphasized, other verb tenses were intermixed such as the past and present progressive. The students responded with flexibility to rapid shifts in verb tense.

EXHIBIT 14

FAMILY VOCABULARY

husband		uncle
wife		aunt
		nephew
mother	parents	niece
father		cousin
		mother-in-law
son	children	father-in-law
daughter		son-in-law
		daughter-in-law
brother		sister-in-law
sister		brother-in-law
grandmother	grandparents	
grandfather		
granddaughter	grandchildren	
grandson		

Review the future tense. In this review the instructor would cue a future action by saying, "Alfredo and Eva are going to walk to the center of the room." Then before the action took place, the instructor asked, "What are they going to do, Jaime?"

In addition to the format for the future tense illustrated in this class, other instructors have used a format in which the future tense was imbedded in the conditional such as:

If Edgar walks to the center of the room, Valorie will stand on the chair, but if Edgar draws a funny face on the chalkboard, Maxine will erase it.

Notice that what will happen is contingent upon a decision by the student, Edgar.

New commands. Even though the students had over 130 hours of training, new vocabulary was still internalized through the imperative. The new items were "shut, knock, ring, sweep and watch." The instructor would utter a command, then execute it herself as a model.

Get the broom and sweep the floor.
Knock on the door.
Ring the door bell.
Watch me as I walk to the door and knock on the door.

Then the new vocabulary was used in the context of the future tense.

In one minute, Alfredo is going to sweep the floor.
Jaime, is Alfredo going to cut his hair? ***Answer:*** "No, he is going to sweep the floor."

Field trip to a house.† The class was divided into two groups, each of which visited a different house. The instructor led one group and an assistant led the other. The students could respond with enormous range and flexibility in a home setting. First the instructor directed a chain of behavior, then individual students reversed roles and produced English to move the instructor and peers. Here is a sample from an almost infinite number of possible utterances.

Open the first drawer of the cabinet; take out the knives, forks, and spoons; then go to the dining room and set the table.
Open the refrigerator and take out a coke and pour the coke into a glass.

Individual students could be directed so rapidly that everyone was in motion simultaneously performing some action that resulted in an integrated pattern such as setting the table for dinner.

†As preparation for the visit to a home, try the **TPR Student Kit: The Home.** (See page 5-11.)

The Forty-Fifth Class

Review of the future tense. The instructor asked questions about future events which required a short or long answer from students. For typical questions as follows, students invented possible answers:

What is Jaime going to do?
What is Maria going to ring?
Who's going to ring the bell?
Is Maria going to ring the bell?

Pancho Carrancho with verb cards. Each student was given a card with a verb printed on it. When a student's turn came, the individual invented a sentence in the future tense that contained the specific verb the student was holding.

The instructor began with, "Pancho Carrancho is going to ring the doorbell." The first student said, "No, Pancho Carrancho is not going to ring the bell; he is going to watch the girls." The next student said, "No, Pancho Carrancho is not going to watch girls; he is going to wash the dishes."

The future tense with the Michigan Cue Cards. Each student was given a card with a different place. Then the instructor would ask a question about a future event and the student responded making reference to the "place" card. For example: Where are you and Miguel going? ***Answer:*** "We are going to the post office." Where is Eva going? ***Answer:*** "She is going to the park."

The Forty-Sixth Class

Role Reversal. Individual students played the role of teacher and asked questions of other students.

Field trip to a house. This was another visit with about 15 students going to one house with the instructor and the rest going to another house with an assistant. The students were directed in a variety of activities as:

Take the vacuum cleaner from the closet, turn it on and vacuum this rug.
Pick up the duster and dust the bookcase.
Make the bed.
Sit on the sofa and rest.
Water the plants.

Reading. The students were given a copy of Exhibit 15 which contained all the vocabulary internalized in the field trips to a home.

EXHIBIT 15

HOUSE

1. *Living Room*

bookcase
pillow
shelf - shelves
couch - sofa
carpet - rug
coffee-table
lamp - floor lamp
ashtray
candle
curtains
drapes

2. *Bedroom*

dresser
drawer
bed
bookcase
shelf
desk
closet
pillow

3. *Kitchen*

kitchen table
refrigerator
freezer
stove
oven
sink
pots - pans
counter
cabinet
faucet
blender

4. *Bathroom*

towels
soap
mirror
toilet paper
toilet
sink
shower
bath tub

The Forth-Seventh Class

Verb review. This was a fast-moving review in which all verb forms were randomly presented in a mixture of directions and questions. Examples would be:

Juan, what is Jaime wearing today?

Eva, what did Jaime wear yesterday? What did you wear yesterday?

Miguel, tell us the clothes you plan to wear tomorrow.

What do you think Delores is going to wear tomorrow?

House review. The instructor asked each student to tell about something they experienced in the houses they visited. Examples would be:

I saw a vacuum cleaner.

I swept the floor with a broom.
Eva washed the picture window.
Jaime washed dishes.

As each student uttered an observation, the instructor wrote on the chalkboard a vocabulary item from the house experience.

Introduction of "there is." The instructor said, "In this box there is a blue plate. In my pocket there is a kleenex. In this vase there is a little water."

The Forth-Eighth Class

Review vocabulary learned in the house. Again using Exhibit 15, the instructor read each item twice; then individual students made up a sentence using a particular vocabulary item.

Review of "there is." The students listened as the instructor asked and answered questions using "there is" as a constituent. For example:

Is there a piece of chalk on the floor? ***Answer:*** "Yes, there is."
Is there a knife on the plate? ***Answer:*** "No, there isn't."
Is there a refrigerator in this room? ***Answer:*** "No, there isn't."
Is there a hand on my shoulder? ***Answer:*** "No, there isn't."

Then the instructor continued, still answering her own questions while the students listened.

Is there a book or a piece of chalk on the floor? ***Answer:*** "A piece of chalk. There's a piece of chalk on the floor."
Is there a lawyer in this room? ***Answer:*** "Yes, there is. There's a lawyer in this room. Edelia is a lawyer."

The Forty-Ninth Class

Continuation of "there is." The instructor "warmed up" the students with the following:

On the table there's a box.
In the box there's a broom.
Under the box there's a book.
Next to the box there's a napkin.

Then there was a series of questions to which the student was expected to respond with "Yes, there is." or "No, there isn't." For instance, the instructor asked:

Is there a box on the table?
Is there a piece of chalk in the box?

Next, the students were cued with an example to show that the instructor wanted an *expanded response* to each question. The pattern is illustrated as follows:

Is there a box or a magazine on the table? ***Answer:*** "There's a box on the table."

What else is on the table? ***Answer:*** "There's a glass on the table."

Adjectives. Students described themselves in three sentences using descriptive words which were written on the chalkboard. For example, one student said, "I'm a mother. I'm beautiful. I'm intelligent."

Another said, "I'm tall. I'm friendly. I'm kind."

Words written on the board included tall, short, man, woman, student, teacher, housewife, lazy, kind, nice, friendly, pretty and so forth.

The Fiftieth Class

Review of "there is." This was a fast-moving review which went like this:

There is a refrigerator in this room. Jaime, is there a refrigerator in this room? ***Answer:*** "No, there isn't," or "No, there is no refrigerator in this room."

There is a clock on the wall. Delores, is there a clock on the wall? ***Answer:*** "Yes, there is," or "Yes, there is a clock on the wall."

Introduction of "there are." This was a logical transition from the prior activity. Examples would be:

There are men and women in this room. Are there men and women in this room, Juan? ***Answer:*** "Yes, there are men and women in this room."

There are cars in this room. Are there cars in this room, Eva? ***Answer:*** "No, there are no cars in this room."

A guest speaker. A guest speaker from the Chamber of Commerce gave a presentation about places of interest in the city and the talk was illustrated with colored slides. The students were attentive, seemed to understand most of what was said, and were pleased with their progress.

The guest speaker was a test of reality. The students were delighted that they could follow the narration of someone other than the regular classroom instructor.

Reading. The instructor read each sentence in Exhibit 16, which was distributed to the students. Then each student read a sentence which was a review of the future tense.

EXHIBIT 16

FUTURE TIME

I'm going to sleep.	We're going to sleep.
You're going to sleep.	You're going to sleep.
He's going to sleep.	They're going to sleep.
She's going to sleep.	
It's going to sleep.	

. . . .

I'm not going to sleep.	We aren't going to sleep.
You aren't going to sleep.	You aren't going to sleep.
He isn't going to sleep.	They aren't going to sleep.
She isn't going to sleep.	
It isn't going to sleep.	

. . . .

Am I going to sleep?	Are we going to sleep?
Are you going to sleep?	Are you going to sleep?
Is he going to sleep?	Are they going to sleep?
Is she going to sleep?	
Is it going to sleep?	

Review of "there is" and "there are." The singular and plural forms were mixed in a fast-moving review with utterances as:

Is there a tall man and a short woman in this room? ***Answer:*** "Yes, there is a tall man and a short woman in this room."

Are there people and cats in this room? ***Answer:*** "There are people but there are no cats in this room."

Introduction of "can." The instructor used "can" in a sentence, then demonstrated. For example, she said:

I *can* touch my nose. Watch me.

I *can* shake hands with Juan. Watch.

I *can* lift this chair and put it on the table. Watch me.

Can you lift this chair, Jaime? ***Answer:*** "Yes, I can lift that chair." Then show us.

Can you touch your toes, Luke? ***Answer:*** "Yes, I can touch my toes." Then show us.

More with opposites. The instructor contrasted opposites in commands such as:

Maria, walk to the chair *near* you but run to the chair *far* from you.

Jaime, pick up the *thick* book and give it to me; then get the *thin* book and throw it to Maria.

Get the picture of the *fat* girl and put it next to the picture of the *skinny (thin)* boy.

Other opposites that the students practiced in commands were high-low, old-new, easy-difficult, old-young, strong-weak, and narrow-wide.

The Fifty-Second Class

Review of opposites. The instructor used the imperative to review opposites in commands such as: "Miguel, find the picture of an *old* man and a *young* man and give both to Eva!"

Introduction of "I can't . . . because." Since the students had demonstrated that they had internalized the form of "can," the transition to "can't" was smooth. For example, the instructor began with utterances as:

I can't touch the ceiling because it's too high.

I can't pick up this table because it's too heavy.

I can't throw this chair because it's too heavy.

Then the instructor asked questions as follows:

Can you touch the ceiling? ***Answer:*** "No, I can't."

Why can't you touch the ceiling? ***Answer*** "Because it's too high."

What can't you touch? ***Answer:*** "The ceiling, the light, the top of the window."

An imaginary car. An imaginary sedan was simulated by arranging two chairs side by side behind two other chairs facing the class. Then students were directed with commands as:

Open the doors of the car and everyone get in.

Strap on your seat belts.

Roll down the windows.

Who is the driver? Jaime?

Jaime, start the car. Release the emergency brake. Shift into gear and go for a ride.

At this point, without prompting from the instructor, the four students in the imaginary car moved their chairs forward in unison. When the instructor said, "Turn right," they turned their chairs in the appropriate direction and continued to move in unison. Then "Turn left," and they maneuvered their chairs left. Other commands were:

Stop the car.
Roll up the windows.
Open the doors.
Everyone get out, close the doors and lock them.
Maria, open the trunk and Juan, get out the tire.

The Fifty-Third Class

After Exhibit 17 was distributed to the students, the instructor read each sentence twice. Then individual students would read a sentence while another student acted out the appropriate behavior.

EXHIBIT 17

Shirou, open up the car door.
Sit behind the wheel.
Close the door.
Elaine, Ramiro, and Pablo, get in the car also.
Turn the key.
Push in the clutch and drive forward.
Put your hand out the window.
Turn left.
Now, go straight.
Elaine, tell Shirou to stop at the supermarket.
Pablo, tell Shirou not to stop at the supermarket but to go to the clothing store.
Put on the brakes.
Shirou, tell them all to close their mouths.
Now drive into the gas station.
Tell the attendant to fill the tank.
Tell him also to wash the windshield, and check the tires.

Slides of a gas station. † The instructor narrated each slide by saying, "I drove my car into this gas station. The attendant said, 'May I help you?' I said, 'Yes, please give me regular gas.' He said, 'Shall I fill it up?' I said, 'Yes.' Then he said, 'Would you like me to check the tires?' and I nodded my head. Then he checked under the hood as you can see in this slide."

Role play a gas station transaction. The instructor played the gas station attendant and a group of students drove their imaginary car into the station. The verbal interaction followed what had been seen on the slides, but there were unexpected student utterances as, for example, when one passenger asked the attendant, "While I am in the men's room, please wash the windows of the car."

Exhibits 18-22 are other situations that were used to practice not only reading, but changes in verb tense. For example, Miako read aloud from Exhibit 18, "Stand up," and Shirou, who was the actor in this situation, stood up. Then the instructor said, "Jeffe, what did Shirou do?" The expected answer was, "He stood up."

If you want to practice with the present progressive, then it would work like this: Juan reads, "Walk to the car" and Shirou walks to the imaginary car while the instructor says, "Wing, what is Shirou doing?" The expected answer is, "He is walking to the car."

If you want an exercise with the future tense, the procedure could be this: You say, "Next, Shirou will walk to the car," and Pablo reads from Exhibit 18, "Walk to the car."

If you want the students to practice writing, try this: A student reads from Exhibit 18, "Stand up," and Ramiro, who is the actor, stands up. Now you say, "Write down on your paper what Shirou did."

†For more practice with cars, which students can do **at their seats,** try the **TPR Student Kit: The Gas Station.** (See page 5-11.)

EXHIBIT 18

DRIVE THE CAR

1. Stand up.
2. Walk to the car.
3. Take out your keys.
4. Unlock the car.
5. Open the door.
6. Get in.
7. Put the key in the ignition.
8. Put your foot on the accelerator.
9. Start the car.
10. Release the brake.
11. Drive the car.
12. Stop!
13. Go ahead.
14. Red light. Slow down.
15. Stop.
16. Wait for the light to change.
17. Drive the car again.
18. Put on the turn signal for a left turn.
19. Turn left.
20. Put on the turn signal for a right turn.
21. Turn right.
22. Pull over.
23. Stop.
24. Turn off the motor.
25. Take out the keys.
26. Open the door.
27. Get out.
28. Close the door.

EXHIBIT 19

Go to the Kitchen and Have a Coke

1. Stand up.
2. Go to the kitchen
3. Open the refrigerator.
4. Take out a bottle of Coca Cola.
5. Close the refrigerator.
6. Walk to the cabinet.
7. Open the cabinet.
8. Take out a glass.
9. Close the cabinet.
10. Walk to the drawer.
11. Put down the glass.
12. Open the drawer.
13. Take out the bottle-opener.
14. Open the bottle.
15. Pour the coke into the glass.
16. Put the bottle-opener back.
17. Close the drawer.
18. Put down the bottle.
19. Pick up the glass.
20. Walk to the table.
21. Sit down at the table.
22. Drink the Coke.
23. Relax.

EXHIBIT 20

Go to the Bank

1. Go to the bank.
2. Open the door and go in.
3. Walk to the window.
4. Wait in line.
5. Move up.
6. Move up again.
7. Go to the window.
8. Give a check to the teller.
9. Say, "Please cash this check for me."
10. Pick up your money.
11. Walk to the door.
12. Open the door and walk to your car.

EXHIBIT 21

Just Looking

1. Go to the store.
2. Open the door and go in.
3. The salesman says to you, "May I help you?"
4. *Answer,* "No thanks, I'm just looking."
5. Walk around and look around.
6. Stop in front of the pants.
7. Pick up a pair of pants.
8. Look at them.
9. Put them back.
10. Go to the door.
11. Open it and go out.

EXHIBIT 22

Take the Bus

1. Stand up.
2. Go to the door.
3. Open the door.
4. Go out.
5. Close the door.
6. Walk to the bus stop.
7. Wait for the bus.
8. Get on.
9. Put the money in the box.
10. Ask the driver for a transfer.
11. The driver gives you a transfer.
12. Look for a seat.
13. Find a seat.
14. Walk to the seat.
15. Sit down.
16. Look out the window.
17. What do you see?
18. Pull the cord.
19. Stand up.
20. Walk to the door.
21. Hold on.
22. Get off.
23. Wait for the other bus.
24. Get on.
25. Give the transfer to the driver.
26. Look for a seat.
27. Find a seat.
28. Walk to the seat.
29. Sit down.

SELECTED REFERENCES

Asher, J. J. "A symbolic logic theory of perception." Unpublished monograph, San Jose State College, 1959.

Asher, J. J. "A neo-field theory of learning the 1+n language." Unpublished monograph, San Jose State College, 1960.

Asher, J. J. "Sensory interrelationships in the automatic teaching of foreign languages." Final Report of Sept. 1, 1961, Title VI Project Number 578 (Grant Number 7-04-091) of the National Defense Education Act of 1958. Research supported by a grant from the Office of Education, U. S. Department of Health, Education, and Welfare.

Asher, J. J. "Sensory interrelationships in the automated teaching of foreign languages." (Abstract) *Perceptual and Motor Skills,* 1962, 14, 38. (a)

Asher, J. J., and Fallentine, B. C., "The high velocity process of logic in verbal learning." Unpublished manuscript, San Jose State College, 1962. (b)

Asher, J. J. "Evidence for 'genuine' one-trial learning." *International Review of Applied Linguistics,* 1963, vol. 1/2, 98-103. (a)

Asher, J. J. "Toward a neo-field theory of problem solving." *The Journal of General Psychology,* 1963, 68, 3-8. (b)

Asher, J. J. "Toward a neo-field theory of behavior." *Journal of Humanistic Psychology,* 1964, 4, 2, 85-94. (a)

Asher, J. J. "Vision and audition in language learning." Monograph Supplement IV, 19, *Perceptual and Motor Skills,* 1964, 19, 255-300. (b)

Asher, J. J. "The strategy of the total physical response: An application to learning Russian." *International Review of Applied Linguistics,* 1965, 3(4), 291-300.

Asher, J. J. "The learning strategy of the total physical response: A review." *The Modern Language Journal,* 1966, 50(2), 79-84.

Asher, J. J. "The total physical response approach to second language learning." *The Modern Language Journal,* 1969, 53(1), 3-17. (a)

Asher, J. J. "The total physical response technique of learning." *Journal of Special Education,* 1969, 3(3), 253-262. (b)

Asher, J. J. "Implications of psychological research for second language learning." 157-186 in Dale L. Lange and Charles J. James, eds., *Foreign Language Education: A Reappraisal (Britannica Reviews of Foreign Language Education; Volume 4).* Skokie, Illinois: National Textbook Company, 1972. (a)

Asher, J. J. "Children's first language as a model for second language learning." *The Modern Language Journal,* 1972, 56(3), 133-139. (b)

Asher, J. J. "The Nava adventure: American students assimilate into a Mexican village." Unpublished paper, San Jose State University, 1973.

Asher, J. J. Kusudo, J., and de la Torre, R. "Learning a second language through commands: The second field test." *The Modern Language Journal,* 1974, 58(1-2), 24-32.

Asher, J. J. "Children learning another language: a developmental hypothesis." *Child Development,* 1977, 48, 1040-1048.

Asher, J. J. "Motivating children and adults to acquire a second language." *SPEAQ Journal,* 1979, Vol. 3, Nos. 3-4, 87-99.

Asher, J. J. "Fear of foreign languages." *Psychology Today,* August, 1981, 52-59. (For a *complimentary copy,* write or call: Sky Oaks Productions, Inc., P.O. Box 1102, Los Gatos, Ca. 95031.)

Asher, J. J., and Price, B.S. "The learning strategy of the total physical response: Some age differences." *Child Development, 1967, 38 (4), 1219-1227.* [Reprinted in *Child-Adult Differences in Language Acquisition.* (eds.: Krashen, S.D., Scarcella, R.C., and Long, M.). Rowley, MA: Newbury House Publishers, Inc., 1981.]

Asher, J. J., "The extinction of second language learning in American schools: An intervention model." In *The Comprehension Approach to Foreign Language Instruction.* H. Winitz (ed.) Rowley, MA: Newbury House Publishers, Inc., 1981.

Asher, J. J. "Comprehension training: The evidence from laboratory and classroom studies." In *The Comprehension Approach to Foreign Language Instruction.* H. Winitz (ed.) Rowley, MA: Newbury House Publishers, Inc., 1981.

Asher, J. J., and Garcia, R. "The optimal age to learn a foreign language." *The Modern Language Journal,* 1969, 53, 334-341. [Reprinted in *Child-Adult Differences in Language Acquisition.* eds., Krashen, S. D., Scarcella, R. C., and Long, M.). Rowley, MA: Newbury House Publishers, Inc., 1981.]

Asher, J. J. and García, R. "The optimal age to learn a foreign language." *Citation Classics,* March 24, 1986, Vol. 18, No. 12.

Asher, J. J. "The total physical response: theory and practice." In *Native Language and Foreign Language Acquisition.* H. Winitz ed.) Vol. 379, 324-331. *The Annals of the New York Academy of Sciences,* 1981. (For a *complimentary copy,* write or call: Sky Oaks Productions, Inc., P.O. Box 1102, Los Gatos, Ca. 95031.)

Asher, J. J., "Keynote presentation to the 59th Bi-annual Conference of the Foreign Language Association of Northern California at West Valley College, Saratoga, California — April 17, 1982. (For a *complimentary copy,* write or call: Sky Oaks Productions, Inc., P.O. Box 1102, Los Gatos, Ca. 95031.)

Asher, J. J. "Comprehension training: The 'outrageous' hypothesis that works." JALT Newsletter, Sept. 1, 1983, Vol. VII, No. 9 & 10. (For a *complimentary copy,* write or call: Sky Oaks Productions, Inc., P.O. Box 1102, Los Gatos, Ca. 95031.)

Asher, J. J. "The total physical response: Some guidelines for evaluation." Published by the *Indiana University Linguistics Club,* 1985. (For a *complimentary copy,* write or call: Sky Oaks Productions, Inc., P.O. Box 1102, Los Gatos, Ca. 95031.)

Asher, J. J. "Excellence for most of our students in the 'school' of the year 2000: A plan." Published in the *1986 Yearbook* by the New York State Association of Foreign Language Teachers. (For a *complimentary copy,* write or call: Sky Oaks Productions, Inc., P.O. Box 1102, Los Gatos, Ca 95031.)

Blakeslee, T. R. *The Right Brain.* Garden City, New York: Anchor Press/Doubleday, 1980.

Benson, D. F., and Zaidel, E. (eds). *The Dual Brain: Hemispheric Specialization in Humans.* New York: The Guilford Press, 1985.

Bühler, C., and Hetzer, H. *Testing children's development from birth to school age.* New York: Farrer & Rinehart, 1935.

Carroll, J. B. "Wanted: A research basis for educational policy on foreign language teaching." *Harvard Educational Review, 1960,* 30, 128-140.

Carroll, J. B. "Some neglected relationships in reading and language learning." *Elementary English,* 1966, 43, 577-582.

Carroll, J. B. "The foreign language attainments of language majors in a survey conducted in U.S. colleges and universities." Final Report for Contract OE-4-14-048 U. S. Office of Education. Cambridge, MA: Labor for Research in Instructional Graduate School of Education, Harvard University, 1967.

Chui, Glennda. "Single gene may be to blame for heart attacks, researchers say." *San Jose Mercury News,* June 21, 1986.

Davidson, Patricia S. "Rods can help children learn at all grade levels." *Learning,* 6, 86-88, November 1977.

Davies, N. F. "Receptive versus productive skills in foreign language learning." *The Modern Language Journal,* 1976, 60(8), 440-443.

Davies, N. F. *Putting receptive skills first: An investigation into sequencing in modern language learning.* (Mimeo). 1978. University of Linköping, Department of Language and Literature, Linköping, Sweden.

DeRoche, E.F., and Bogenschild, E. G. *400 Exciting and Ready-to-Use Math Motivators.* West Nyack, NY: Parker Publishing Company, Inc., 1977.

Dye, J. C. *The use of body movement to facilitate second language learning for secondary school students: Listening and speak-ing — A teacher's guide.* Doctoral dissertation, Division of Foreign Language Education, New York University, 1977.

Ervin, S. M. "Imitation and structural change in children's language." In E. H. Lenneberg (ed.), *New directions in the study of language.* Cambridge, MA: MIT Press, 1964.

Fallentine, B. C. *Experimental validation of constructs within the theory, "A neo-field theory of learning the 1+n language."* Unpublished master's thesis, San Jose State College, 1961.

Fleming, J. N. *The development of an ESL placement test.* Advanced student project in linguistics, San Jose State University, San Jose, CA. January, 1973.

Friedlander, B.Z., Jacobs, A.C., Davis, B. B., and Wetstone, H. S. "Time-sampling analysis of infants' natural language environments in the home." *Child Development,* 1972, 43, 730-740.

Gary, J. O. "Delayed oral practice in initial stages of second language learning." In M. K. Burt and H. C. Dulay (ed.), *New directions in second language teaching, learning and bilingual education.* Washington, DC: TESOL, 1975.

Gary, J. O., and Gary, N. "Comprehension-based language instruction: Theory." In *Native Language and Foreign Language Acquisition.* H. Winitz (ed.) Vol. 379, 332-342. *The Annals of the New York Academy of Sciences,* 1981.

Gary, N., and Gary, J. O. "Comprehension-based language instruction: Practice." In *Native Language and Foreign Language Acquisition.* H. Winitz (ed.) Vol. 379, 343-357. *The Annals of the New York Academy of Sciences,* 1981.

Gauthier, Robert. Tan-Gau — a natural method for learning a second language. *Teacher's Guide to accompany the Tan-Gau Method.* Toronto: W.J. Gage.

Gazzaniga, M. S. "The split brain in man." *Scientific American,* August, 1967, 217, No. 2, 24-29.

Gazzaniga, M. S., Le Doux, J. E., and Wilson, D. H. "Language, praxis, and the right hemisphere: Clues to some mechanisms of consciousness." *Neurology,* 1977, December, 1144-1147.

Gesell, A., and Thompson, H. "Learning and growth in identical infant twins: An experimental study by the method of co-twins control." *Genetic Psychology Monographs,* 1929, 6, 1-124.

Gonzalez, Burnette M. *Asher's Total Physical Response: An Effective Means of Teaching a Second Language (Mimeo).* July, 1976. Describes the dramatic results of teaching Spanish and French to 300 Junior High school students. Also tells of action-oriented training materials developed for French, German, Latin, Russian, and Spanish. Available from the author at the Parkway School System, 455 North Woods Mill Road, Chesterfield, MO 63017.

Gouin, Francois. "The Art of Teaching and Studying Languages," 5th Edition, London: George Philip and Son, 1894.

Hilgard, Ernest R. *Divided Consciousness: Multiple Controls in Human Thought and Action.* New York: John Wiley & Sons, 1977.

Ingram, F., Nord, J. R., and Dragt, D. "A program for listening comprehension." *Slavic and East European Journal,* 1975, 19(1), 1-10.

Jacobsen, T. L. and Asher, J. J. "Validity of the concept constancy measure of creative problem solving." *The Journal of General Psychology,* 1963, 68, 9-19.

Knowles, Frank. Coloured rods, a calculator and decimals. *Mathematics Teaching,* No. 86, March, 1979.

Kohno, J. M. and Suenobu, J. *Pleasureland of English.* Osaka, Japan: Osaka Educational Books Co., 1976.

Krashen, S. D. "The monitor model for second-language acquisition." In *Second Language Acquisition and Foreign Language Teaching.* (ed. R. Gingras) 1978, Arlington, Virginia: Center for Applied Linguistics.

Kunihira, S., and Asher, J. J. "The strategy of the total physical response: An application to learning Japanese." *International Review of Applied Linguistics,* 1965, 3(4), 277-289.

Larsen-Freeman, Diane. *Techniques and Practices in Language Teaching.* New York: Oxford University Press, 1986.

Lawson, J. H. "Should foreign language be eliminated from the curriculum?" In J. W. Dodge (ed.), *The case for foreign language study.* New York: Modern Language Association Materials Center, 1971.

Mesic, P. "Superlearning." *Spring Magazine,* May, 1982, 44-47. (For a *complimentary copy,* write or call: Sky Oaks Productions, Inc., P.O. Box 1102, Los Gatos, Ca., 95031.)

Nord, J.R. "A case for listening comprehension." *Philologia,* 1975, 7, 1-25.

Nord, J. R. *Shut-up and listen, a case for listening comprehension* (Mimeo). Learning and Evaluation Service, 17 Morrill Hall, Michigan State University, East Lansing, Michigan 48824.

Nord, J.R. "Developing listening fluency before speaking: An alternative paradigm." *System,* 1980, Vol. 8, No.1, 1-22.

Nord, J. R. "Text talk or tape talk." *Philologia,* 1980, 12, 1-33.

Nord, J. R. "Three steps leading to listening fluency: A beginning."In *The Comprehension Approach to Foreign Language Instruction.* H. Winitz (ed.) Rowley, MA: Newbury House Publishers, Inc., 1981.

Osborn, A. F. *Applied Imagination.* New York: Scribner's, 1957.

Palmer, H., and Palmer, D. *English Through Actions.* London: Longman Group Limited, 1970.

Postovsky, V. A. *The priority of aural comprehension in the language acquisition process.* Paper presented at the 4th AILA World Congress, August 25, 1975. The Defense Language Institute — West Coast, Monterey, CA. [Reprinted in *The Comprehension Approach to Foreign Language Instruction.* H. Winitz (ed.) Rowley, MA: Newbury House Publishers, Inc., 1981.]

Reeds, J. A., Winitz, H. & Garcia, P.A."A test of reading following comprehension training," *International Review of Applied Linguistics,* 1977, 15(4), 307-319.

Richards, I.A. *Design for Escape.* New York: Harcourt, Brace, and World, Inc., 1968.

Swaffar, J. K. & Woodruff, M. S. "Language for comprehension: Focus on reading. A report on the University of Texas German Program." *The Modern Language Journal,* 1978, 62, 27-32.

Swann, H., and Johnson, J. *Prof. E. McSquared's Original, Fantastic and Highly Edifying Calculus Primer, Part 1.* Los Altos, California: William Kaufmann, Inc., 1975.

Swann, H., and Johnson, J. *Prof. E. McSquared's Original, Fantastic and Highly Edifying Calculus Primer, Part 2.* Los Altos, California: William Kaufmann, Inc., 1976.

Terrill, T. *The Natural Way.* Oxford: Pergamon, 1982.

Webb, Marion R., and Tabery, Julia J. *Audio-Motor Units for Use in Teacher Training Institutes in Spanish (Mimeo).* October, 1976. Action-oriented materials were developed to train 100 teachers in Spanish. Available from the authors at the Houston Baptist University, 7502 Fondren Road, Houston, Texas 77074.

Wertheimer, M. *Productive Thinking.* New York: Harpers, 1959.

Winitz, H., and Reeds, J. *Comprehension and problem solving as strategies for language training.* Hague, Netherlands: Mouton, 1975.

Winitz, H. *Comprehension and learning.* Paper delivered at the 1978 TESOL convention in Mexico City, Mexico. Available from the author, Speech and Hearing Science Laboratory, University of Missouri, 5216 Rockhill Road, Kansas City, Missouri 64110.

Winitz, H. "Nonlinear learning and language teaching." In *The Comprehension Approach to Foreign Language Instruction.* H. Winitz (ed.) Rowley, MA: Newbury House Publishers, Inc., 1981.

Winitz, H. "Use and abuse of the developmental approach." *For Clinicians, By Clinicians, Articulation and Language* (in press).

Winitz, H. "Input considerations in the comprehension of first and second language." In *Native Language and Foreign Language Acquisition.* H. Winitz (ed.) Vol. 379, 296-308, *The Annals of the New York Academy of Sciences, 1981.*

Winitz, H. "Native and second language learning: Implications for foreign language teaching. *Die Unterrichtspraxis* (in press).

Wollitzer, P. A. Foreign language and international studies in selected Bay Area high schools: A preliminary assessment, 1983. Report published as a joint project of The World Affairs Council of Northern California, 312 Sutter Street, San Francisco, CA 94108.

Woodruff, M. S. *Comprehension-based Language Lessons: Level I.* Los Gatos, CA: Sky Oaks Productions, Inc., 1986.

PART VI

A Conversation with Dr. James J. Asher about Total Physical Response (TPR) and Education

REPRINTED WITH PERMISSION FROM THE IDEAS FOR EXCELLENCE NEWSLETTER, FALL 1996

James J. Asher is the originator of Total Physical Response (TPR), which is a stress-free approach to second language acquisition. As part of TPR, teachers physically and verbally model commands for students who are then required to respond with appropriate actions. Through TPR, students develop receptive language before expressive language emerges. Thus, speech production is the result of comprehension and language acquisition and not the cause. Dr. Asher has published numerous books and articles and assisted in the production of several documentary films. He has been widely recognized for his teaching excellence, including being named outstanding professor at San Jose State University, and he was recently interviewed about his educational research for an upcoming episode on NOVA for PBS. Dr. Asher is presently on sabbatical leave and graciously agreed to share his reflections about TPR and education with the editors of the IDEAS for Excellence Newsletter.

Question: In the past 30 years, other models of second language acquisition have appeared and disappeared, but TPR continues to be used in thousands of classrooms throughout the world to help children and adults acquire another language. How do you explain the longevity of TPR? What is TPR's secret?

Dr. Asher: I think there are three elements that explain the success of TPR. First, it is *aptitude free.* This means that the approach is effective for everyone in the normal curve of ability, not just those with high academic ability. Students who are having difficulty in school shine in TPR classes because for the first time in their lives, they experience the thrill of being "A" students. Second, as has been demonstrated in study after study, TPR works with both children and adults. There are *no age barriers* to acquiring a second language. Third, TPR is *stress-free* because it is, to use Leslie Hart's colorful term, "brain compatible." In comparison, "brain antagonistic" approaches start with production ("Listen and repeat after me!") or memorization ("Memorize this dialog.") or explicit grammar instruction ("Here is the explanation of the grammar feature for today."). These direct approaches are stressful for most people learning a new language.

Question: What makes the TPR approach "brain compatible"?

Dr. Asher: The answer has to do with the way in which the brain and nervous system are wired to acquire language. The wiring schemata is visible when you observe infants acquiring their first language. What you will observe is unique "language-body conversations" between the caretaker and the baby. These transactions start immediately after birth with utterances like this:

Look at Daddy! Look at Daddy! Look at Daddy!

The baby's eyes turn in the direction of the voice. In response, the caretaker exclaims with great excitement, "She's looking at me! She's looking at me!" Later, as the infant develops, the directions become more complex:

Take my hand!
Don't spit up on your shirt!
Pick up your toy and put it on the table!

I call these transactions "language-body conversations" because the caretaker speaks and the baby responds with an appropriate physical action such as looking, smiling, pointing, grasping, holding, turning, or walking. The child's physical response signals understanding, which makes these transactions true conversations.

Babies are silent except for babbling for about two years, but during this critical period the infant is internalizing the sounds and patterns of the strange, new language. Only after the child internalizes an enormous sample of the language does speaking occur.

In the recorded history of the human race and in all cultures, we find no deviation from this sequence for language acquisition. In all countries, you will find thousands of hours of language-body conversations between caretakers and infants before the rudimentary appearance of utterances such as "Mommy" or "Daddy." Production always lags far behind comprehension, and it remains that way for many, many years.

Question: But does this work the same way for a second language?

Dr. Asher: The neural blueprint does not change with age. The sequence is the same for all ages. Surprisingly, children and adults can acquire the sounds and patterns of a target language in a fraction of time because their range of physical responses is vast compared with infants. And, when TPR is the mode of instruction, there is a kind of age inversion with adults outperforming children, and older children (sixth, seventh, and eighth grades) outperforming first, second, and third graders. However, studies are consistent in showing that children younger than puberty have the advantage of being accent-free in speaking a second language.

Question: What are the "best ways" to use TPR with students at a particular language level?

Dr. Asher: If you are teaching students who are in the initial stage of language acquisition (sometimes called preproduction), you should definitely use TPR because the sounds and patterns of the new language can be internalized rapidly through language-body conversations. Additionally, long-term retention is extraordinary, which gives both students and teachers keen motivation day after day. No other learning model is concerned with the motivation of the teacher, but if teachers are not excited about what they are doing, they cannot orchestrate a spell-binding learning experience for students.

Even before students reach Level 2, the production stage, speech will appear spontaneously. Of course, it will not be perfect, but gradually it will shape itself in the direction of the native speaker, especially for children. High school students and adults will be intelligible, but they will have at least some accent.

Question: Is TPR still of value after students have made the transition to speaking, reading, and writing?

Dr. Asher: Yes. My recommendation is to use TPR to help students internalize any new grammatical feature or vocabulary item. Then proceed to use the item in conversations, story telling, instruction, and so forth. For example, a textbook in another language will shock most students because it is "crawling with alien creatures." The left side of the student's brain is whispering sabotaging messages such as, "Oh, oh! Nothing in this book looks familiar! You don't understand any of this. You probably never will! This looks difficult! You are going to have a terrible time with this book! Better get out now, if you can!"

The solution is to comb the book to list all adjectives, adverbs, verbs, and nouns that students can internalize with TPR. Do this before your students ever open the book. Then when students open the book for the first time, they encounter only "friendly creatures." This strategy transforms a "fearful" textbook into an attractive book that is a challenge to students.

Question: Can you give an example of how you might do that?

Dr. Asher: Let's take the vocabulary item "crooked." You can TPR the item with directions in the target language such as, "Luke, make a crooked arm." "Elena, make a straight arm." "Jaime, go to the board and draw a crooked tree." "Maria, run to the board and draw a straight tree." For details on how to TPR hundreds of vocabulary items that are common to most FL/ESL textbooks, I recommend Stephen Mark Silver's ***The Command Book.***

Question: How about grammatical features?

Dr. Asher: Eric Schessler's excellent book, ***English Grammar Through Actions,*** (which is also available in Spanish or French) demonstrates how to TPR 50 grammatical features in any of those languages. For example, try the possessive case with directions such as, "Bill, give John's book to Mary." (Bill performs the action.) "Hank, touch Herb's pencil." (Hank performs the action.) "Sally, put Eric's paper on Jean's desk." (Sally performs the action.)

Question: Does TPR have applications in school programs other than language acquisition?

Dr. Asher: I'm glad you asked that because I have just completed a new book, ***The Super School of the 21st Century,*** that shows how TPR can be applied to improve every feature in today's schools. But first, you must understand that TPR is powerful because it is a brain-switching device. Students who are "academically gifted" can brain-switch on their own to move information from the left to the right brain and back again for immediate understanding.

Those with engineering aptitude, for instance, can visualize objects in three-dimensional space and they can, in their imagination, rotate an object to see it from many different angles. Others of us need some assistance, which is where the frontier of computer technology called virtual reality comes into play. This technology will create on the screen what engineers can see in their imaginations. Remember, those concepts in mathematics, physics, and chemistry are in motion. Now, for the first time in the history of education, using computer simulation, we can enable every student to see those "mysterious" concepts move on the computer screen. When you see them move, you understand immediately how they work.

Question: Any closing thoughts you would like to share?

Dr. Asher: I would like to express my appreciation for the support and encouragement from thousands of fine teachers worldwide. Their feedback about what does and does not work in the classroom has been invaluable.

To receive a complimentary catalog of TPR publications, write, fax, e-mail, or call:

Sky Oaks Productions, Inc.
P.O. Box 1102, Los Gatos, CA 95031
Phone: (408) 395-7600
Fax: (408) 395-8440 • E-Mail: TPR World@aol.com

The Application of TPR to Higher Order Thinking Skills

EXPERIENCES OF CLASSROOM TEACHERS

Increasingly, teachers are recognizing the tremendous potential of using TPR to successfully develop students' higher order thinking (H.O.T.) skills to native and non-native speakers at all levels of language production. Here are some creative ideas about how to use this approach with your students:

Jan Boomer, an ESL teacher in Coppell, Texas who uses the *Carousel of IDEAS* program, suggests extending the lesson on fruits and vegetables by adding a TPR-based, H.O.T. activity. After students are familiar with the vocabulary, Boomer explains to them that some fruits and vegetables grow on the ground while others grow high above the ground. She models this form of classification by giving commands and placing pictures of fruits and vegetables in appropriate piles. In watching and imitating her actions, Boomer's students learn classification skills that are transferable to other academic areas.

TPR can also be used effectively in ESL and subject area classrooms to introduce new knowledge and concepts. Students grasp abstract concepts more easily when they begin with concrete objects and actions. About one-fifth of **Diane Preston's Kindergarten class in San Lorenzo, California** consists of non-native English speakers. She developed a TPR-based lesson on patterning and sequencing that is effective for the entire class. She asks her students to bring teddy bears to class and begins the lesson by classifying the bears as either "dressed bears" or "bare bears." She then demonstrates a sequencing pattern (e.g., "AB") for students by arranging the bears in a specific sequence one dressed bear, one bare bear, one dressed bear, one bare bear, and so on, using TPR commands to involve students in the activity. Preston's lesson varies as students experiment with different patterns.

Preston also uses TPR to teach her students the concept of Venn diagrams. After students draw pictures of their bears, Preston creates two large Venn circles on the floor with string. She then names two characteristics of the pictures, such as "This bear is brown and has a bow." Preston models where to place each picture appropriately in the Venn diagram and then gives commands for students to place their pictures in the diagram. Through TPR, these pre- and early production students learn analysis and grouping and are able to access a fairly advanced mathematical concept.

Dr. Connie Williams, a teacher-trainer, uses the TPR-based *Let's Celebrate!* program to teach students about cultural events such as Las Posadas. Williams introduces the concept of *how* Las Posadas is celebrated by using pictures and commands (e.g., "Look outside at the people holding candles." "Invite the guests to come in for the night." "Show them the Las Posadas nativity scene." "Break the piñata filled with candy and treats."). Once students understand *how* Las Posadas is celebrated in the United States, they are prepared to learn why it is celebrated. Williams involves students in making their own mini-books with copies of the pictures and commands and engages them in a pictorial of the background story of Las Posadas. Through these activities, students develop language skills and also discover the genesis, traditions, values, and similarities and differences of important cultural events.

Joyce Nutta, instructor of foreign language education at the University of South Florida, asserts that TPR is an effective technique in developing both language and H.O.T. skills because it employs *authentic* learning. Instead of being "buried in textbooks," students actively interact with the material and with one another. TPR allows students, regardless of their stage of language acquisition, to readily assimilate new levels of knowledge.

To make her lessons relevant and meaningful for intermediate and advanced students, Nutta uses a language experience approach. This approach includes these students giving the commands and working closely with beginning students. More advanced students are encouraged to write new stories and commands, which Nutta then helps them to correct or adjust. Her lessons cover job site training in various vocations, "emergency" lessons such as learning about CPR using a mannequin, and a "community helpers" lesson that includes a visit from local firemen. Nutta's TPR lessons are structured to develop students' higher order cognitive skills such as assessing a situation, task analysis, classifying information, and making quick decisions under stress.

Students need H.O.T. skills in order to succeed academically and in their lives. Using TPR to teach higher order thinking skills to your students really works! If you have ideas you would like to share about using TPR to teach H.O.T. skills to your students, please write us and we will share them in a future edition of *IDEAS for Excellence Newsletter,* 480 Atlas Street, Brea, California 92621-3117. Phone: (800) 321-4332.

PART VII

From My Mail Bag

CORRESPONDENCE WITH TEACHERS IN THE FIELD

Subject: TPR Student Kits

From Jim Baird

Dear Dr. Asher,

I just wanted to tell you how much I'm enjoying the TPR Student Kits I recently ordered. I have enlarged on your student kit idea with this innovation:

My classroom has a wall-to-wall white board and I have used it to create complete communities and an entire country with cut- outs and markers (wish I had stick-on cities).

Students are required to drive, walk (with their fingers), fly, hop, run etc. between buildings or cities, pick up things or people and deliver them to other places. They can fly into an airport and rent a car and drive it to another city where they can catch a flight or a boat, all kinds of possibilities. Sure is fun!

Jim Baird
ghc@ocsonline.com

Subject: Degree of Body Movements and Language Learning

From Jim Baird

Dear Dr. Asher,

I am thoroughly enjoying your books. I am curious about the relationship of degree of body movement to the internalization of new material. There is lots of body movement that obviously cannot take place in the confines of a classroom (hence the reason for your student kits). Can one learn just as well if no significant body effort takes place?

There is a big difference for example between moving a chair several feet with your arms and legs and moving a small picture of chair a few inches using two fingers. It would appear the more one gets physically into the action the more effective the internalization. Is that a valid assumption?

Thank you again,
Jim Baird

Answer from James J. Asher

Dear Mr. Baird,

From our observation of students, the movement of fingers to simulate walking for example, seems as effective as actual walking but definitive research has yet to be done. This would be an excellent research project for a master's thesis or a doctoral dissertation. Thanks for your inquiry. —JJA

<u>Subject</u>: **Helping Immigrant Workers Acquire a Second Language**

From Jim Baird

Dear Dr. Asher,

I just rented one of your videos and have become more excited about TPR than ever!

I am a volunteer ESL teacher at a literacy center in our town in Georgia. My classes vary from 9 to 27 students. Each new class contains 25 to 50% new students. Half the class shows up 30 to 45 minutes late. As you can see, I have a problem.

Some of this chaos can be explained by the character of Dalton. It is 20-30% Hispanic and they are here to make carpet. There is no unemployment; there are more jobs than people. Many of my students work full time. If they are not working they are caring for children whose parents are working. Our town produces half of all the carpet sold in the world..

My question is, how can I use TPR when my attendance is so brief and so interrupted? My students love the process, but if they go back to Mexico to tend to a problem or change their work schedule they lose subsequent exposure to reinforce what they are learning. I feel I must produce encapsulated lesson plans that have no carry over from one class to another.

I would appreciate any advice and specific recommendations on what materials to order from your catalog. I'm ready to get into TPR 100%!

Three extra questions and I won't bother you again (for a while).

1. What in your opinion is the maximum size a TPR class can be?
2. Is there any reason TPR can't be used with just one student?
3. Can TPR be used to teach "how to ask" questions?

Thank you very much,
Jim Baird

Answer from James J. Asher
Dear Mr. Baird,

TPR is ideal for your unique situation for two reasons: First, your students will have long-term retention and second, TPR is non-linear. A student can enter the flow of activity at any point and within minutes, tune into the meaning of the "noises" coming from the instructor's mouth.

Answer from: Joan Christopherson
Dear Jim,

I'm one of the TPR Practitioners Dr. Asher sent your query to. I'll attempt to answer each of your questions.

1. Maximum size… I have used TPR in classes as small as 3 and as large as 40 with equal success given the lack of individual attention given to those in the class of 40.

   I have used it with kids as young as 4 and with adults taking French for conversation at the community college.
2. I have also used it with an exchange student I had in my home a couple of years ago whose English wasn't what it was purported to be in the exchange organization's information about the boy. It helped him a lot.
3. In the school I last taught (Mountlake Terrace High School), we used a system called Roll Call to teach many grammatical structures. It is not exactly TPR, but because it is comprehension-based (which is what makes TPR so successful) Dr. Asher has given his blessing to its use.

For roll call, I would ask a volunteer to do different things, then I would say to the class, "Ask what Mary is doing"— eating, making a face, etc." Then when I call a student's name, the student would ask, "Mary, what are you doing?"

Another variation: "Ask what Mary was doing." The student I call upon asks: "Mary, what were you doing?" Still another variation is: "Ask what Mary will be doing next."

They will try to be original in their responses, thinking that is the point of your activity where your actual point is getting the entire group to ask a question using the same basic structure and have everyone there hear an answer with different content but the same structure over and over until it sounds right to them. Be ready for some entertaining answers.

Joan Christopherson - garyc@wolfenet.com

PS. If you would like the Roll Call handout I give at TPR Seminars, I would be glad to send it to you, if you'll send me your address.

<u>Subject</u>: TPR works like a charm with Japanese children but the school's owner wants them to learn the "hard way." What do I do?

From Danny Becker

Dear Dr. Asher,

I read the books in the TPR Starter Kit and tried it out in my first little kids class in Japan. The children are ages 3 through 13. It was too successful. Did all that stand up, sit down, and walk business. And by popular demand the command "run" was introduced and necessity had me introducing "STOP." I had great fun and so did the kids. Maybe too much. The owner of the school wants to observe my next classes, and wants me to stick to the class outline which is ALM of course.

Now that I am turned on to the TPR method, I feel guilty at putting these kids through the ALM. I can see the distress all over their faces. The kids were easy to convince, parents and administrators are going to be another thing. Any ideas?

More specifically: Material or references which will help me turn an ALM text into some fun TPR? Ramiro Garcia's book is great for a full course, but something geared more to taking over with TPR...

Very truly yours,

Danny Becker
danorin@tkc.att.ne.jp

Answer from James J. Asher

Dear Mr. Becker,

You are not alone in your dilemma. It is not easy to arouse people from their "dogmatic slumber." One strategy is to invite the director of your school, parents and others in for an evening in which you show off your kids with a "fireworks display" of complex English that they understand with TPR. Be sure to have food and other refreshments for the visitors. If you are clever, you can lure adults from the audience to participate showing that they too are capable of a quick understanding of English.

You are on the right track! Gradually, step by step, you can introduce more and more TPR into the program. For example, use the ALM text to your advantage. Here is how: Comb the book for all vocabulary that you can TPR. Organize your search under nouns, verbs, adverbs, adjectives, and prepositions. Then before your students see a chapter, TPR the vocabulary in that chapter. The result is that instead of being frightened by looking at alien creatures (mysterious vocabulary in the chapter) they are enjoying the discovery of friends—that is, vocabulary they have already internalized.

<u>Subject</u>: Dyslexia

From Abigail Marshall,
Information Services Director
Davis Dyslexia Association International

Dear Dr. Asher,

I am the webmaster for the Dyslexia, the Gift website and editor of our quarterly newsletter, The Dyslexic Reader (circulation 5,000). I found out about TPR because it is the method used in my son's high school; my dyslexic son has astounded everyone because his favorite subject is French and he is getting A's. Most dyslexic kids have a tough time learning languages, so I think that our readers (mostly teachers, parents & adult dyslexics) might be very interested in TPR.

Abigail Marshall
Information Services Director
Editor, Dyslexic Reader
1601 Old Bayshore Highway #245 • Burlingame, CA 94010
Davis Dyslexia Association International
Our Web Site: http://www.dyslexia.com

<u>Subject</u>: Correspondence from Italy

From Ferrari Chiara
Dear Dr. Asher,

As a project to complete my college degree, I would like to interview you about TPR. Here are some questions that I have not seen in your books:

Q. In Italy there are only a few books that speak about TPR and if they do, they devote to it only a couple of pages. As a consequence, Italian FL teachers acquire a quite limited view of TPR that is reduced to a verbal stimulus followed by an action, such as *Jump*, *Walk to the door*, but they don't know that you, in collaboration with some teachers, have developed other teaching techniques that range from TPR Storytelling to games such as Pancho Carrancho, TPR Bingo, etc., including assessing techniques. They don't know almost anything about the large number of experiments that prove your theories about language learning.

A. The answer here is for a progressive Italian book distributor to import all of our TPR books for the sale to Italian educators.

Q. As a psychologist, why did you decide to devote yourself to the study of foreign language teaching?

A. I wanted to focus my research upon an interesting unsolved problem in complex human learning. The acquisition of another language has a notorious attrition rate of 95%. Something is obviously wrong, seriously wrong! What can be done to repair it? Experimental psychology has resulted in thousands of studies that explore human learning. Surely this body of information must have some important contributions for foreign language learning.

Q. Which do you think are the most important factors in language learning: genetic factors or environmental factors?

A. Obviously both are important, but TPR is powerful because it is perhaps the only tool now available that is relatively aptitude-free. This means that most students in the normal range of ability have a high probability of success. Instead of 95% failure, we have 95% success. The reason that TPR works so well in the hands of a talented teacher is that it is "brain compatible" rather than, as Leslie Harte describes so much of education, "brain antagonistic."

Q. If you had to summarize TPR in a few words what would you say?

A. TPR replicates in the classroom the process by which all infants in all places on earth acquire their native language so gracefully.

Q. Research about TPR shows that this power tool can produce better results compared with the audio-lingual or the grammar-translation method. How do you explain these results?

A. Audio-lingual and grammar-translation use half the brain—usually the wrong half at the wrong place in language training. Hence these approaches are "brain antagonistic." These approaches can be extremely effective at more advanced levels if the practitioner has a sophisticated understanding of the left-right brain lateralization model.

Q. At what age can people start learning a foreign language through TPR?

A. Start in preschool because the research is clear that if the second language learning begins before puberty, there is the maximum probability that the person can acquire a near-native pronunciation. After puberty, the probability of achieving a near-native pronunciation is almost zero even if one lives in another country for 50 years. With TPR as the foundation, every student is capable of acquiring basic fluency in multiple languages before leaving elementary school and enjoy an additional bonus of speaking with a near-native pronunciation.

Q. Some people think TPR can only be applied with children or beginner students of a foreign language. How is it possible to use it in advanced courses?

A. TPR is an essential tool at all stages for anchoring, with minimal effort from the teacher and the student, any novel feature in the target language including vocabulary and grammar. Once the new feature (new to the student) is anchored in the right brain, then the instructor can successfully switch to traditional left brain activities which include dialogues, patterned drills, skits, grammar explanations and so on. The instructor's task is to bounce the information back and forth creatively from one side of the student's brain to the other.

Q. People think that TPR can be limited because it is based on only one technique of language-body conversation composed of a verbal stimulus followed by an action. How is it possible to provide variety in a TPR course?

A. Read James J. Asher's ***Learning Another Language Through Actions*** and Ramiro Garcia's ***Instructor's Notebook: How to apply TPR for best results.***

Q. When would you advise the teacher to use TPR? When would you advise them not to use TPR?

A. Use TPR to establish a foundation for all other activities in the target language. Don't use it if you don't understand how it works. Don't use it if you are satisfied with the results you are now getting with whatever strategy you are using.

Q. Are there any unanswered problems about TPR?

A. Sure. The research possibilities are many and interesting. I have suggested these in detail elsewhere. Again, see my book, ***Learning Another Language Through Actions*** and also explore our website which is www.tpr-world.com

One interesting research issue is to explore the optimal mix of activities at each stage of second language acquisition. Another is to explore the effectiveness of short-term goals that are of keen interest to students (How to direct a taxi to a restaurant? How to ask directions to the hotel? How to buy a train ticket? etc.) rather than teacher goals of "covering the chapters in a textbook."

Q. In which country is TPR meeting with success?

A. In no country has TPR been unsuccessful in the hands of a talented teacher.

Q. Do you know at what stage is the knowledge of TPR in Europe and especially in Italy?

A. My impression is that Europe may be twenty years behind, probably because foreign language teachers do not read the research journals. They may tend to believe that they already have "the answer." You cannot learn what you think you already know. Teacher education programs are especially negligent in their cursory presentation of TPR to beginning teachers.

TPR in thousands of classrooms worldwide is the most helpful power tool that any beginning teacher (or veteran teacher) can have hooked to their educational tool belt. For example, Jim Martinez who heads the Top School of Languages in Brazil, told me that before they discovered TPR, their attrition rate was 80%. Now it has dropped dramatically to 2%.

Q. Can TPR be applied to other school subjects?

A. Yes, I am working upon applications to the universal language of mathematics which has an attrition rate that matches foreign language learning. In America, we spend more money on remedial mathematics than all other forms of math education combined. This can be turned around. For the latest on TPR applications to mathematics and all other school subjects, read my book: ***The Super School of the 21st Century.***

Q. Is there any experimental research in this field?

A. Of course. See scores of references in my book ***Learning Another Language Through Actions.*** My own ten-year program of experimental work was supported by research grants from the U.S. Office of Education, the U.S. Office of Naval Research, the Department of Defense, and the State of California.

Q. What are you working on at the moment?

A. Novel applications of TPR that enable children and adults to enjoy rapid and stress-free understanding of mathematics including computer programming.

Q. Do you think it useful to present any further aspects of your research to Italian readers?

A. The greatest contribution to Italian education is to translate the books I have mentioned into Italian for sale in Italy.

Good luck with your project —JJA

Yours sincerely,
Ferrari Chiara
chiara@dsc.it

Subject: TPR Chat Groups

From R.A. Oldaker
Dear Dr. Asher,

I was wondering if there are any people on AOL who regularly meet to share imperatives (commands) from the world's languages and who discuss classroom strategies using Total Physical Response. I am interested in employing the method as much as possible in my German classes at our university. I have ordered a number of materials from your publishing company in Los Gatos, California. The "storytelling" books (written by others) that I have seen would not appeal to my students, so I am looking for intermediate and advanced picture books that are more appropriate as far as content is concerned and that can be used as a springboard for in-class activities. However, I have not been successful in finding what I need.

R. A. Oldaker
raowvup@aol.com

Answer from James J. Asher
Dear Professor Oldaker,

We suggest posting your inquiry on the bulletin boards of various foreign language newsgroups such as FL Talk. The e-mail address is: fltalk@listserv.acsu.buffalo.edu Your local reference librarian can help you locate other appropriate groups. —JJA

Subject: How to Erase an Accent

From Beth Thompson
Dear Dr. Asher,

Q. A friend who is a special education elementary teacher took a leave of absence to go to Laos and teach ESL to doctors and nurses who had no English background. She had already been trained in TPR and chose this method for her class. She felt it was extremely successful. She even used the method to teach vocabulary on advanced anatomy and medical terms.

My friend explained that the theory behind TPR is that people must first learn to listen, then to speak, just as they did with their first language. Is it easier for adults to pick up correct phonetic speech if they are not pressured to speak at the beginning? Are there any studies on this?

A. Yes, there are a number of studies which you will find in the reference list of my book, ***Learning another Language Through Actions***. Most studies corroborate this conclusion: If one starts the study of a second language before puberty, the probability is almost certain that the student can acquire a near-native, if not native pronunciation. After puberty, the probability is almost certain that the student will have at least some accent no matter how many years one may live in the foreign country. Puberty seems to be a biological marker. Cross the marker and you can expect to master a second language but always with a discernible accent.

Q. My friend's experience gave me the key on how to write my assignment. My problem? I live in a rural community (I commute to the University) and I cannot find any authentic TPR material to adapt. There are some community education ESL classes in another town, but they aren't using TPR. Do you know of any website that has some TPR material for one lesson that I could use for my class? I am especially interested in a lesson that is making the transition between only listening to some speaking.

A. You will find scores of TPR lessons in Asher's ***Learning Another Language Through Actions*** and Garcia's ***Instructor's Notebook***. There is no one lesson that will take students from listening to speaking. After about 10 to 20 hours of TPR instruction, most students are ready to speak.

Q. Also, a question on other research on the TPR method. I am specifically interested in why some adults learn to speak phonetically correctly, and others, while fluent in speaking and listening, cannot make themselves understood because they mispronounce English sounds so badly.

A. You will find the explanation again in Asher's ***Learning Another Language through Actions***.

Q. Hopefully TPR will be covered in my ESL methods class next fall, but I would like to know resources about research and theory to prepare for it.

A. Unfortunately, most language methods courses offer only a cursory presentation of TPR.

Beth Thompson
bthompsn@mnic.net

Subject: How to Help Management Personnel Acquire Spanish

From Margarita E. D. de Baker

Dear Dr. Asher,

I have been teaching Spanish in a local carpet industry for the past five years with a combination of methods including TPR, which I borrowed from my elementary Spanish teaching experience.

I have always enjoyed teaching Spanish using the TPR methodology, but have never used it exclusively until now. I am continually designing and redesigning the Spanish courses for the company, trying always to reach the goal of preparing their management personnel to communicate as effectively as possible in Spanish to their Mexican employees.

As I browsed the Net in search of professional information to help me, I found your Web page and ordered your materials.

After reading both Asher and Garcia's books I decided to take the plunge and go 100% TPR. I am currently teaching a Level I (24 hour) and Level II (24 hour) Spanish course. Each level meets four hours a week for 6 weeks.

Can you link me up with anyone else who is using TPR in an industrial setting? All your resources are elementary, secondary, or night-class adult oriented.

Margarita E. D. de Baker
hmbaker@ocsonline.com

Answer from James J. Asher

Ms. Baker,

Here is a suggestion: Post your request on the bulletin boards of various FL/ESL newsgroups on the web. For example, try FL Talk. To send e-mail: fltalk@listserv.acsu.buffalo.edu —JJA

<u>Subject</u>: I want to teach myself a foreign language

From: Bruce Daniels

I am interested in learning Hebrew. Do you have programs, materials, etc. for self-study? I currently can read Hebrew but want to be able to converse.

Thank you,
Bruce Daniels
dandf@kc.net

Answer from James J. Asher

Dear Mr. Daniels:

For self-study cues, please see the Q & A section of my book, ***Learning another Language Through Actions.*** If you have a tutor, I explain step by step how to acquire another language on your own with a tutor using my TPR Student Kits. Also, call private schools in your area that teach Hebrew. Be sure to ask them whether they use TPR in their instruction. Good luck! —JJA

Subject: How "play" is related to TPR

From: Richard Ehrlich

I recently read about Noam Chomsky's work on a human's innate ability to acquire language. I was especially interested in the fact that he said that one needs to be stimulated for advanced language acquisition.

After reading about TPR, I realized that there may be a direct connection with someone's ability to play and the development of language acquisition. After all, play seems to be innate among children in that they seem to know how to play without being taught; they then learn about words and language through play.

What do you feel is the role of "play" in one's innate ability to learn language? What is your opinion of the role of play in TPR for language acquisition? How does TPR relate to Chomsky's innate language acquisition ability?

Richard Ehrlich
English/Writing Teacher
Ehrlich_R@popmail.firn.edu

Answer from James J. Asher
Dear Mr. Ehrlich,

"Play" is the essential element in TPR. When we play, we are tuned into the right brain. Children outperform adults in acquiring a second language because children in a foreign country zip into the language when they interact with playmates. By comparison, their parents struggle to acquire the alien language word-by-word sitting in rows of schoolroom chairs. The mistake is "sitting" which disconnects the target language from the student's body. The intimate interaction between language and body movements is the secret of TPR.

We demonstrated using Russian, that when adults have the same opportunity to "play" as children, they outperform children of all ages (except for pronunciation). The research is summarized in my book, ***Learning another Language Through Actions.*** Chomsky's innate language acquisition hypothesis can perhaps be tested when gene mapping is completed. What do you think? —JJA

Subject: Where can I contact Spanish teachers in my area who are tuned into TPR?

From: Frederick A. Pysher in Northern Pennsylvania

Q. I don't know where to contact Spanish teachers in my area. My purpose is to perfect my application of the "Total Physical Response" for the benefit of my students in the middle school environment. I have been teaching Spanish for the past 30 years primarily using the traditional approach. Recently I had the pleasure of experiencing TPR in the classroom by way of observing a young Spanish teacher in Salamanca, New York. I am convinced that TPR is a more user-friendly approach.

A. Click on the web. Post a note on the bulletin boards of FL/ESL newsgroups. To locate these newsgroups, consult with your reference librarian. Almost all libraries, even in small communities, invite library-users to use the libraries' computers to find anything on the web. —JJA

Subject: TPR in Mongolia

From: Brian Hogan

Thank you so much for your excellent TPR materials which I use exclusively for teaching English to my Mongol students. They have made my class very successful and fun! I began to envy my Mongol students their ease of English acquisition and asked my Mongol instructor tutor to please use TPR to teach me Mongolian. He plugged us into a Mongolian translation of Cabello's ***TPR in First Year English*** and we now have eight American students in the pilot class..."

In a follow-up progress report...

We translated and adapted where necessary about 20 lessons into Mongolian. I trained two Mongols to teach the TPR to a group of about eight American adults and another group of children. It went great for about 10 lessons. Everyone felt they learned a lot, but logistics killed the class. ...finding a time when all could attend ... was difficult, and finally too much. But I would say that the material worked well for Mongolian.

My Mongolian students learning English via TPR learned well, after they got past it being "too fun."

Brian Hogan
hogan@writeme.com

Subject: I want to create a curriculum using only TPR

From: Al King

Dear Dr. Asher,

I am the only Spanish teacher at a private high school in

Oklahoma. I teach Spanish 1 and 2 and have as much flexibility as I desire in selecting curriculum and instructional methodology. Currently I am experimenting with various TPR techniques and materials that I have purchased from Sky Oaks. I have the majority of the Sky Oaks books.

However, next year I would like to totally revamp our curriculum and design it according to the TPR approach. What would you suggest if you were in my position and could design any type of program you wanted?

Al King
lulu@ionet.net

Answer from Dr. Jules Mandel

Dear Mr. King,

I'm Jules Mandel, retired Los Angeles District FL Specialist and a firm believer in the value of TPR to develop listening comprehension. What a lucky person you are! Having total control over a high school Spanish curriculum. And how fortunate to have become an Asher-ite.

Some considerations: At the High School level, you need to consider the learning modalities of your students, many of whom are visual learners. This means that they won't be satisfied not to have something visual to refer to when they're not in class. Therefore a textbook of some sort, could be a syllabus of your own design or a commercial item, would be of help for those kids. The other two modalities-kinesthetic and audio—will lap up TPR.

However, it is certainly possible and I think that other classroom teachers who've taught via TPR more recently and over a longer period of time will be able to give you more specific how-to's. At your level, though, it'll be necessary to get the kids to write what they hear and see as you model it, AFTER having practiced a given sequence or sequences to a good degree of automaticity.

If you choose to use a textbook, you can always approach a new unit/chapter/module with TPR strategies combined with competency-based instructional techniques: storylines, realia, loads of visuals, etc. Getting the kids to generate materials is a natural for a TPR teacher. And your kids will be able to handle class business—asking permission, borrowing materials, explaining needs—mucho mejor en español que los de otros maestros en las escuelas vecinas. Let me know what you find out from others, and what you decide to do. —Buena suerte!

E. Jules Mandel, Ph.D. • JMandel70@aol.com

<u>Subject</u>: TPR in Finland

From: Terttu Iiskola

Dear Professor Asher,

I have a daughter, who has difficulties in learning Swedish as a second language. I have heard about TPR-method. Do have any TPR-material in Finnish or Swedish? Do have any TPR-material on computer? I would really appreciate Your answer as soon as possible... Thank you for your help!

Terttu Iiskola
info@anaheimfinland.fi

Answer from James J. Asher
Dear Ms. Iiskola,

We cannot offer you TPR lessons in Swedish or Finnish, but if you have access to a tutor for your daughter, I have some suggestions. First, read my book, ***Learning another Language Through Actions,*** to understand how TPR works. Then you guide the tutor, lesson by lesson.

I would recommend that you train your tutor in how to TPR the vocabulary that your daughter will encounter in each lesson at school. Confer with the teacher to find out when each chapter in the book will be "covered" in class, then prepare your daughter. Help her internalize the vocabulary in advance through TPR. This makes the book user-friendly. An excellent resource is Stephen M. Silvers, ***The Command Book: How to TPR 2,000 vocabulary items in any language.*** I also recommend: Eric Schessler's ***English Grammar Through Actions*** as a model for how to TPR grammatical features in Swedish or Finnish. —JJA

<u>Subject</u>: Is Mathematics a Foreign Language?

From: Brian Brady
Dear Dr. Asher,

I enjoyed your book ***Brainswitching*** for many reasons, but mostly for the connections it makes between learning a language and learning mathematics. As a math instructor who "works" at teaching students foreign languages like algebra, geometry, and calculus; and who "plays" with learning French, Spanish, and German himself, I am continually reminded of how similar the skills are that are needed to progress in these two areas. I have a two part question:

Q. First, are you aware of any colleges/universities that blend the study of mathematics with foreign languages, particularly for under-prepared students at 2-year colleges?

A. No, but it is a great idea. As you may know, in America we spend more money on remedial mathematics than all other forms of math education put together. The problem, as I see it, is that in math and in foreign languages we play to half the brain, usually the wrong half. The result is "brain antagonistic" instruction that creates the illusion of "difficulty" which then translates into the damaging conclusion by the students, "Well, I guess I am no good at mathematics..."

Q. Second, between the growing emphasis on problem-solving skills in mathematics on the one hand, and the acting-out techniques used in TPR on the other, there might be some interesting ways to work on student deficiencies in both math and foreign languages at the same time. What do you think?

A. I think you are on to something. One of the great tragedies in education is the disconnecting and compartmentalizing of subject areas. Each specialty then becomes sacred territory guarded by the academic tribal warriors. Cross into it at your own risk. As the folks who live along the bayou are fond of saying to would-be trespassers, "Bones don't float."

Brian Brady

Instructional Specialist in Mathematics,

University of Cincinnati - Clermont College

Brian.Brady@uc.edu

bradybn@email.uc.edu

<u>Subject</u>: Math as a Foreign Language...

From: Susan Patel

Dr. Asher:

On your website (www.tpr-world.com), I just read your article "Math as Foreign Language."

I'm one of those students who just hates math. The big ordeal in my life is that math is just not up my academic alley. I excel in all other subjects, but math, which is required in order to achieve my ultimate goal: to be an M.D. The irony is that I have yet to meet a doctor that has said "Yeah, my undergraduate courses in algebra/calculus has helped me out in my career." I surmise these difficult (in my eyes) math courses must be a weeding out process— sort of

a way of getting the *crème de la crème*. In any case, I would like to see algebra switched over as an elective, but I just can't see it happening any time soon.

Susan Patel
sujan5@hotmail.com

Answer from James J. Asher
Dear Ms. Patel,

I empathize with you. Mandatory algebra and/or calculus for everyone is like the 19th century mandatory Latin for everyone. Latin was assumed to be *good for you* and *absolutely necessary to success in your life's work* and *invaluable in understanding the English language*. It was assumed (and later shown in research to be false) that skill in Latin would generalize to *skill in thinking* and *skill in problem solving*. I challenge the premise that requiring mathematics is a legitimate strategy for, as you expressed it, "a way of getting the *crème de la crème*." Certainly *statistics* is relevant for a physician since one must be able to read, understand, and evaluate research data in all fields of medicine. Algebra is helpful in understanding statistics, but not absolutely necessary since applied research statistics is, as one mathematician expressed it, "a novel application of arithmetic."

I would support declassifying algebra from "required" to an "elective." Before any mathematics beyond arithmetic (which, incidentally, is exciting because of the hidden implications for understanding the universe), I recommend an elective which I call, *Mathematical Appreciation*. The student needs to be electrified with the romance of mathematics to excite a passion for exploring the how-to-do-it skills. We are extraordinarily successful with electives in *Art Appreciation* and *Music Appreciation*. It is time now for *Mathematical Appreciation*. For more details, read my book: ***The Super School of the 21st Century***.

<u>Subject</u>: Using TPR in 2nd language training of Police Officers

From: Chris Spader

Q. I have been approached about teaching a group of police officers beginning Spanish (30 hours). If I did it I would want to use TPR, but feel quite overwhelmed as I have not done it in the past. Any suggestions?

A. TPR is the ideal approach for second language learning by police officers, fire fighters, and emergency room personnel. Dr.

Sam Slick from the University of Southern Mississippi in Hattiesburg tells me that he experienced remarkable success using TPR in the training of police officers given a short training session of only two days.

His strategy: For the first day, he directed the action of the police officers with commands in Spanish that were typical of street patrol such as: "Open the car door... Get out of the car slowly... Face away from me... Place your hands on the back of your head... walk backwards towards me... etc. The next day, using a list printed in Spanish, each officer practiced uttering a direction to another officer who played the role of defendant. The officers internalized a remarkable repertoire by the end of the second day. In their evaluation, they wrote that this was one of the most enjoyable and productive training seminars they have ever experienced.

Chris Spader
dspader@juno.com

Subject: Adapting TPR to Self-Directed Language Learning

From: David Ker

Dr. Asher,

I am working on a paper called "Adapting TPR to Self-Directed Language Learning" which applies TPR methods to one-on-one language learning during field linguistics. I have attached a summary at the bottom of this message in hopes that you might be able to offer guidance or comments...

Adapting TPR to Self-Directed Language Learning (Unpublished Extract, 2/19/98), Copyright 1998 by David Ker

INTRODUCTION

One of the most helpful methods for teaching a second language is called "Total Physical Response" or just TPR. The originator of this method is Dr. James J. Asher, and his book, ***Learning Another Language Through Actions*** has caused practically a revolution in teaching methods for second languages. The purpose of this paper is to discuss TPR as it applies to learning another language in the field and suggest ways of adapting the methods found in ***Learning Another Language Through Actions*** to field linguistics where much language learning takes place through self-directed language learning, hereafter referred to as SDLL.

TPR: A SUMMARY

By using TPR, teachers seek to teach students a new language using methods that more closely mimic the ways children actually learn their mother tongue. Two of the key concepts are: delaying speaking and tying comprehension to physical responses. Traditional methods have been just the opposite. Learners have been required to mimic an instructor almost from the first day of class. Also, classroom methods have tended to place the student in an inactive role, sitting at a desk, listening to the instructor, and reading a book or filling in an exercise sheet. TPR de-emphasizes the role of speaking in early stages, using physical responses to indicate comprehension. Anyone with experience learning or teaching a second language intuitively sees the advantages of TPR over traditional methodology. And classroom results prove that TPR is simply a better way to learn.

LANGUAGE LEARNING OVERSEAS

For someone with a background in TPR methods it can be frustrating attending a language learning class overseas. It is uncommon to find a teacher using TPR-style methods in class. Far more usual is to find yourself in a classroom, sitting at a desk along with several other students, while the teacher directs lessons from the chalkboard. Frustration with traditional classroom learning can lead a learner to experiment with individual sessions or in-home tutoring...

For more on SDLL, contact: David and Hilary Ker - Wycliffe Bible Translators. Mail: Alameda Conde de Oeiras 26 R/C, Nova Oeiras 2780, PORTUGAL. Missionaries to Mozambique - In Portugal for Language Study. Permanent E-mail Address: David.Ker@sil.org or Hilary.Ker@sil.org

<u>Subject</u>: TPR for Preschoolers

From: Gloria Briesmaster

Dear Dr. Asher,

I just finished reading your book ***Learning Another Language Through Actions.*** I found it fascinating. I am from Spain. I taught Spanish to English speaking adults in Spain for several years. Now I live in New England. In our neighborhood there are many toddlers that stay home with their moms. Their moms envy my children because they are bilingual. Therefore I thought that I could invite those toddlers to come to my house and listen to me speak Spanish. After reading your book I am convinced that TPR would be the best way to do it. My question is: Has TPR been used with toddlers before? Assuming that the answer is *yes,* is there a book or manual for teachers of toddlers? When I read the lessons at the end of your book, I see that there are things that I will not be able to do with toddlers, like ask them to write something, or draw something, etc. Would it be OK just to skip the parts that they cannot do. What do you think about teaching songs in the new language? Would that be considered right side brain activity or left side? Would you encourage to teach songs in Spanish to toddlers as a positive way to teach the language? I want to thank you in advance for all your help and look forward hearing from you soon.

Gloria Briesmaster
briesmaster@juno.com

Answer from James J. Asher

Dear Ms. Briesmaster,

Your instincts are right on target! Music and singing along with TPR are right brain activities. Since TPR lessons are non-linear, you can select only those lessons that fit your situation with the preschoolers.

I recommend an excellent little book developed especially for preschool children by Nancy Marquez. The title is ***Learning With Movements*** and it is available in English, Spanish or French. Keep me posted on your progress with the children.

Also see Todd McKay's new books, ***TPR Storytelling for Children in Elementary and Middle School*** (for details, see the ad pages in the back of this book). —JJA

Subject: Is Translation Harmful?

From: Martin Colborn

Dr. Asher,

I know that in your book you do not advocate translation to the student's first language. Is there research that supports the idea that translation is a hindrance rather than a help, or do you simply see translation as unnecessary? I am talking particularly about abstract concepts. Does translation harm the acquisition process?

Martin Colborn
mcolborn@usd223.k12.ks.us

Answer from James J. Asher

Mr. Colborn,

In the beginning stages of second language acquisition, translation seems to result in slow-motion internalization of the target language. The reason is: The student is burdened with an additional task—a task that is unnecessary to understanding of the target language.

In more advanced stages, occasional translation is not harmful. A better strategy, in my opinion, is to explain the abstraction or idiom in simple terms using vocabulary that the student has already internalized. Example: "Don't let it throw you!" What does this mean? It means, "Don't get upset." —JJA

Subject: Using TPR with Latin

From: Leslie Noles

Dr. Asher,

I am a devotee of TPR in foreign language acquisition! I have taught Latin for nine years and during the last four years I have successfully used TPR combined with the Reading Method. What a novel idea for teachers of a language that used to be taught the old fashioned way: decline and conjugate! BBBAAAAAHHHH.....

I am now training teachers to troubleshoot technology and have discovered that a huge "language" barrier exists. I plan to use TPR in my training...

Leslie Noles
lnoles@esc14.net

Practical Applications Of the Right-Left Brain!

Recent breakthroughs in brain research demonstrate how to move information from one side of the brain to the other. TPR is a classic example of brainswitching—challenging students to process information in a new and different way.

In this easy-to-read book, you will discover how to use brainswitching to improve motivation, and help your students learn "difficult" subjects such as foreign languages, mathematics, and science. Other exciting applications include: problem solving, work, play, counseling, and interviewing.

THE SUPER SCHOOL

OF THE 21ST CENTURY

BY JAMES J. ASHER

HOW TO GET THE EDUCATION YOU WANT FOR YOUR STUDENTS FROM PRESCHOOL THROUGH HIGH SCHOOL

James J. Asher shows how the magic of **TPR** can be applied to improve every feature of today's schools! Here is a partial list of what you'll find:

- How to prepare every pupil to be a "good student" *before* they step into the classroom. This **TPR** technique is used by Warner Brothers Studios to prepare people to be day players in the movies.
- How to use **TPR** to persuade parents and students to be your most enthusiastic supporters!
- It cost NASA billions of dollars to develop simulators used in the training of astronauts. Now you can have powerful simulators to train your students in the sciences and mathematics—and you can have these simulators for under a hundred dollars each.
- Something happens in the 6th grade that fixes each student's reading rate at about 300 words per minute. A simple remedy can improve one's reading rate to 1,500 words per minute and beyond.
- We now spend more money on remedial mathematics than all other forms of math education combined. Millions of dollars can be saved in remedial work by knowing when to play to each side of the brain.
- Some offbeat paths to finding answers, including an Internet tool called "Gopher."

...and much, much more!

RECENT REVIEW

"Asher's book is a survival kit for everyone who works in public or private education from preschool through high school.

—A *tour de force* of exciting new concepts that are successful in the average classroom with average students, making sure that each student will either get the job of their choice, or significantly enhance the quality of their life—which Asher calls 'gracious adult living.' " —Dr. Robert J. Pelligrini

1995 winner of the Austen D. Warburton Award for Scholarly Excellence

Triple Expanded 4th Edition!

—Best Seller—

For over 25 years, Ramiro Garcia has successfully applied the Total Physical Response in his high school and adult language classes.

This Triple-expanded Fourth Edition (over 300 pages) includes:

- ✓ Speaking, Reading, and Writing
- ✓ How to Create Your Own TPR Lessons.

And more than 200 TPR scenarios for beginning and advanced students.

- ✓ How to Create Your Own TPR Lessons.
- ✓ TPR Games for all age groups.
- ✓ TPR Testing for all skills including oral proficiency.

In this illustrated book, Ramiro shares the tips and tricks that he has discovered in using TPR with hundreds of students. No matter what language you teach, including ESL and the sign language of the deaf, you will enjoy this insightful and humorous book.

New! Just off the press! THE SEQUEL!!!

Ramiro's brand-new companion book to the Instructor's Notebook!

- ✓ Hundreds of TPR exercises your students can enjoy at home
- ✓ Catch-up exercises for students who have missed one or more classes.
- ✓ Review of the classroom TPR experience at home
- ✓ Helps other members of the student's family to acquire another language.
- ✓ Helps the teacher acquire the language of the students with exciting self-instructional exercises!

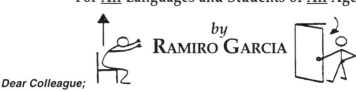

TPR Bingo©

Sky Oaks Productions, Inc.
P.O. Box 1102
Los Gatos, CA 95031-1102

was created by Ramiro Garcia, author of the best-selling *Instructor's Notebook*. In 20 years of applying the Total Physical Response in his high school and adult Spanish classes, **TPR Bingo** is the game that students want to play over and over.

TPR Bingo has playboards for forty students. One side of a playboard has 9 pictures so that you can play **TPR Bingo** with beginning students and when the playboard is turned over, there are 16 pictures for bingo with advanced students.

Here's how **TPR Bingo** works: You call out a direction in the target language such as "The man opens the door." Students listen to the utterance, search for a matching picture and if it is on their playboard, cover it with a chip. You may order the game in *English, Spanish, French* or *German*.

When students listen to the instructor utter directions in the target language, they are *internalizing comprehension*. But, as they advance in understanding, individual students will ask to play the role of the caller which gives students valuable practice in *reading and speaking*. Incidentally, as students play **TPR Bingo**, they internalize numbers in the target language from 1 through 100.

As Ramiro says, "Try this game with your students. You will love it!"

More TPR Lessons in Spanish, French, German, and now English!

Actionlogues

by Jody Klopp

For all **ages** and all levels, **25 TPR units** such as: getting ready for work, making a sandwich, working in the yard, going on a date, building a fire, driving a car, playing sports, etc.

A **native speaker** reads each command on a cassette.

CASSETTE INCLUDED!

Each action is **instantly understood** by looking at a **photograph** (396 of them) which demonstrates the action.

Every action may be pantomimed at the student's desk.

- The **Actionlogues** and **audio cassette** enable each of your students to study **TPR** successfully at home.
- Your students will **internalize** 160 verbs through actions.
- The **short length** of each unit makes **Actionlogues** valuable as a supplement to traditional FL programs.
- Perfect for adults who wish to acquire another language at their own pace, and in the comfort of their own home.

English Grammar Through Actions
Spanish Grammar Through Actions
French Grammar Through Actions

Dear Colleague:

When I present **TPR** Workshops, the most frequent question is, **"The total physical response is fine for commands, but how can it be applied to other grammatical features?"**

In **English Grammar Through Actions,** Eric Schessler demonstrates how **TPR** can be applied successfully for **stress-free** acquisition of grammatical features such as:

Abstract Nouns
Adjectives
Adjectives - Comparison
Adverbs
Articles
Conjunctions
Demonstratives
Expletives
Past Perfect
Past tense of **Be**
Possessive Case and **Of** expressions
Possessive Pronouns
Prepositions of Place
Prepositions of Time
Present Continuous
Future - to be going to
Future - Will
Have - Present and Past
Interrogative Verb forms
Manipulatives
Object Pronouns
Past Continuous
Present Perfect
Simple Past
Simple Present
Singular/Plural Nouns
Subject Pronouns
Tag Questions
Wh - Questions

For students acquiring Spanish or French with **TPR**, Eric has also prepared the books **Spanish Grammar Through Actions** and **French Grammar Through Actions**.

Sincerely,

James J. Asher

NEWS FLASH!

The popular TPR book, **Learning With Movements** by Nancy Márquez is available in **English, Spanish,** and now **French**.

The unique features are:

- A marvelously **simple format** which allows you to glance at a page and instantly generate one direction after another to move your students rapidly in a logical series of actions.
- An **initial screening test** will give you a realistic concept of each student's skill.
- After each lesson, there is a **competency test** for individual students.
- Recommended for preschool and elementary students in **any language**, including the sign language of the deaf.

Hot off the press in your choice of *English, Spanish,* or *French!*

Dear Colleague:

I want to share with you the **TPR Lessons** that my high school and college students **thoroughly enjoy** and **retain** for weeks—even months later. My book has...

- A script you may follow step-by-step including a list of props needed to conduct each class.
- A command format that gives students **instant success**. (Students show their understanding of the target language by responding to directions uttered by the instructor. **Production** is delayed until students are ready and feel comfortable.)
- Grammar taught implicitly through the imperative.
- Tests for an evaluation of student achievement.

TOTAL PHYSICAL RESPONSE IN THE FIRST YEAR
By
FRANCISCO L. CABELLO
with William Denevan

Sincerely,

Francisco Cabello

Look, I Can Talk!

Student Book for Level 1

in English, Spanish, French or German

High School, College, or Adults!

by Blaine Ray

with Greg Rowe and Greg Buchan

Here is an effective **TPR** storytelling technique that **zooms** your students into *talking, reading,* and *writing.* It works beautifully with beginning, intermediate and yes — even advanced students.

Step-by-step, Blaine Ray shows you how to tell a story with **physical actions,** then have your students *tell the story to each other* in their own words **using the target language**, then **act** it out, **write** it and **read** it.

Each **Student Book for Level 1** comes in your choice of *English, Spanish, French* or *German* and has

- ✔ 12 main stories
- ✔ 24 additional action-packed picture stories
- ✔ Many options for retelling each story
- ✔ Reading and writing exercises galore.

Blaine ***personally guarantees*** that each of your students will eagerly tell stories in the target language by using the **Student Book.**

To insure rapid student success, follow the thirteen magic steps explained in th **Teacher's Guidebook** and then work with your students story-by-story with the easy-tc use **Overhead Transparencies.**

The Exciting Sequel!

Look, I Can Talk More!

Student Book for Level 2

in English, Spanish or French

by Blaine Ray

with Joe Neilson, Dave Cline, Carole Stevens, and Christopher Taleck

Keep the excitement going with this sequel for your level 2 students. Ten main storie with many spin-off mini-stories for variety. The drawings are superb and **Overhea Transparencies** may also be ordered. Your students will love it!

Now...

Look, I'm Still Talking!

Student Book for Level 3

in English, Spanish or French

New!

Fluency Thru TPR Storytelling

Dazzle Your Students!!

Show them several of James J. Asher's Classic Video Demonstrations as an exciting and stress-free introduction to your TPR instruction!

You and your students will be inspired by seeing these exciting video demonstrations of TPR. Each video cassette is unique, and shows different stress-free features of TPR instruction — *no matter what language you are teaching,* including English as a Second Language or the Sign Language of the Deaf. ***(Each video is narrated in English.)***

Children Learning Another Language: *An Innovative Approach*©

VHS, Color, 26 minutes, shows the excitement of children from K through 6th grades as they acquire **Spanish** and **French** with **TPR.** (ESL students will enjoy this too!)

If you are searching for ways that motivate children to learn another language, don't miss this classic video demonstration. The ideas you will see can be applied in your classroom for any grade level and for any language, including English as a second language.

A Motivational Strategy for Language Learning©

VHS, Color, 25 minutes, demonstrates step-by-step how to apply **TPR** for best results with students between the ages of 17 and 60 acquiring **Spanish**. Easy to see how **TPR** can be used to teach any target language.

See the excitement on the faces of students as they understand everything the instructor is saying in Spanish. After several weeks in which the students are silent, but responding rapidly to commands in Spanish, students spontaneously begin to talk. You will see the amazing transition from understanding to speaking, reading, and writing!

Strategy for Second Language Learning©

VHS, Color, 19 minutes, shows students from 17 to 60 acquiring **German** with **TPR**. Applies to *any* language!

Even when the class meets only two nights a week and no homework is required, the retention of spoken German is remarkable. You will be impressed by the graceful transition from understanding to speaking, reading, and writing!

Demonstration of a New Strategy in Language Learning©

VHS, B&W, 15 minutes, shows American children acquiring **Japanese** with **TPR**. Applies to *any* language! You will see the first demonstration of the **Total Physical Response** ever recorded on film when American children rapidly internalize a complex sample of Japanese. You will also see the astonishing retention one year later! Narrated by the Originator of TPR, James J. Asher.